TAKING
★ ON THE
SYSTEM

TAKING ★ ON THE SYSTEM

RULES FOR RADICAL CHANGE IN A DIGITAL ERA

MARKOS MOULITSAS ZÚNIGA

A CELEBRA BOOK

Celebra
Published by New American Library, a division of
Penguin Group (USA) Inc., 375 Hudson Street,
New York, New York 10014, USA
Penguin Group (Canada), 90 Eglinton Avenue East, Suite 700, Toronto,
Ontario M4P 2Y3, Canada (a division of Pearson Penguin Canada Inc.)
Penguin Books Ltd., 80 Strand, London WC2R 0RL, England
Penguin Ireland, 25 St. Stephen's Green, Dublin 2,
Ireland (a division of Penguin Books Ltd.)
Penguin Group (Australia), 250 Camberwell Road, Camberwell, Victoria 3124,
Australia (a division of Pearson Australia Group Pty. Ltd.)
Penguin Books India Pvt. Ltd., 11 Community Centre,
Panchsheel Park, New Delhi - 110 017, India
Penguin Group (NZ), 67 Apollo Drive, Rosedale, North Shore 0632,
New Zealand (a division of Pearson New Zealand Ltd.)
Penguin Books (South Africa) (Pty.) Ltd., 24 Sturdee Avenue,
Rosebank, Johannesburg 2196, South Africa

Penguin Books Ltd., Registered Offices:
80 Strand, London WC2R 0RL, England

First published by Celebra,
a division of Penguin Group (USA) Inc.

First Printing, September 2008
10 9 8 7 6 5 4 3 2 1

Copyright © Markos Moulitsas Zúniga, Inc., 2008
All rights reserved

CELEBRA and logo are trademarks of Penguin Group (USA) Inc.

LIBRARY OF CONGRESS CATALOGING-IN-PUBLICATION DATA:
Moulitsas Zúniga, Markos, 1971–
    Taking on the system: rules for radical change in a digital era/Markos Moulitsas Zúniga.
        p. cm.
    ISBN 978-0-451-22519-1
    1. Radicalism. 2. Protest movements. 3. Social action. 4. Political participation. 5. Blogs—political aspects.
I. Title.

    HN49.R33M68 2008
    322.4—dc22   2008012312

Set in Electra
Designed by Ginger Legato

Printed in the United States of America

PUBLISHER'S NOTE
While the author has made every effort to provide accurate telephone numbers and Internet addresses at the time of publication, neither the publisher nor the author assumes any responsibility for errors, or for changes that occur after publication. Further, publisher does not have any control over and does not assume any responsibility for author or third-party Web sites or their content.

For Elisa, Eli and Ari.

And for Saul Alinsky.

The tactics may change, but the soul of the radical endures.

"Do what you can, with what you have, where you are."

—Theodore Roosevelt

"Conflict is the essential core of a free and open society."

—Saul Alinsky

★ CONTENTS ★

TAKING ON THE SYSTEM

★ PROLOGUE ★

You can't change the world without conflict.

Whether you want to change Capitol Hill or Capitol Records, the corporate tower or the ivory tower, conflict must precede change, because in most of the big institutions of our society, we have too many entrenched elites who refuse to give up their power without a fight.

Traditionally, these self-appointed and unaccountable gatekeepers have purported to operate in the public interest, but they are grossly out of touch with the public. Rather than empower people, they designed rules to keep the rabble out of their inner sanctums, where our ideas wouldn't infect their decision-making process. Whether it was record label executives, or Hollywood studio moguls, or editors and producers in the media, or the clubby D.C. politicians, consultants, and lobbyists—many built walls to protect the sanctity of their turf.

Only people with the proper pedigree—rich parents, friends in high places—were invited into the club. The value of an opinion or idea was determined by the social status of the person expressing it. Passion was considered uncouth. Youth was seen as a drawback. And the gatekeepers were stationed at the entryways to the halls of power.

The results? A sick body politic and a homogenized culture. A disengaged citizenry, cynical and despondent over its inability to effect change, and a powerful elite unhampered and unchallenged in the dogged pursuit of its own interests over those of society at large.

But all that is changing. Technology has unlocked the doors and facilitated a genuine democratization of our culture. No longer content to sit on the sidelines as spectators, a new generation of *participants* is taking an active role in our culture and democracy. This has left the traditional gatekeepers and the elites they guard with few choices. Some are embracing this democratization, welcoming the new participants. Others are simply tolerating the interlopers, acknowledging the process as an inevitable evolution in our culture. Then there are those digging in their heels, and fighting a losing battle to protect their domain.

There is nothing inherently evil about being a traditional gatekeeper, only in seeking to muzzle the new voices rising up from the ground. Like mine, for example.

★   ★   ★

In 2002, I sat down and wrote these first three sentences on a silly little site I had dubbed *Daily Kos* ("Kos" being my U.S. Army nickname): "I am progressive. I am liberal. I make no apologies." To say I had no idea where those ten words would lead is an understatement. From that genesis, *Daily Kos* has morphed into one of the most heavily trafficked blogs in the world, and certainly the most influential political blog in the United States today.

I started the site for a simple reason—I felt ill-served by the undemocratic gatekeeping mentality so prevalent in our society. At that time, the United States seemed to be on an inexorable march toward war with no avenue for dissent. There was an assumption by the powers that be that the rest of the citizens couldn't think for ourselves. That we needed self-appointed so-called experts to tell us what to think, what to do, and what we should—or should not—know. For far too long, these gatekeepers controlled the national conversation.

Daily Kos exists because, quite simply, we had a dramatic market failure on our hands. If the gatekeepers wouldn't offer the news and viewpoints I craved, well then, I'd have to take matters into my own hands. Yet I saw no template to work from. If I looked to progressive politics, all I saw was a movement splintered into "issue silos"—environmentalists, pro-choice groups, labor unions, civil libertarians, trial lawyers, ethnic and racial identity groups, all of them screaming that their issue was the most important, and sabotaging each other in pursuit of donor money and legislative priorities. And given the woeful state of the Democratic Party circa 2002, it was clear their approach was a failure. I would have to look elsewhere to channel my energy and activism.

But everywhere I turned, I ran up against gatekeepers. You know them. In media, they are the editors and producers. In politics, they are the party machinery and establishment elite. In music, they are the music label executives. In film and video, they are the Hollywood hierarchy. In the book world, it's the publishing houses. If you wanted to be an active agent in our culture, it was impossible to do so without one of those gatekeepers anointing you with their approval. And most of the time, these gatekeepers saw you as a nuisance. Who needs young whippersnappers shaking up their cozy, safe, predictable worlds?

The comfortable and established are more invested in holding their positions of privilege than in risking new ways of writing, thinking, innovating, exploring, and governing. Hence, we have been cursed with a system that doesn't always reward the greatest talents. It is mostly a cultural and political aristocracy, not a meritocracy. Forget trying to change anything, because to change the world, you had to be a "somebody." And most of us don't get to be "somebody." I sure as heck wasn't back then.

But Katie Couric was. At the time, she was hosting the *Today* show on NBC, judiciously reporting on the drumbeats emanating from a White House preparing for war on Iraq. Anyone who disagreed with the administration's war footing faced vicious attacks. In this post-9/11 environment, criticizing the administration on anything, even domestic policy, was viewed as giving "aid and comfort" to our enemies.

Couric, now anchor of the *CBS Evening News*, characterized the tenor of the time, at the National Press Club in late September 2007: "The whole culture of wearing flags on our lapel and saying 'we' when referring to the United States and, even the 'shock and awe' of the initial stages, it was just too jubilant and just a little uncomfortable. And I remember feeling, when I was anchoring the *Today* show, this inevitable march toward war and kind of feeling like, 'Will anybody put the brakes on this? And is this being properly challenged by the right people?' And I think, at the time, anyone who questioned the administration was considered unpatriotic and it was a very difficult position to be in."

Like Katie Couric, I remember thinking, "Of course the expert journalists in our professional media will fact check this rush to war and put the brakes on it!" But unlike Couric, I didn't host one of the top-rated shows on network television. At a time when the country desperately needed a free, fair, and independent media to save it from what would become—predictably—a tragic and costly disaster, the media became an appendage of the White House propaganda machine.

I remember feeling alone and isolated. Even so-called reasonable and serious progressives sounded neither reasonable nor serious, nor—for that matter—progressive. The most obvious questions were not being asked: Why were we abandoning our war against al-Qaeda in Afghanistan to invade a country that had nothing to do with 9/11? If Vice President Dick Cheney and then Defense Secretary Donald Rumsfeld knew exactly where the WMDs were in Iraq, why didn't they pass that info over to the UN weapons inspectors? The unanswered questions were endless.

So those of us in the hinterlands—lost, forgotten, and marginalized— had a choice to make. If the media was AWOL and the Democrats were rolling over and playing dead, we could accept it and go on with our lives—or we could take up the fight.

Newfangled internet technologies gave us our spark. I wrote those ten words and launched *Daily Kos*. Others spoke out on their own podiums on the internet. And across the country, something new was being born. Our little medium was in its infancy, an insignificant speck in the media landscape. Back in 2002, when our audiences numbered in the hundreds and not millions, we lonely and disparaged bloggers didn't stand a chance against the media giants cheerleading the war. Our courage was lost in the numbers; those with the traditional media megaphones had no courage.

Some of them, like the *Time* magazine columnist and TV pundit Joe Klein, engaged in a bit of revisionist history, claiming they had always opposed the war in Iraq. Industrious bloggers pored over Klein's 2002 and 2003 writings, finding not a single critical or cautionary note about Iraq in the thousands of words he had written. Like Couric, his supposed opposition remained unspoken.

As for Couric, she knew that Saddam Hussein had nothing to do with 9/11. She knew we'd been whipped up into a false patriotism to mask the administration's shameful rush to war. And she knew Bush had run a disastrous war campaign.

She had no problem saying those things during her Press Club interview. Yet she never said them on the air. In that Press Club interview, she said: "I feel totally comfortable saying any of that at some point, if required, on television." Think about that: *if required*. This is what modern media has been reduced to—the notion that journalists reporting what they know to be the truth isn't a requirement, it's an option.

★   ★   ★

I grew up in El Salvador, and when I was nine, my family fled the country to avoid its vicious civil war. As a teenager, I was short, skinny, barely spoke English, looked far too young for my age, and liked to read and play with computers. I was a true nerd, joining the Model United Nations club and running to the library during lunchtime to escape abusive schoolmates.

I was five feet seven and weighed just 111 pounds when I joined the United States Army in 1989. I served my nation during the Gulf War, and in return, my nation provided me with a college education, self-confidence, and a sense of duty to my fellow Americans. Those who wore combat boots looked out for each other and took responsibility for them. I entered the army a Republican, but emerged a Democrat.

So there I was in the early '90s, a newly minted Democrat—but an inconsequential one. I got a solid education at Northern Illinois University, thanks to the GI Bill and financial aid from the state of Illinois. I got two degrees with three majors in four years, and headed off to law school at Boston University. After law school, I switched gears and headed west. I ended up in California with a new wife, working a good but unremarkable job. People like me spent hours talking about politics, but it mattered little in the greater scheme of things. As much as I wanted to play a bigger role in our democracy, I saw no open doors. I didn't have the money to buy my way in, and I didn't have the pedigree to get an invitation.

So I was left with a couple of unpalatable options: I could lick stamps in a dingy campaign office, I could watch a thirty-second television spot, and I could vote. That was it. Like so many others, I was unsatisfied being a passive consumer. I wanted to do my part to improve the world, but didn't know how. There were no role models. No heroes. No guidelines. No success stories to mimic. That's when I set up my own little website and called it *Daily Kos*, now a cog in a vast people-powered movement working to reshape our country and our culture.

In tactics and process and strategy, this new movement is unprecedented. Yet, in terms of its overall mission, its cultural zeitgeist, it is the successor of many movements before us that spurred great societal advances—universal suffrage, the rise of organized labor, civil rights legislation.

Traditionally, it took great leaders like Saul Alinsky to build mass movements and accomplish major changes. Credited with the whole concept of grassroots organizing and using stock holdings to force progressive change at publicly traded corporations, Alinsky is best known for his work organizing the "Back of the Yards" neighborhood in Chicago popularized by Upton Sinclair's novel *The Jungle*. He was the consummate hell-raiser, a hero to radical activists everywhere.

Yet his 1971 book, *Rules for Radicals*: *A Pragmatic Primer for Realistic Radicals*, was an ode to practicality, common sense, and rational activism. "We will start with the system because there is no other place to start from except political lunacy," he wrote. "It is most important for those of us who want revolutionary change to understand that revolution must be preceded by reformation. To assume that a political revolution can survive without the supporting base of a popular reformation is to ask for the impossible in politics."

The book received a warm reception from mainstream observers and liberals, but was harshly derided by the Left. Christopher Lasch, reviewing it in the *New York Review of Books*, wrote that Alinsky, "having divested his movement of any suspicion of 'ideology,' having substituted 'citizens' for 'workers' and interests for classes, and having exalted process over objectives, was free to define 'participation' itself as the objective of community organizing—of politics in general." Todd Gitlin, in the *Nation*, complained that Alinsky had "no transcendent vision of a society worth living in." That is, he was not an ideologue.

Those complaints are surprisingly familiar to me and others like me in this new world of online activism we have dubbed the "netroots." Peter Beinart, the former editor of the *New Republic*, wrote in August 2007: "It's no secret that Moulitsas cares more about victory than ideology. He's said it repeatedly. But it's worth pausing for a moment to recognize how re- markable this ultra-pragmatism is." Such pragmatism is no more remark- able today than it was in Alinsky's day. Fact is, then as today, far too many people mistake "big picture" activism designed to empower individuals as lacking an ideological base. Each "leader" is expected to have all the answers—the vision, the values, and the specific policy statements. Del- egating policy papers to, say, the *experts* on those topics is frowned upon. Beinart says that I care more about winning than ideology, but he fails to understand this: I care about winning *because* of my ideology.

No one should ever tell people what to believe. I don't. That is the old "top-bottom" view of activism that I categorically reject. People can deter- mine for themselves what they'll work for, and once they've found some- thing they're passionate about, whatever that might be, they now have the tools to be effective advocates for change.

Waxing poetic on the best progressive education policy or enlightened foreign policy is irrelevant when in a powerless minority. All the ideology in the world is useless without the practicality to attain power. The Amer- ican conservative movement learned this lesson in the '60s and '70s, and built a machine that has dominated American politics for the past two decades. And even if Republicans get swept out of power, the institutions they built will last for generations.

Witness the jokers Alinsky described having to deal with as he fought to empower and mobilize regular citizens in the '60s:

> "What is the alternative to working 'inside' the system? A mess
> of rhetorical garbage about 'Burn the system down!' Yippie yells
> of 'Do it!' or 'Do your thing.' What else? Bombs? Sniping? Silence
> when police are killed and screams of 'murdering fascist pigs'
> when others are killed? Attacking and baiting the police? Public
> suicide? 'Power comes out of the barrel of a gun!' is an absurd ral-
> lying cry when the other side has all the guns [. . .] Militant
> mouthings? Spouting quotes from Mao, Castro, and Che Gue-

vara, which are as germane to our highly technological, computer-
ized, cybernetic, nuclear-powered, mass media society as a
stagecoach on a jet runway at Kennedy airport?"

Where are those "yippies" today? Extinct or marginalized, far from the
levers of power or centers of influence. Today, as in Alinsky's time, the
ideologically pure and their idealistic slogans are of no consequence if
they remain in the political and cultural wilderness.

Alinsky's *Rules for Radicals* was, in essence, a set of guidelines for his
generation's activists—how, when, and where to engage political enemies
for maximum political effect. The subsequent years, however, haven't
been kind to Alinsky's brand of activism, or the tactics he espoused. To be
blunt, the '60s are over—regardless of any lingering hippie nostalgia or of
any out-of-touch conservatives ranting about "communist Democrats."
And while the challenges facing Americans in the '60s can seem superfi-
cially similar to those today—an unpopular war fought by an unpopular
president with rampant corporatism threatening the very fabric of our democracy—the times have changed dramatically. We need new tactics and
new strategies.

Alinsky died the year after publishing *Rules for Radicals* at the age of
sixty-three. As I conceived and wrote this book, I often fantasized about
meeting and interviewing him. I would've loved to get his thoughts on this
brave new (virtual) world of ours. There's something heartening about a
tome for a new generation of activists published almost a century after
Alinsky's birth and written by this young turk born the same year Alinsky's
seminal work was published.

★   ★   ★

We are living in a time when technology is breaking down barriers, empowering the isolated, arming the powerless, and educating the ignorant.
The tools and tactics to enact social change have evolved dramatically
in even the last short decade. We're entering an era of dramatic democratization.

We were once expected to simply sit quietly and let the gatekeepers decide what we should watch, what we should think, and what we should do. Now technology is making it possible for us to take charge of our own lives. Whether it's blogs, podcasting, social networking sites like MySpace or Facebook, wikis or YouTube, people are quickly adopting myriad communication technologies emerging from the internet and using them to become active participants in their culture.

Rather than rail against the media, we are becoming the media. Rather than bitch about the political establishment, we are taking it over. Rather than despair about the quality of Hollywood movies, we are becoming filmmakers. Rather than complain about corporate music, we're making our own.

We are the first generation that has direct, individual access to the world and to the emerging technologies. We are the first generation that can bypass the old-world gatekeepers to communicate to the masses—that is, *with each other*. And we won't let anyone filter or alter or censor those communications.

We have the technology and the collaborative spirit to find each other, pool our talents, and press for real systemic change. No longer content with being spectators, we are becoming players. No longer content to merely receive messages, we now send them as well. No longer content to be media consumers, we now are creating.

As we become conscious of our own collaborative power, we are taking charge of our culture and our politics, not because someone gave us permission, but because we—like I did that lonely day I started *Daily Kos*—have roused ourselves from a restless sleep and realized that no permission is necessary. There are no legitimate guardians of the gate and no one barring us because we don't have the right pedigrees or the right connections.

So millions are taking matters into our own hands. We are seizing the tools, finding our voice, exploring mediums, building communities, engaging in conversations, connecting with new friends, discovering that we are not alone. We are challenging ourselves to organize, collaborate, respond, and innovate. While the gatekeepers question our credibility, we are systematically building it the old-fashioned way—we're earning it.

Some of the most important changes, however, go beyond mere bits and bytes and tools. As the culture evolves to embrace what some derisively label as the "Cult of the Amateur" (otherwise known as "regular people"), the gatekeepers are flailing, trying to determine their role in a world where the tectonic plates of power are shifting.

In his day, Alinsky's actions were designed to change the behavior of those gatekeepers, because he was under no illusion that they could be replaced or eliminated. The tools to do so did not exist. Today's activism is not only designed to influence the gatekeepers, but also to bypass or simply eliminate them.

The gatekeepers won't cede power without a fight. So we need a new set of rules for today's cultural and political battleground.

CHAPTER 1

THE NEW INSURGENTS

To create long-lasting change in a democracy, you must shape public opinion by making your voice heard, your ideas clear, and your cause visible. In today's world, that means you must manage modern media—not just its technology, but its gatekeepers, too, by bypassing, crushing, or influencing them.

I t was February 2003 and there was a sense of inevitability across the nation—and abroad—that the United States was on a headlong course toward war against Iraq. Nevertheless, people from all over the world refused to be passive spectators to the impending horror, and on the weekend of February 15–16, millions participated in antiwar marches. Huge crowds turned out in New York (100,000–500,000), San Francisco (200,000), London (750,000 to 2 million), Rome (almost 3 million), and in hundreds of other cities across the United States, the Middle East, and Europe.

But something funny happened here in the United States. All of that hell-raising and chanting of antiwar slogans in public places barely registered in the media landscape. Nightly television newscasts gave the protests a minute or two. Newspapers noted that a bunch of people protested the war, and then quickly moved on to more pressing business. After the initial coverage, what little reaction there was in the traditional media was negative, such as the February 19 column in the *Washington Post* by Michael Kelly, a former editor of the *New Republic* and the *Atlantic Monthly*:

> "Of course, not all the marchers can be counted as 99.9 percent pure moralists. Some—perhaps many—marched out of simple reactionary hatred: for the United States, for its power, for its paramount position in a hated world order. London's paleosocialist Mayor 'Red Ken' Livingstone, a featured speaker at that

city's massive demo, comes to mind. His enlightened argument against war consisted chiefly of calling George W. Bush 'a lackey of the oil industry,' 'a coward' and 'this creature.' [. . .]

"To march against the war is not to give peace a chance. It is to give tyranny a chance. It is to give the Iraqi nuke a chance. It is to give the next terrorist mass murder a chance. It is to march for the furtherance of evil instead of the vanquishing of evil. This cannot be the moral position."

The war began on March 20, and on April 3, Michael Kelly became a casualty himself when he was killed while traveling in a Humvee with the Third Infantry Division, covering the war he so passionately supported.

What Kelly wrote about the antiwar protests seems to have been shared by a large number of the journalists working in the major media outlets in the United States at the time, as their one-sided coverage suggests. Generally starved of media attention, the marchers' efforts were for naught. Perhaps never before had so many people in the streets been so ineffective. Not in their inability to prevent the war, which was preordained and unstoppable, but in their inability to make even a ripple in the media world and register their objections with the public consciousness. An ABC News poll taken right after the protests showed 63 percent of Americans favoring the war. Ten days later, that number was 65 percent.

What happened? How could so many be so ignored? How could such mass discontent have so little influence on the public debate?

The old philosophical riddle asks, "If a tree falls in the forest and no one is around to hear it, does it make a sound?" Discussing the modern-day efforts at social and political change, we might ask ourselves, "If an act of protest takes place and no one records it, does it make any difference?" What happened on that February weekend was simply that the media gatekeepers decided that antiwar voices were not important or "serious" according to the terms of the media narratives—this was a war against evil, for instance—that dominated the national conversation at the time. Trapped in a 1960s mind-set, the powers that be in the media saw the war opponents as unclean hippies out of touch with harsh reality, and well outside of the mainstream. War supporters were the grown-ups, given a megaphone denied to the others. With that simple decision, the debate became a one-sided affair, the outcome predetermined without input from the public.

And here we arrive at a foundational rule of this book: Without the media, little can be accomplished. If you cannot influence the flow of information, you cannot effect change on any substantial scale. That's not to say it is absolutely impossible to make a difference without media attention, but to foster radical and long-lasting change, activists must be seen and heard widely and be part of the public discussion.

The most effective activism is a function of its times and is directly related to the condition of the contemporary media. Time and place do matter, but the principle remains the same: the more widely you can communicate your vision, express yourself, and disseminate information, the better the chances that you may actually change hearts and minds.

Thomas Paine, the eighteenth-century revolutionary author and intellectual, used pamphlets to promote the cause of independence among the American colonists. In 1776, he authored *Common Sense*, which is credited with inspiring George Washington and John Adams to join the cause. The next year, he wrote *The American Crisis*, galvanizing the ragtag revolutionaries in their early, difficult times with words of hope and courage:

> "These are the times that try men's souls: The summer soldier and the sunshine patriot will, in this crisis, shrink from the service of their country; but he that stands it now, deserves the love and thanks of man and woman. Tyranny, like hell, is not easily conquered; yet we have this consolation with us, that the harder the conflict, the more glorious the triumph. What we obtain too cheap, we esteem too lightly: it is dearness only that gives every thing its value."

In 1930, Mahatma Gandhi launched his first campaign of civil disobedience—the Salt March to Dandi—by making extensive use of global newsreel teams. The Salt March was designed to catch the British off guard by protesting the salt tax as a burden to poor Indians, an apparently minor issue in the larger context of the Indian independence movement.

Ignored at first by colonial British rulers, who considered his actions of no real consequence, Gandhi convinced newsreel teams to capture the planning and execution of the 248-mile march. That they did, and more, and worldwide audiences got firsthand views of the repressive actions the British took to try and squash the rapidly growing nonviolent movement. The United Press International correspondent Webb Miller reported on May 21, 1930:

> "Not one of the marchers even raised an arm to fend off the blows. They went down like ten-pins. From where I stood I heard the sickening whacks of the clubs on unprotected skulls. The waiting crowd of watchers groaned and sucked in their breaths in sympathetic pain at every blow. Those struck down fell sprawling, unconscious or writhing in pain with fractured skulls or broken shoulders. In two or three minutes the ground was quilted with bodies. Great patches of blood widened on their white clothes. The survivors without breaking ranks silently and doggedly marched on until struck down."

The story horrified worldwide audiences and is credited with swaying world opinion against British rule of India. *Time* magazine named Gandhi the 1930 "Man of the Year" and compared his actions to the American patriots at the Boston Tea Party. The world would not have heard about the British brutality and the passions of the marchers had it not been for Gandhi's deft use of newsreel technology.

By the 1960s, the newsreel was obsolete, replaced with direct television broadcasts, and in the United States that meant primarily the three television network newscasts: NBC, ABC, and CBS. Introduced in the late 1940s, television was quickly adopted by the masses, with 90 percent of American homes having a television set by the early 1960s. While CBS pioneered the television newscast in 1948, it wasn't until 1963 that the network and its rivals—NBC and ABC—expanded their newscasts from fifteen minutes to thirty minutes. By 1969, 85 percent of television viewers had one of the three network newscasts on during their scheduled half hour, according to a report from the Project for Excellence in Journalism.

American activists in the 1960s seeking radical change soon realized that they needed access to that new medium to beam their messages directly into the nation's living rooms. Spurred by opposition to the U.S. war in Vietnam, college students learned to create spectacles tailor-made to attract television news cameras and still photographers. Street theater actions like sit-ins, campus takeovers, and rowdy, anarchic protests were surefire ways to make the all-powerful media gatekeepers pay heed and bring attention to their cause. Their colors were bright, the signs provocative, and the fashions scandalous. It was a very visual form of protest designed for a very visual medium.

At the 1968 Democratic National Convention in Chicago, protesters used such tactics to highlight the absurdity of a nomination process that ignored the will of the people in favor of the party's insider elite. In one memorable scene, protesters mocked the undemocratic process by performing a nomination ceremony for a pig, the animal being later hauled away by police as cameramen and photographers captured the absurdist images for posterity. As delegates inside the convention hall voted on the nomination, matters outside were quickly reaching a boiling point. Protesters and police engaged in pitched street battles, providing far more compelling visuals than anything inside the convention hall. The convention forgotten, the media followed the drama and beamed the brutal images directly into living rooms all around the country. Even though the number of protesters at any one place was small, maybe a few thousand, the television images artificially amplified their numbers and their significance. And the constant playing and replaying of those images ensured that the Chicago riots would permanently sear themselves into the nation's memory as a reminder of the 1960s civil unrest.

In fact, those riots are so embedded in our nation's psyche that they still define what "activism" should look like today. Post-boomer kids have grown up hearing how they are "apathetic" and "uninvolved" because of their failure to "take it to the streets" like the boomers did in the '60s.

To be clear, those 1960s activists were trailblazers whose tactics and actions were finely tuned for the media of their era, but today's media landscape is much more complex and presents a completely different challenge for activists. The big three network news shows have steadily lost 1 million viewers in each of the last twenty-five years, despite our nation's steady population growth; today, only 7.7 percent of Americans are watching the nightly news, according to the Project for Excellence in Journalism. Cable news has eaten into that audience, as news-centric networks like CNN, MSNBC, CNBC, and Fox News have arrived on the scene. Television is now fragmented with hundreds of channels micro-targeting consumers. We have not just regular radio, but satellite radio as well. Immigrant communities are creating their own media outlets, with ethnic newspapers, radio, and television growing rapidly even as their "mainstream" colleagues suffer declines. But most dramatically, we have the internet and myriad technologies that have essentially democratized media creation. The internet has become a power unto itself, fragmenting audiences into ever thinner slices of the once-simple media pie.

And hence the paradox—the internet and the democratizing of our culture make it easier to reach the masses, yet reaching the masses has never been more difficult. Rather than three gatekeepers at the head of ABC, CBS, and NBC controlling access to the American public, we now have innumerable gatekeepers in charge of their own little segments of the mass audience.

The changing media landscape offers new opportunities as much as it offers new challenges, and chief among those opportunities is the mother lode of modern activism—the ability to dislodge "conventional wisdom" on any given topic.

"Conventional wisdom" (or CW) refers to ideas and explanations generally accepted as the truth by the public, the gatekeepers, and the decision makers. Effecting societal change often requires changing the conventional wisdom on issues, especially when the "wisdom" isn't so wise. For instance, the conventional wisdom on the stock market says that Republican administrations are good for the market, while Democratic ones are not. A December 2007 survey of Wall Street investment professionals showed that 22 percent listed "Democrats in the White House" as their top worry for 2008, more so than global unrest (15 percent), U.S.

economic growth (15 percent), and even a terror attack (13 percent). Yet in reality, since 1948, Democratic administrations have delivered 15.25 percent gains in the market compared to 9.53 percent for Republican ones, according to Jeremy Siegel, a finance professor at the Wharton School of the University of Pennsylvania and a Kiplinger columnist. Sometimes, "wisdom" like this is simply unsupported by evidence and is based more on "feel," or intuition, such as the notion that file-sharing software is the primary cause of a decline in revenues at the record labels and Hollywood movie studios, or that the number-one killer of women is breast cancer when it's actually cardiovascular disease.

Whoever defines the "truth," the conventional wisdom, controls the terms of the debate. Note that Galileo ended up under house arrest the final years of his life for disputing the religious consensus that the sun revolved around the earth. On the other hand, Christian conservatives demanding the teaching of "intelligent design" in public schools have an uphill battle given the scientific consensus on the legitimacy of the theory of evolution. In American politics today, the notion that Democrats are weak on national defense issues is so strongly ingrained that even Democrats seem to believe it. Meanwhile, George W. Bush used a rhetorical sleight of hand in his 2000 presidential campaign to turn negative CW about his party into a personal virtue, calling himself a "compassionate conservative" (as opposed to the rest of his mean-spirited party).

When there's widespread conflict surrounding an issue, consensus can't form. Take the abortion question, for example: because there are authentic differences in view about abortion among large segments of the public, no conventional wisdom can coalesce. In fact, the only conventional wisdom on abortion may be that there will never be a consensus on the issue. One of the goals of the global warming deniers has been to fight the formation of any consensus on the issue. It doesn't matter that the evidence is clear and there is general agreement within the scientific community. By touting phony evidence to counter that scientific consensus, these contrarians hope to prevent the emergence of a broader, popular consensus that would generate the political will to aggressively combat global warming.

So how can activists influence the conventional wisdom on any issue?

Once the exclusive province of elite gatekeepers, shaping conventional wisdom is becoming a far more democratic affair, thanks to the networking nature of the internet. And while the ability to establish CW is currently (and likely always will be) beyond the capabilities of citizen activists, they now have the ability to play an important role.

In the aftermath of the 2004 presidential election, Peter Daou, internet guru to the John Kerry and Hillary Clinton presidential campaigns, set out to map the limits of the progressive blogosphere's power. While Daou focused on progressive blogs, what he found is quite relevant to all citizen media, whether in politics or elsewhere. Published on *Salon* in September 2005, Daou's article, "The Triangle: Limits of Blog Power," remains one of the most insightful and influential analyses on the ability of citizen media to effect change. Explaining that "blog power on both the right and left is a function of the relationship of the netroots to the media and the political establishment," Daou painted a triangle with blogs along one side, the traditional media on another, and the political establishment on the third.

> "Simply put, *without the participation of the media and the political establishment, the netroots alone cannot generate the critical mass necessary to alter or create conventional wisdom.* This is partly a factor of audience size, but it's also a matter, frankly, of trust and legitimacy. Despite the astronomical growth of the netroots . . . and the slow and steady encroachment of bloggers on the hallowed turf of Washington's opinion-makers, it is still the Russerts and Broders and Gergens and Finemans, the [*Wall Street Journal, Washington Post,* and *New York Times*] editorial pages, the cable nets, Stewart and Letterman and Leno, and senior elected officials, who play a pivotal role in shaping people's political views. That is not to say that blogs can't be the first to draw attention to an issue, as they often do, but the half-life of an online buzz can be measured in days and weeks, and even when a story has enough netroots momentum to float around for months, it will have little effect on the wider public discourse without the other sides of the triangle in place." [Emphasis in the original.]

So in order to create or change conventional wisdom, the Daou Triangle posits that citizen media must enlist both the political establishment (or ruling establishment in other verticals, like the Hollywood studios or record labels) *and* the traditional media to its cause.

> "Should we conclude, then, that the inability of bloggers on the left and right to alter or create conventional wisdom means that they have negligible political clout? If the netroots can't change CW without the mass media and the political establishment, and if the mass media and the political establishment can change CW without the netroots (which seems undeniable), then isn't the blog world a relatively powerless echo chamber? The answer, of course, is no.
>
> "Bloggers can exert disproportionate pressure on the media and on politicians. Reporters, pundits, and politicians read blogs, and, more important, they care what bloggers say about them because they know *other* reporters, pundits, and politicians are reading the same blogs. It's a virtuous circle for the netroots and a source of political power. The netroots can also bring the force of sheer numbers to bear on a noncompliant politician, reporter, or media outlet. Nobody wants a flood of complaints from thousands of angry activists. And further, bloggers can raise money, fact check, and help break stories and/or keep them in circulation long enough for the media and political establishment to pick them up.
>
> "Consequently, bloggers, though unable to change conventional wisdom on their own, are able to use these proficiencies and resources to persuade the media and political establishment to join them in pushing a particular story or issue."

In early 2005, the Bush administration embarked on an effort to "save" Social Security, claiming the cherished social program was in danger of insolvency. Their plan? Privatize the program by allowing younger Americans to invest part of their Social Security benefits in the stock market, conveniently providing a bonanza for the Republicans' Wall Street constituents. The progressive blogs erupted in immediate opposition, with economists like Duncan Black (a.k.a. *Atrios*) and Brad DeLong pushing back on the economic policy front while Joshua Micah Marshall of *Talking Points Memo* worked on the political fronts. The initial conventional wisdom inside the D.C. Beltway was that Democrats had to "compromise" to find a "solution" to the "crisis," and with the Democratic Party dazed and demoralized after its crushing 2004 loss, it seemed as if capitulation was inevitable. However, bolstered over time by allies in the labor movement and other progressive groups, and by bloggers pushing their analyses into the traditional media, the Democratic Party found its backbone. What had been a fringe position—the bloggers' claim that "there is no crisis"— eventually became the party's position. With a united Democratic front facing down Bush, the media awarded the victory to the Democrats, helping ratify the new conventional wisdom.

Activists can put pressure on either the media or the political side of the triangle, or *both*. They can work to enlist the power brokers in order to bring the traditional media along; they can work to enlist the traditional media in order to bring the power brokers along; or they can work both sides and maximize their chances of success. Gandhi worked the media as a way to craft a conventional wisdom (the British are oppressing the Indians) that ultimately helped convince the British government to grant India its independence. It's what antiwar protesters did in the 1960s as they engaged in actions designed to generate media coverage to try and turn the nation against the war. Once the conventional wisdom became "the American people oppose the war," it was increasingly difficult for the American government to continue waging it. And it's what those unsuccessful antiwar protesters were hoping to do in February 2003 as they expressed their loud dissent in streets around the world.

But this is not an era for street protests. The traditional media won't cover the mundane, routine, predictable, or familiar. Forty years of organized protests and marches for every conceivable cause—wars, abortion, black pride, gay pride, and so on—have desensitized not just the press but the broader public to the street spectacle. Been there, done that. It's the reason that no one blinked twice at the millions who hit the streets to protest the Iraq war in 2003. Today's citizen activists have far more tools at their disposal to pressure both the traditional media and ruling establishment to effect change. Activists were once hostage to the mass media conglomerates, but they can now create their own media outlets. Promoting a cause used to require deep pockets to finance expensive marketing and PR campaigns, but now there are myriad low-cost or no-cost ways to get the message out.

While activism was once predicated on influencing the media gatekeepers, we can now build campaigns that simply bypass those gatekeepers, or campaigns that can damage or destroy them. And while "influencing" is still the path of least resistance, and the preferred course of action with any campaign, merely the *threat* of bypassing or crushing the existing gatekeepers makes them more amenable to being influenced.

BYPASS THE GATEKEEPERS

In June 2000, the musician Courtney Love wrote a widely distributed exposé of the record labels' greed on *Salon*, skewering industry executives as "pirates" and making an impassioned case on behalf of the musicians. The economic model of the music industry has always been tough on musicians, dramatically favoring the record labels at their expense. But few knew just how bad things were.

Love started with some math, assuming a "bidding-war band that gets a 20 percent royalty rate and a million-dollar advance." Half of that million was spent recording the album, while their manager got a 20 percent commission on the remaining half million. After paying their lawyers and business manager, the rest of the four band members split the remaining $350,000, which came out to about $45,000 each after the government took its bite from taxes. Love then assumed the album turned out to be a huge hit, selling 1 million copies. The band would make two videos, splitting the half-million-dollar tab for each video with the label. They'd get $200,000 in tour support and $300,000 in promotions, all of which had to be paid back. And remember that $1 million advance? That had to be paid back as well, leaving the band owing a total of $2 million to the record label. With a royalty rate of $2 per album, the band would net $2 million from its 1 million album sales, essentially breaking even. Meanwhile, the label would gross $11 million on the album, and after $4.4 million in expenses, make a cool profit of $6.6 million. "[T]he band may as well be working at a 7-Eleven," wrote Love. "Of course, they had fun. Hearing yourself on the radio, selling records, getting new fans and being on TV is great, but now the band doesn't have enough money to pay the rent and nobody has any credit. . . . Worst of all, after all this, the band owns none of its work."

Then came the file-sharing networks in the late 1990s and early 2000s, adding additional strain to a system that was already broken. In the same article, Love wrote:

> "Somewhere along the way, record companies figured out that it's a lot more profitable to control the distribution system than it is to nurture artists. And since the companies didn't have any real competition, artists had no other place to go. Record companies controlled the promotion and marketing; only they had the ability to get lots of radio play, and get records into all the big chain stores. That power put them above both the artists and the audience. They own the plantation.
>
> "Being the gatekeeper was the most profitable place to be, but now we're in a world half without gates. The Internet allows artists to communicate directly with their audiences; we don't have to depend solely on an inefficient system where the record company promotes our records to radio, press or retail and then sits back and hopes fans find out about our music."

That was the year 2000. Now nearly a decade later we are indeed in "a world half without gates." With the continued growth in legal and illegal downloading, record industry profits have been taking a nosedive ever since 2000. As the former Talking Heads frontman David Byrne pointed out in his January 2008 *Wired* magazine article, music purchases reached their apex in 2000 with $17 billion in sales (in inflation-adjusted 2006 dollars) and it's been all downhill since then—$12.9 billion in 2003, $10.6 billion in 2006, and a projected (and likely too optimistic) $9.1 billion in

2012. Unlike the panicking music industry, Byrne wasn't pessimistic about the numbers:

> "What is called the music business today, however, is not the business of producing music. At some point it became the business of selling CDs in plastic cases, and that business will soon be over. But that's not bad news for music, and it's certainly not bad news for musicians. Indeed, with all the ways to reach an audience, there have never been more opportunities for artists."

For the past decade, the record industry has been acting like a jilted lover, lashing out and blaming everyone else for its troubles. First it blamed the revenue collapse on customers for using free swapping sites like Napster and Limewire. Napster was sued out of existence, yet in a world where digital files can easily be swapped between friends and larger communities, no amount of lawsuits could stem the tide. The number of targets was too great, and suing ten-year-old girls proved a PR disaster. Then the business tried to implement "digital rights management" (DRM) protections to CDs to prevent digital distribution of their music, which proved both a technical *and* PR disaster, as the "locked" CDs refused to play in certain CD players. This made a mockery of copyright law that allowed consumers to make a small number of copies for personal use.

What was really taking place—under the record companies' radar—was a smart revolt by consumers. The music labels and retailers insisted on being gatekeepers to the music, forcing consumers to accept the industry's terms for how they would buy the music and how they could use it once they'd bought it. Now, consumers had to figure out ways to bypass those gates. They weren't going to pay obscenely inflated prices for a CD with one or two good songs and they weren't going to let the labels determine the media in which they would listen to those songs. Fed up with the high cost and unwieldiness of physical media (that is, CDs), music fans were opting for the format that offered the greatest portability (small digital media players like the iPod). They bypassed the retailers by directly getting the music the most convenient way—by downloading it, either paying 99¢ per song to iTunes or getting music for free from peer-to-peer

networks like Limewire. It took a while, but eventually this reality began
to dawn on the music industry. As the January 10, 2008, edition of the
Economist reported:

> "In 2006, EMI, the world's fourth-biggest recorded-music com-
> pany, invited some teenagers into its headquarters in London to
> talk about their listening habits. At the end of the session the EMI
> bosses thanked them for their comments and told them to help
> themselves to a big pile of CDs sitting on a table. But none of
> the teens took any of the CDs, even though they were free. 'That
> was the moment we realized the game was completely up,' says a
> person who was there."

And it wasn't just the consumers who tired of the record labels' gatekeeping. The artists themselves started to realize that they have alterna-
tives, as evidenced by Radiohead's release of their 2007 album, *In
Rainbows.*

After six successful albums and legally free of any major label commitments, Radiohead pondered their options as they mapped out their next
album. Recording an album, once a cost-prohibitive proposition, could
now be done at a home studio with a few microphones and a laptop computer using free or inexpensive software. The web had proven itself a via-
ble distribution model and an accessible one at that. Radiohead had a
rabid fan base to boot, hungry for the band's first album in four years. Why
not bypass the record label entirely and sell directly to the fans? There was
one big challenge to consider—like all digital media, any songs they distributed online could be freely swapped by anyone, endangering the
band's efforts to earn its fair share for their work.

So Radiohead arrived at an ingenious solution—put the music on serv-
ers and let fans download it for whatever they thought the music was
worth. They could even pay nothing. In just the first week after its October
10 release, roughly 1 million fans downloaded *In Rainbows*, paying an
estimated average of between $5 and $8 each. "In terms of digital income,
we've made more money out of this record than out of all the other Radiohead albums put together, forever—in terms of anything on the Net," the

Radiohead frontman Thom Yorke told David Byrne for the *Wired* magazine interview. "And that's nuts." Just as important, Yorke waxes poetic
about Radiohead's ability to remove a gatekeeper between the group and
its fans: "I think there's a lack of understanding [between what kids want,
and what the record labels deliver]. It's not about who's ripping off whom,
and it's not about legal injunctions, and it's not about DRM and all that
sort of stuff. It's about whether the music affects you or not." As Courtney
Love wrote in her *Salon* piece, "Record companies don't understand the
intimacy between artists and their fans. They put records on the radio and
buy some advertising and hope for the best. Digital distribution gives everyone worldwide, instant access to music."

The record labels always thought the delivery mechanism was the
medium—the album, the CD, the digital file—when in fact the power is
in the music itself. When the music was tied down to physical media, the
power rested in the hands of the record labels. But the democratization of
media now means that musicians can once again *own* their own music.
It means that the labels no longer have a say in who gets to hear that
music.

Sometimes, it means that fans get to decide these things.

In Sheffield in the UK, the band Arctic Monkeys formed in 2002, a
year after a couple of the band's teenage members received electric guitars
as Christmas presents. They began playing local gigs in 2003, and as a way
to promote their efforts, they burned a few CDs to give away at shows.
Those CDs were limited in number, so their fans ripped the music back
on their computers and began sharing the files among themselves. Band
members were thrilled. "We never made those demos to make money or
anything," the drummer Matt Helders told the online magazine *Prefix-
mag.com* in a November 2005 interview. "We were giving them away free
anyway—that was a better way for people to hear them. And it made the
gigs better, because people knew the words and came and sang along."

Soon, fans had set up a MySpace page for the band, uploading the files
and getting the word out about their work. Arctic Monkeys didn't have a
record label and were not doing any real marketing on their own, yet they
were being asked to play at gigs farther and farther away from home. Record label execs flocked to their shows, yet the band left instructions to

turn them away at the door. "Before the hysteria started, labels would say, 'I like you, but I'm not sure about this bit, and that song could do with this changing . . .' We never listened. And once it all kicked off we didn't even worry about it anymore. In London, the kids were watching the band and the record companies were at the back watching the kids watching the band," Alex Turner, the band's frontman, told his interviewer.

In June 2005, they signed with a small independent label. Their first single debuted at number one in the UK. Their second single, released a few months later, followed suit. Their first album, *Whatever People Say I Am, That's What I'm Not*, released in January 2006, became the fastest-selling album in UK history, selling 363,735 copies in the first week alone—success paved by the frenetic file sharing and online promotions of the band's zealous fans.

Amazingly, as the *Prefix* interview shows, the band never really knew what its fans were doing online, and doesn't seem to understand their crucial role in the band's success. Here's an exchange from the *Prefixmag. com* interview:

PM: Are you guys Internet users?

ARCTIC MONKEYS: Only to email or whatever; iTunes, stuff like that. But none of us really knew how to. It was a guy at college who made the Web site. We had tried putting music on the site, but it didn't work properly. People couldn't listen to it properly.

PM: I notice you have a pretty popular site on MySpace.

ARCTIC MONKEYS: We don't know about that, either.

PM: So that's not you guys?

ARCTIC MONKEYS: No, no. The other day someone said to us, "I looked at your profile on MySpace." I said, "I don't even know what MySpace is." [When we went number one in England] we were on the news and radio about how MySpace has helped us. But that's just the perfect example of someone who doesn't know what the fuck they're talking about. We actually had no idea what [MySpace] was.

Not only did the fans bypass the record label executives, they bypassed the band as well. Rather than depend on their favorite band to promote themselves, the fans did it for them. And while these fans didn't run fancy music publications or have the money to advertise the band in traditional venues, they did have access to new media tools—peer-to-peer file-sharing networks, social networks like MySpace, and other such online tools. The traditional gatekeepers can only watch as their iron grip on the business crumbles around them.

As music fans begin bypassing the record labels, there's a very real danger that many of those labels will be driven out of business, while the rest struggle to survive and adapt to stave off extinction. It is a karmic comeuppance for an industry far too quick to exploit its artists and customers, but the execs won't be driven out by a torch-wielding mob hell-bent on revenge. Instead, the labels will suffer the indignity of neglect and irrelevance as technology and changes in our culture render them obsolete.

And it's not just music. These new empowering technologies are allowing "amateur" filmmakers to use inexpensive video and editing equipment to create content, then post it on sites like YouTube for free and instant worldwide distribution. The free ad website *Craigslist.com* has singlehandedly busted the newspapers' monopoly of classified advertising and, along with it, one of their biggest revenue sources. Bloggers have taken to web publishing tools to create instant publications costing a few bucks, at most, and have built publications that rival their traditional media counterparts in the celebrity, political, and technology worlds. And with their rapid ascent and large audiences, many of these bloggers have managed to make an impact once reserved for establishment gatekeeper voices, with a fraction of the staff and overhead of the old media. The advent of the digital era has allowed anyone creative and resourceful enough to simply bypass the traditional gatekeepers. But sometimes more drastic action is required.

CRUSH THE GATEKEEPERS

When progressive bloggers emerged on the political scene in the early 2000s, they were motivated by two fundamental notions: that the Republican Party, driving under the influence of its neocon and evangelical wings, was steering the nation onto treacherous pathways; and that the Democratic Party, disproportionately influenced by the corporatists inside its big tent, was losing its populist and progressive soul. There were plenty of dragons to slay inside the Democratic Party, but the corporatists were a particularly insidious bunch.

They founded the Democratic Leadership Council (DLC) in the late 1980s to combat what was seen as a dangerously obsolete "Jesse Jackson wing" of the party—the remnants of the labor-urban New Deal coalition that had led Walter Mondale to a historical loss in 1984, and then delivered a just slightly better defeat in 1988 under Michael Dukakis. Co-founded by Bill Clinton before his presidential run, the organization was a creature of its times—a vehicle to reinvigorate a party that had clearly lost entire geographic swaths of the country as well as key demographic groups like white males, the so-called Reagan Democrats.

Assuming that liberalism was dead and conservatism on the rise, the DLC promoted "a third way"—neither traditional liberalism nor old-fashioned conservatism, but a hybrid, an amalgam of the party's traditional social liberalism and the GOP's business-friendly approach. The math made sense—labor unions were in dramatic decline while business interests were inundating the Republican Party with enough funds to utterly drown out Democratic efforts. Meanwhile, Republicans had built a vast direct-mail, small-dollar donor operation that overwhelmed pathetic efforts by the Democrats. The money disparity loomed large. If the status quo persisted, the Democratic Party might be doomed for generations. The DLC was nominally a think tank, but its close ties to corporate America gave it the ability to steer donations from big business to its preferred candidates. In a cash-starved party, this was a very big deal.

Meanwhile, the *New Republic* magazine, while not directly related to the DLC, worked in concert to promote not just the Democratic Party's corporatist wing but also a more hawkish and militaristic foreign policy. Founded in 1914, the magazine once represented, as the author Eric Alterman wrote in the June 18, 2007, edition of the *American Prospect*, "the voice of re-invigorated liberalism—a cachet that was perhaps best illustrated when the dashing, young President Kennedy had been photographed boarding *Air Force One* holding a copy." However, under the tutelage of Likudnik hawk Marty Peretz, the magazine became more inviting to right-wing voices like Charles Krauthammer and Fred Barnes while regularly providing cover for conservatives, as Alterman further noted:

> "The Reagan White House had 20 copies messengered every Thursday afternoon. And no wonder. Nothing gave conservatives more pleasure than to begin an argument, or a speech, or, oftentimes, a joke with the words, 'Even *The New Republic* agrees. . . .' For those liberals who refused to come along for the ride—who continued to pay heed to old-fashioned ideas like the primacy of diplomacy, human rights, and fair elections—well, history, according to Krauthammer-authored editorials, would prove that they had made 'Central America safe for Communism.' They could whine in *The Nation* or hold candlelight vigils with Central American nuns, whatever. History, argued the *TNR* neocons, had left them behind, and that was that. But by insisting on its liberal bonafides while endorsing conservative causes, *TNR* offered the Reaganites badly needed intellectual cachet, as then-editor [Hendrik] Hertzberg regretfully admitted in the early '90s."

In other words, the weekly magazine was a neocon in liberal clothing. In the 1990s, the conservative writer Andrew Sullivan took the helm of the publication and led it through an era of scandal (including putting Stephen Glass, who turned out to be a serial fabricator, in charge of fact checking) and in an ever more conservative direction. Among other things, Sullivan used his publication to trumpet Charles Murray's *The Bell Curve*—a racist and methodologically flawed tome published in 1994 arguing that blacks were less intelligent than whites—giving Murray ten thousand words to make his case in a cover story. Following Sullivan, *TNR* was edited by the late Michael Kelly, already noted in the opening paragraphs of this chapter as a virulently antiliberal neocon. The magazine's Iraq war coverage was downright belligerent in its support of the war and its opposition to critics of the war, labeling them un-American with a zeal rarely matched by extreme right-wing publications.

With the DLC inside and the *New Republic* outside, the Democratic Party was being heavily pushed to the right, chasing the Reagan Democrats and leaving behind its progressive values and the disenfranchised communities it had traditionally represented. As a result, the "center" of American politics, defined by conventional wisdom as that "middle ground" between the two major parties, continuously drifted right. So much so, in fact, that a little-known governor from a small state—Howard Dean of Vermont—rose to front-runner status in the 2004 Democratic primary by promising to represent "the Democratic wing of the Democratic Party." That rallying cry galvanized the rank-and-file activists of the party and the netroots and fueled the people-powered progressive movement. That such a declaration—"the Democratic wing of the Democratic Party"—was immediately understood and resonated so well that it became a revolutionary call to arms was testament to how far the party had strayed from its progressive roots.

As a result, the DLC and *TNR* both felt threatened with an insurrection and an outraged Democratic base wanting their party—and their values—back. They were alarmed at the antiwar bent of these new insurgents, convinced that the nation wouldn't support anything but the most aggressive and hawkish pro-war Democrats. So those gatekeepers pushed back with a vengeance. In Howard Dean they saw the return of their old, vanquished enemy—liberals, anticorporatists, peaceniks, and the Jesse Jackson wing of the Democratic Party. Fearful that their influence inside the party was at stake (and it was), these corporatists launched a full-throated assault against Howard Dean. Never mind his pro-gun record and an indisputable history of responsible budget management (once lauded by the DLC itself), Dean was branded a threat to the Democratic Party, or, at least, *their* Democratic Party. The *New Republic* gleefully joined in the anti-Dean attacks, even hosting a regular feature titled "Diary of a Dean-o-Phobe."

The corporatists got what they wanted when Dean's campaign crashed and burned. But they also got something they didn't want—new enemies within the Democratic Party. The *New Republic* and the DLC had both used their megaphones to thwart the modernization of the Democratic Party, but they were no longer the only ones using amplified sound.

The rapidly growing progressive netroots closely watched the party's corporatist forces kneecap Dean, and they realized that before they could take on Republicans, they would first have to work to clean out their own house. They responded on two fronts. The first was to build a people-powered candidate-funding mechanism. The DLC had become a muscular force by helping funnel corporate donations to candidates. But Dean's campaign had pioneered the raising of small-dollar contributions via the internet using websites and allied blogs, and through what had quickly emerged as the most effective fund-raising tool in politics, the email list. What had taken conservatives decades to build, Dean had built in less than a year. And while some observers fretted that this success was somehow exclusive to Dean, the reality was soon apparent—Democrats finally had a medium that favored their style and that of their supporters. Small-dollar Democratic donors were happy to support Democrats who promised to reform a sick party. Reformist, noncorporatist, populist Democrats could now raise at least part of their requisite stash from noncompromised sources, weakening the DLC's stranglehold on the party.

The second response was a media assault on both the DLC and the *New Republic*. Every time the DLC would stick its head up anywhere, it would get whacked by bloggers. Every time the *New Republic* wrote yet another tiresome antiprogressive screed, bloggers (including me) would fire off responses and urge their readers to cancel subscriptions. For example, on June 22, 2006, the *TNR* writer Jason Zengerle accused me of controlling access to advertising revenues to other blogs, thus using that threat to keep the progressive blogosphere under my supposedly iron fist. The charges were patently ridiculous and wholly unsupported by the facts, but it was also a terrible affront to every independent blogger Zengerle had accused of being afraid of me. "[T]hat's pretty much par for the course for the Joe Lieberman Weekly," shot back Jane Hamsher of the blog *Firedoglake*. "They have the journalistic ethics of gutter snakes and as their circulation spirals into the tank they seem to be growing quite desperate." The blogger Billmon was vicious in his response: "Actually, the real reason I haven't posted anything about this idiotic affair up until now is that it's been just that: idiotic. At times, scanning the feeble slurs over at *The New Republic*'s 'blog,' the Plank, really has been like reading a bad Monty Python parody. I mean, the idea that Kos could use his influence, such as it is, to intimidate Left Blogistan into a quivering reign of fear is simply laughable—a paranoid fantasy that wandered away from FreeRepublic. com and was adopted by some silly little Ivy League boys who've decided they like how Karl Rove plays the game and want to get in on the fun."

For the *New Republic*, this relentless and sustained mocking was particularly damaging. In a world where progressive media voices were scarce—essentially *TNR* and three other opinion magazines—it was much easier to build an audience and thrive. The rise of the blogosphere gave political junkies a much wider variety of reading material. With the *New Republic*'s brand tarnished by the relentless netroots attacks as well as its more obvious blunders, like its rabid support for the Iraq war, its circulation began to suffer. The results were dramatic—a proud and influential weekly opinion journal with a circulation of 101,651 in 2000 was reduced, in four short years, to publishing every two weeks with a circulation of 61,675, or roughly a 40 percent decline, according to the Audit Bureau of Circulation. Its ability to influence the public debate had been greatly diminished.

The DLC didn't fare any better. Its role in the national debate became that of contrarians—called upon by reporters to attack the rising people-powered Democratic movement. Unable to influence the public debate, they became the proverbial old guy angrily shaking his fist and yelling at the kids to get off his lawn. After 2004, we set out to make the organization radioactive, and settled on a strategy of targeting their list of members who were elected officials. The list had long been a way for candidates to prove their corporate-friendly policies when soliciting campaign contributions from corporate interests, while the DLC got to brag about its influence in the party with the big-name Democrats it could claim as its allies. It was a win-win proposition for both sides, and we set out to change that.

I first noticed that list when, after the 2004 elections, the DLC had included Sen. Barack Obama on its DLC/New Democrats directory of elected officials. This was an odd addition since Obama had certainly not run a corporatist campaign (he had raised $3 million from the DLC nemesis MoveOn in his Senate run), and had already shown antipathy to the organization. When Obama was declared one of "100 Democratic Leaders to Watch" by the DLC in 2003, it spurred an angry article in the weekly online magazine *The Black Commentator* by Bruce Dixon:

> "This is not the Barack Obama that Illinois progressives would like to support. It is not the Barack Obama who can win a primary or general election in a season where the President kicks off his campaign from the deck of an aircraft carrier impersonating Top Gun. It's not the Barack Obama who can win in the year that Republicans will wind up their convention at Ground Zero NYC, the second week of September 2004, screaming 'Terror!' at the top of their lungs. Unless Barack Obama recovers his lost voice, he will have no answer.
>
> "Instead, Obama seems to be listening to the voice of DLC founder and CEO Al From, who in February declared to so-called New Democrats, 'Your most formidable opponent isn't Bush or your fellow contestants for the nomination. Your real enemy is the ghost of Democrats past.' Those 'ghosts' are the 'activists' and 'special interests' of the Democratic Party—the very same code words that Republicans use for Blacks, unions and advocates of Obama's own, cherished 'altruism.'"

Unbidden, Obama responded to that piece on June 19:

> "I read with interest, and some amusement, Bruce Dixon's recent article regarding my campaign, and his suggestion that per-

haps my positions on critical issues facing this country are somehow being corrupted by the influence of the Democratic Leadership Council (DLC). . . .

"Since my mother taught me not to reject a compliment when it's offered, I didn't object to the DLC's inclusion of my name on their list. I certainly did not view such inclusion as an endorsement on my part of the DLC platform.

"In sum, Bruce's article makes nice copy, but it doesn't reflect the reality of my campaign. Nor does it reflect my track record as a legislator. In the last three months alone, I passed and sent to the Illinois governor's desk 25 pieces of major progressive legislation, including groundbreaking laws mandating the videotaping of all interrogations and confessions in capital cases; racial profiling legislation; a new law designed to ease the burden on ex-offenders seeking employment; and a state earned income tax credit that will put millions of dollars directly into the pockets of Illinois' working poor."

That letter spurred a second article on the *Black Commentator* titled "Not 'corrupted' by DLC, says Obama." It was clear that in deed and in word, Obama had little in common with the DLC. Yet after 2004, there he was on their members' list. After bloggers made some noise about the inclusion, Obama requested the DLC take him off their list and they complied. But three months later, they once again tried to slip him through. On March 15, 2005, I brought attention to the fact, drawing an angry response on the DLC blog:

"[Markos] even took the trouble to dig down in our web page—bypassing a few hundred thousand pages of policy work, which is what we do to pass the time while waiting for the next call from Fox News—and discover that Sen. Barack Obama is still listed in our database! Scandal! (He's in there because he recently joined the Senate New Democrat Coalition, all of whose members are in our database, which is about as controversial as a phone book)."

Yet a few hours later, they were forced to retract:

> "UPDATE: Turns out I was misinformed about Obama's being
> a member of the Senate New Democrat Coalition. The misunder-
> standing was based on the two different meanings of New Demo-
> cratic Senators, but we were wrong about that, and have removed
> his name from our Directory. Still love the guy, though."

Sensing blood, netroots activists began contacting politicians on the
list demanding that they ask to be taken off. Three weeks later, on April 7,
the blogger Bob Brigham, a prime organizer of this campaign, noticed
the DLC had updated its directory. Dozens of names had disappeared.
"Sure some politicians were term limited and many lost their seats (after
taking DLC advice?). But many up and coming politicians have decided they want nothing to do with the DLC strategy of attacking Democrats
through triangulation," he wrote. "Congressman [Tim] Ryan's name disappeared. California gubernatorial candidate Phil Angelides is no longer
on the list. Arizona Governor Janet Napolitano has no need for the DLC.
Hell, even [Colorado Senator] Ken Salazar would rather stand with
Obama than the DLC."

It was a stunning victory—elected officials no longer saw the list as a
painless way to curry favor with special interests. The campaign continued
until, at some undetermined point (sometime between September 2005
and the end of that year), the DLC decided the list wasn't worth the trouble to itself or its members and eliminated it completely. Not only did we
eradicate a credentialing system for Democrats seeking corporate cash,
but without that impressive list of big-name Democrats, it was harder for
the DLC to name-drop its way to greater influence.

By 2006, the DLC was down but not quite out. When the online publication *AlterNet* asked me that June to write a piece on "the demise of the
DLC," I wrote "No thanks" in response. "Frankly, I think it's still a little
early to write this piece." At that moment, we were locked in a battle with
the DLC—we had targeted their patron saint, the Connecticut senator
Joe Lieberman, in the Democratic primary, who was being opposed by the
businessman Ned Lamont. An angry DLC responded in its magazine:

"In many respects, the purge-Lieberman movement is more a test for its proponents than for its object. Internet-based liberal activists have a lot to offer the Democratic Party: energy, fundraising prowess, a commitment to open debate, and a healthy skepticism about the orthodox liberal interest groups and consultants who rarely look beyond the Beltway.

"But if they want to be a serious and permanent element in progressive politics, they should resist the temptation to indulge themselves in mean-spirited vengeance against Democrats like Joe Lieberman who proudly defend the Clinton legacy and warn against counter-polarization."

The patronizing tone aside, this was perhaps the first admission by the DLC that the new "internet-based liberal activists" actually had a place in the Democratic Party. But that realization had come too late, and it was born out of strategic weakness. We weren't about to call off the fight. In addition to Lieberman, we also targeted another DLC protégé in the Montana Senate race, State Auditor John Morrison, who had the backing of the Democratic establishment and was considered a DLC rising star. His opponent was Jon Tester, a term-limited state senate president and farmer from eastern Montana who had the unqualified support of both the Montana and national progressive netroots. That gave us two clear proxy U.S. Senate primary battles between people-powered candidates and those championed by the DLC and its corporatist allies. It was a naked power play, and a risky one. Both DLC candidates were better known, better funded, and had access to the establishment machines.

When the primaries were done, we had emerged twice victorious. Tester beat Morrison 61 percent to 35 percent and Lamont beat Lieberman 52 percent to 48 percent. Lieberman would go on to win as an independent in November 2006, but for our purposes, the message had been sent—there was no place for DLC candidates in the Democratic Party. We had left the DLC weakened and bereft of much of its former influence. After years of prominent elected Democrats serving as chairmen of the DLC, the group had to settle for former representative Harold Ford in

2007, fresh off losing a 2006 Senate campaign in Tennessee. It was an apt metaphor for what the DLC had become.

If there was any doubt of the waning of the DLC's power inside the Democratic Party, it was put to rest at the DLC's own annual convention in Nashville in July 2007. Here's how *Politico* reported on it:

> "It's a Democratic prom without a king, a queen or really any of the popular kids, only the star quarterback of yesteryear. Three hundred and fifty politicians will be present, key governors to ambitious state legislators, from almost every state.
>
> "But none of the eight Democratic contenders for the White House are making time for the Democratic Leadership Council convention Sunday and Monday in Nashville, although DLC staffers sought for weeks to woo the candidates."

One week later, essentially the entire Democratic field of candidates showed up in Chicago to meet with bloggers at their annual conference, YearlyKos (now Netroots Nation). The press had a field day with the stark contrast, culminating in a debate on *Meet the Press* between Harold Ford and me on the future of the party. It was not much of a debate; it was an embarrassing sign of a severely weakened organization that no longer carried much weight—the only reason they had been invited on the show was to play foil against a blogger. A blogger! Much like the Jesse Jackson they had vanquished over a decade prior, they had been relegated to the fringes of the Democratic Party.

Directly challenging existing gatekeepers does not necessarily mean they are destroyed and disappear. It means they bleed influence and power. To make that happen, you need to evaluate your target gatekeeper and determine the source of its power, and then supplant it. For the DLC, it was its ability to deliver easy corporate dollars to candidates and elected officials in exchange for fealty to the organization and its business-friendly ideology. For the *New Republic*, it was its influential group of readers. In both cases, the grass roots and the netroots dislodged the gatekeepers and filled in the gaps.

INFLUENCE THE GATEKEEPERS

All power flows through gatekeepers and influencing them has long been a necessity for those seeking change. There are several ways to do that. You can buy that access the way record companies used to do by paying radio DJs to play their artists' music. Businesses and other institutions pay PR firms to garner positive media attention or pay marketing firms to create advertising, buying access to the nation's consumers. Corporate lobbyists and special interest groups wine and dine politicians and stuff their campaign war chests with cash. You can also give the gatekeepers something they need, the way political activists create compelling spectacles for content-hungry media outlets, or the way churches gain the attention of politicians by offering their congregations as ground troops for their campaigns.

But technology has now given us another option: show the influence makers that we can render them irrelevant. Irrelevance is a great motivator for those who would otherwise ignore the barbarians at the gate, as Sony Music learned the hard way when forced to deal with the fans of the singer-songwriter Fiona Apple.

At the age of sixteen, Fiona Apple made a three-song demo tape and passed it on to a friend. That friend gave the tape to another friend, who passed the tape to a producer at Sony Music, and soon Apple had a recording contract. Three years later, her 1996 album, *Tidal*, thrust her into the national spotlight when the song "Criminal" shot up the charts. The debut album ended up selling a whopping 2.7 million copies, establishing her as one of the top-selling acts of the year. In 1999, she released her second album, *When the Pawn . . .* , which did not do as well, but still sold 1 million copies in the United States. Then silence.

It wasn't until 2002 that word got out that Fiona Apple was back in the studio, and that Sony Epic Records would release the work in 2003. By May 2003 the album was finished. Titled *Extraordinary Machine*, it was slated for a July release, but that month came and went with no album hitting the stores. In October, *Entertainment Weekly* quoted Jon Brion, Apple's producer, saying the project had been shelved "due to the label not hearing any obvious singles," though the label insisted the album would be released in February 2004 after some rerecording was finished. That date also came and went and still no word.

Then came the leaks. Two tracks appeared online and spread like wildfire. *Entertainment Weekly* wrote in January 2005 that the tracks were "tantalizing, eccentric art pop," and concluded that "with Apple, the weirder, the better." When *USA Today* asked about her album's release date, Apple replied tersely, "You'll probably know before I do." More light was shed on the holdup by *MTV News* in January 2005:

> ". . . Apple's third record, *Extraordinary Machine*, completed in May 2003, has been gathering dust on Sony's shelves, according to Jon Brion, the album's producer. Label executives allegedly don't consider it commercial enough for release, and thus a long and mostly uneventful silence has followed. [. . .]
>
> "'The record company wants 'Criminal' junior, and Fiona doesn't offer that up,' Brion said. 'She wrote that stuff when she was 16, and she's now in her mid 20s. She's extremely intelligent and writes this beautiful, really emotionally involved stuff that's very musical—lots of chord changes, very involved melodies, intensely detailed lyrics. It's just not the obvious easy sell to them.'"

Apple's fans were a determined bunch and did not take well to the gatekeeping label's efforts to prevent her music from succeeding or failing on its own merits. So they took things into their own hands, first launching the FreeFiona.com website, which pled their case to Epic's executives:

> To: Sony Music
> We, the fans of Fiona Apple, are very upset with your company's decision not to release "Extraordinary Machine," which has been complete since May of 2003. As you can interpret from the number of signatures and the comments that follow, there are many

people who anxiously await this release. Please release Fiona Apple's "Extraordinary Machine."

Sincerely,
The Undersigned

Over thirty-seven thousand fans signed the petition, while the site's author, Dave Muscato, became an unofficial spokesperson for her frustrated fan base. "All the major labels have these researchers who supposedly study what everyone wants to listen to and what we want," Muscato told the *St. Petersburg Times* in a February 2005 report, "but they're wrong. All they know is that pop and hip-hop sell the most. Unfortunately, it's not what everyone wants. They shouldn't make those decisions for all of us. There is so much wonderful music out there that we don't have access to because major labels keep feeding us the same things."

The word about Apple's predicament and Sony's apparent heavy-handedness began to spread and the traditional media picked up on it. The *San Francisco Chronicle* columnist Mark Morford voiced her fans' frustrations, and castigated Sony in a March 2005 column:

"'Extraordinary Machine' is an album that Apple finished over *two years ago*, but which was quickly shelved by the sad corporate drones over at Sony because they didn't 'hear a single' and because it doesn't sound exactly like Norah Jones and because they're, well, corporate drones. They dictate cultural tastes based on relatively narrow and often deeply ignorant criteria related to marketing and money and fear of the new and the different. This is what they do.

"In other words, it was shelved because it's different, unique, a little eccentric, all bells and oompah horns and strings and oddly lovely circuslike arrangements, and you as the co-opted overmarketed oversold listening audience can't really handle anything like that, anything challenging or interesting or distinctive or deeply cool or lacking in prepackaged backbeats that sound just like Kelly Clarkson or maybe 'American Idiot,' even if it comes from a stupendously talented world-class Grammy-winning artist. Right? Isn't that you? Doesn't matter. This is what they believe."

By then, more tracks from the unreleased album were leaked. A Seattle DJ started playing tracks from a bootleg version, and the songs were soon being traded furiously on file-sharing networks. Better-quality versions of some of those tracks were subsequently leaked, and the work received a positive critical response.

In other words, fans were listening to Apple's music, music reviewers were reviewing it, and the record label sat by the wayside, utterly irrelevant to the process. On August 15, 2005, Sony Epic announced that the album would, indeed, be released, and set an October 4 release date. Apple had a new producer, Mike Elizondo, and she later claimed that it was *she* who halted the project, not the label. *Entertainment Weekly* reported on its website in September, 2005:

> "The short version of what really happened, as Apple told *Entertainment Weekly*'s Karen Valby, is that she shelved the album herself; that when she decided to rerecord the tracks with Elizondo, Epic balked; and that, facing the prospect of song-by-song scrutiny from Epic over the rerecording, she quit the sessions altogether. 'So where everybody thinks [Epic] shelved the album, that is actually when I just said, "I quit,"' Apple told Valby. 'It was the only thing I thought I could do.' In March, when unknown fans leaked the Brion version to the Internet in an apparent effort to prod the label to release the album, Apple said, 'I started feeling guilty, because it wasn't the truth. The album hadn't really been shelved. What was I going to do, tell all *these people* to stop, tell them that I had done the quitting? But I quit because I felt that what was going to happen was what they thought was already happening.'"

Nevertheless, the fact remained that the sustained fan effort on behalf of the record convinced Sony Epic to fork over cash for a rerecording of the album and it was finally released that October. Its first-week sales made it Apple's first top-ten album, though sales tapered off quickly. Even then, despite the lack of any hit singles (as the label had argued all along), the album went on to receive "gold" certification, or 500,000 copies sold, and earned her a Grammy nomination. "It was very admirable she has this amazing core of fans," Elizondo told *Billboard* in August 2005. "The way they interpreted it was, the label isn't putting out her record, so we're going to do it for her."

All Fiona Apple's fans needed was the internet. Their petition ensured that Epic executives were aware of the fan demand for the album and their persistence inspired stories in the traditional media. Meanwhile, file-sharing networks allowed her fans to distribute and essentially "publish" the album without the label's permission—or Apple's, for that matter. With the power of the medium harnessed, the very real threat of being bypassed and rendered irrelevant spurred Sony Epic to provide the resources to finish and release the album. The company had been forced to act, influenced by a bunch of fanboys and fangirls.

Influencing gatekeepers isn't just for fans of pop culture—it's big business for big business as well. With the advent of twenty-four-hour business cable networks like CNBC, Bloomberg TV, and Fox Business News, companies are building five-figure in-house TV studios to push their PR into the media, as *Money Management Executive* noted in its September 11, 2006, edition. "In-house studios are more economical than print advertisements and are very time effective," the article stated. "Additionally, they are a great way for firms not close to a television studio to get their name out and their voice heard. It's the perfect way to reach thousands more people. It is literally a billboard, as the company's name is usually situated behind the interviewee."

The political world is actually way ahead of the business community in this sense. While it may not have been the first to do so, the conservative Heritage Foundation think tank is a pioneer in building a state-of-the-art media operation to blast its work into the media and political worlds in an effort to influence key political battles. A profile of Heritage on the *Media Transparency* website reads:

> "According to one analysis of Heritage Foundation operations, the 'delivery system consists of four marketing divisions: Public

Relations markets ideas to the media and the public; Government Relations to Congress, the Executive branch, and government agencies; Academic Relations to the university community, Resource Bank institutions (including state think tanks), and the international conservative network; and Corporate Relations to business and trades.' [. . .]

"As effective, timely and influential as Heritage has been in marketing its policy analyses and recommendations, it does not stop with the mere production and dissemination of its policy products to officials and journalists. Indeed, as Stuart Butler, Vice President of Domestic and Economic Policy at Heritage, acknowledged, 'The unique thing we have done is combine the serious, high-quality research of a "traditional think tank" like the Hoover Institution or Brookings Institution with the intense marketing and *"issue management" capabilities of an activist organization.'"* [emphasis added]

In other words, producing solid research is not sufficient, in and of itself, to effectively influence the public debate. A report does no good if it sits on the shelf. The best ideas are irrelevant without the ability to communicate them to the media and government gatekeepers. And Heritage's operation is the gold standard. Eric Alterman described their operation in his seminal book *What Liberal Media?* (2003) and showed how they are focused like a laser not on the broader public but on those people who ultimately reach the broader public. In other words, they're aiming to influence the most influential people—the gatekeepers:

"Heritage computers are stocked with the names of over 3,500 journalists, organized by specialty. Every Heritage study goes out with a synopsis to those who might be interested; every study is turned into an op-ed piece, distributed by the Heritage Features Syndicate, to newspapers that wish to publish them. Heritage has two state-of-the-art television studios in its offices. Its Lehrman Auditorium is equipped with an advanced communications system for live feeds to TV and radio networks. 'Our targets are the policymakers and the opinion-making elite,' said [Heritage Vice President Burton] Pines. 'Not the public. The public gets it from them.' Heritage provides lawmakers and talk-show guests with colored index cards stating conservative positions in pithy phrases on every imaginable issue. According to Heritage's 'vice president for information marketing,' these cards have been 'wildly successful' with Republicans in Congress for media appearances. They are also a big help for conservative pundits on television, who otherwise would risk embarrassment due to how ill-informed they are on a variety of issues about which they are called upon to argue."

During 2001, Heritage was cited in 159 news items in eighty-one publications, or better than once every three days, according to a study published in the *Journal for Critical Education Policy Studies*. Heritage-penned op-ed pieces were distributed in high-circulation newspapers, and Heritage fellows offered the conservative viewpoint on education policy on television shows. Without its marketing operation, little of this would have been possible. Power indeed stems from the wielding of media to influence the gatekeepers, and on this front, Heritage has few parallels.

Many organizations have followed Heritage's lead. The Republican National Committee built its TV studio in the early 1990s. The Democratic National Committee made a television studio a key addition to its 2003 headquarters redesign, a decade after their Republican foes had done so. The Center for American Progress, a progressive think tank patterned after Heritage, has copied its conservative counterpart's media plans. Other similar organizations have followed suit.

Yet television studios are expensive affairs, out of reach of the average person. It doesn't matter. With technology leveling the media playing field, smaller organizations and individuals can use the internet to promote their messages and actions to a broader audience, targeting and influencing the gatekeepers. The power that so few media gatekeepers monopolized in years past is undergoing radical decentralization, with power devolving to the masses and those who learn to most effectively wield these new media tools to fight for change.

But before we confront the gatekeepers, we must first understand that leaders are not promoted or ordained. We now live in a rapidly evolving entrepreneurial age, and so the first rule is that we must speak our mind, follow our heart, and question all authority. We cannot wait to get permission before we act.

CHAPTER 2

MOBILIZE

Take charge of your message, your strategy, and your effectiveness. Don't wait for orders—seek out your own fellow troops, join or start networks, and be a catalyst for change. Find creative ways to get the word out, in new and unexpected venues, tailored to your local conditions and audience. Above all, be a leader who seeks out others and creates a partnership of leaders.

It was a race that surveys showed Ben Affleck would have lost three to one. Actor-director Affleck was among several potential Democratic candidates tested against the Republican U.S. senator George Allen in Virginia for his 2006 reelection race. None fared well. Allen seemed unbeatable. Word among insiders was that Allen might be headed to the White House in 2008.

The Democratic Party of Virginia looked around and settled on Harris Miller, a lobbyist who had never been elected to public office before. The only time he ran—for a House seat from Virginia in 1984—he had lost. Marc Fisher, a columnist for the *Washington Post*, didn't mince words in describing Miller in a May 30, 2006, column: "Miller is a Republican strategist's dream opponent. He's as charismatic as a toaster, wonkier than Al Gore and as proudly liberal as Al Franken. And at just about the very worst time to be one, he's a *lobbyist*."

The lobbyist comment was particularly relevant because months earlier a scandal surrounding the Republican lobbyist Jack Abramoff had culminated in convictions for him, a congressman, three Bush administration officials, and at least seven others. Miller wasn't just any ordinary lobbyist, either; he was president of the International Technology Association of America, an ardent proponent of outsourcing IT work and recruiting foreigners to fill American jobs, making him anathema to labor unions. The AFL-CIO Executive Director Michael Gildea issued a letter claiming Miller was "truly one of the bad guys. Over and over again on core issues like trade, immigration, overtime protections and privatization of federal jobs, he's not only been on the wrong side, he's been galvanizing corporate efforts against us."

Nevertheless, the Democratic establishment in Virginia lined up behind Miller, who was a business associate of the former popular Democratic governor Mark Warner.

Fund-raising began, and a desultory campaign cranked up.

A lot of progressive bloggers, myself included, were hoping for a better candidate who could help Democrats take the Senate majority in 2006. Then one day a sharp-eyed reader sent me an interview with a former Republican named James H. Webb from the October 30, 2005, edition of the *San Diego Union-Tribune*. Webb was a decorated marine in Vietnam, a former secretary of the navy under Ronald Reagan, an author of seven books, and an early opponent of the Iraq war. But it was the very last question and answer that stood out: Asked if he had considered running for office, Webb said, "I have been talking to people about running for the Senate next year against George Allen, as a Democrat from Virginia. I have a very good life. I'm not sure that I'm going to do that or not but I have been talking to people." I immediately blogged it on *Daily Kos*.

On the other side of the country, Lowell Feld of Virginia, the chief blogger on the progressive blog *Raising Kaine*, saw the *Daily Kos* post and was also intrigued by Webb's comments. More than intrigued, in fact. He was positively excited at the prospect of a Democratic candidate with military credentials who opposed the Iraq war. And he was hopeful that a candidate like Webb might help fuel the Democratic resurgence that had made major inroads in his state in recent years.

Virginia, the home of the former capital of the Confederate States of America, was in the midst of wrenching change. It was being torn in half between its southern portion—with its "deep South" traditional culture—and the fast-growing, tech- and government-centric Northern Virginia, clustered around cosmopolitan Washington, D.C. As a state with a moderate tradition, Virginia had experienced the rise of ideologically rigid Republicans to office, first with George Allen's election as governor in 1993, then with the 1997 election of his successor, James Gilmore, and with GOP gains further down the ballot. In 1999, Republicans saw their first-ever majorities in both chambers of the state legislature. In 2000, Allen knocked off the incumbent Democrat, U.S. Sen. Chuck Robb, and the Virginia GOP appeared to be solidifying its power.

Yet in 2001, Mark Warner halted the Republican advance when he won the governorship back by focusing on rural Virginia, a territory Democrats routinely ceded to Republicans, concentrating instead on their traditional Northern Virginia urban base. Warner's victory was followed in 2005 by his more liberal lieutenant governor, Timothy Kaine, who won an unexpected race to succeed him, while Democrats also picked up seats in the state legislature.

But in the fall of 2005, Democrats couldn't offer up anyone better for that Senate race than Harris Miller. The state party kept its chin up, pointing to Kaine's upset win the previous year. "Tim's victory was a blow to conventional wisdom in Virginia," Kevin Griffis, spokesman for the Democratic Party of Virginia, told the *Washington Post* on December 4, 2005. "It's a good environment for Democrats right now. . . . Washington is a mess. We're going to have a good, credible candidate." Yet all the big names in the state had begged off. Warner had decided to run for president. Former lieutenant governor Donald S. Beyer said he wasn't interested. It just didn't look good for Democrats and optimism was hard to come by.

A January 2006 poll by *Rasmussen Reports* gave Allen a commanding thirty-point lead over Miller. *Rasmussen* had even polled another name being floated in some circles, Ben Affleck, who fared even worse, losing 62 percent to 20 percent in a December 2005 poll. Compounding the perceived folly of taking on the overwhelming favorite, the Allen campaign announced he had raised $6.82 million in 2005, entering 2006 with $6.2 million in the bank—a daunting sum to overcome.

Against such a backdrop, few pretended that Miller was anything but a sacrificial lamb. The state's previously ebullient grassroots and netroots Democratic activists, who'd been stoked by the two consecutive gubernatorial victories and state legislature gains, were forced to admit they lacked a credible challenger. Yet they believed Allen was vulnerable, only if a strong candidate could be found. This core of energized web-based activists had shaken up Virginia politics in recent years and they felt an unacceptable candidate was being foisted upon them. Their successes in the 2005 gubernatorial race left them hungry for more.

So when Lowell Feld saw the Webb quote in the San Diego paper, he didn't just blog about it. He ran with it. While winning the race remained unlikely, a credible and compelling potential candidate had suddenly emerged. It was time to draft him into the race.

Feld wasn't going to sit around and wait for someone else to take charge or lead the way. Feld Googled Webb's name, and the results were encouraging. In addition to his military pedigree and a string of critically and commercially successful books, Webb seemed to have the sort of judgment that was in short supply inside the Beltway.

In the September 4, 2002, edition of the *Washington Post*, the former navy secretary had written an impassioned and prescient op-ed criticizing the impending war on Iraq. The title itself was telling: "Heading for Trouble: Do We Really Want to Occupy Iraq for the Next 30 Years?" Coming from a then Republican former Reagan administration official, the op-ed was a gutsy—and well-written—argument against the Bush administration plans:

> "The issue before us is not simply whether the United States should end the regime of Saddam Hussein, but whether we as a nation are prepared to physically occupy territory in the Middle East for the next 30 to 50 years. Those who are pushing for a unilateral war in Iraq know full well that there is no exit strategy if we invade and stay. This reality was the genesis of a rift that goes back to the Gulf War itself, when neoconservatives were vocal in their calls for 'a MacArthurian regency in Baghdad.' Their expectation is that the United States would not only change Iraq's regime but also remain as a long-term occupation force in an attempt to reconstruct Iraqi society itself."

Pointing out the differences between the invasion of Japan led by Gen. Douglas MacArthur in 1945 and what was being discussed in the Bush White House regarding Iraq, Webb wrote: "In Japan, American occupation forces quickly became 50,000 friends. In Iraq, they would quickly become 50,000 terrorist targets."

Feld knew he had an excellent candidate in James Webb. If only he could persuade him to run, things could look up for Virginia Democrats. In an audacious move, Feld struck up an email correspondence with Webb, whose early interest in taking on Allen was weak, especially with a thirty-one-point deficit in the first poll of the potential contest. Undaunted, Feld proceeded to write a fateful post on his blog on December 20, 2005, titled "Draft James Webb," in which he gave progressives in Virginia reasons to back Webb:

> "This guy is extremely impressive: first in his class at the Marine Corps Officers Basic School in Quantico, Virginia; earned the Navy Cross, the Silver Star Medal, two Bronze Star Medals, and two Purple Hearts in Vietnam; has a JD from Georgetown University; has written six best-selling novels; has even won an Emmy Award as a journalist. Who wouldn't want THAT resume? Also, this is a man who has spoken out against the Iraq war at least since September 2002, when he asked the question, 'Do we really want to occupy Iraq for the next 30 years?' Smart guy!
>
> "Yes, James Webb used to be a Republican, but now he's a Democrat and several of us here at *Raising Kaine* believe he'd be a super-strong candidate against George Allen this coming November. Honestly, we feel that of all the names mentioned as potential Democratic senatorial candidates, James Webb would stand the best chance BY FAR of defeating George Allen, or at least of giving him a heck of a run for his money. [. . .]
>
> "So, how do we convince James Webb to throw his hat in the ring? For starters, we tell him how much *we want him to run*, we let him know how much *we'll HELP him if he runs*, we DRAFT him to run!"

In ten days, 563 people (340 of them Virginians) had signed the Draft Webb petition Feld posted online and had pledged $20,380 to his campaign if he entered the race. More important than that dollar sum—which was paltry in light of the astronomical costs of a Senate campaign—was a promise by 145 people to volunteer for Webb's campaign. These early recruits were energized and committed, the first foot soldiers in what would become a potent army of volunteers. By New Year's Day, the Draft-JamesWebb.com website went up.

Even more remarkable than those online efforts was the "intelligence briefing" Feld and his fellow draft organizers prepared for Webb, titled "Results of the Draft Effort." The report detailed the state of play in the Virginia Democratic Party, offering up the contact names of establishment players for Webb to start wooing, including those of some Miller supporters. The report also included intelligence on the strengths and weaknesses of Miller's campaign. When Miller officially announced his candidacy on January 10, 2006, the draft movement shifted to a new level of urgency, but Webb still was taking his time to make the big decision. On January 18, Feld ran a poll on *Daily Kos* asking if people felt Webb should run—nine hundred people (98 percent of respondents) said he should, and that provided another shot in the arm for the draft organizers.

Then came some bad news when, on January 30, 2006, rumor spread that Webb wouldn't enter the race, creating a near-suicide watch among Feld and his coconspirators. By February 6, the draft website had collected ten thousand signatures and more than $40,000 in pledges. The next day, Webb finally spoke out and announced that he would, indeed, be a candidate. As he later told Feld and Nathan Wilcox for their book, *Netroots Rising*, "Seeing the spontaneous enthusiasm of the 'draft' movement was a very strong motivator for me, particularly as one who had never run for office, and would be running as a Democrat after having served in the Reagan administration."

While the Virginia and national netroots cheered Webb's entry into the race, the establishment media snickered. "Well, Jim Webb is not—at the moment—consulting me on his decision. His candidacy seems to me to be largely based on a group of persistent online activists rather than any real interest in the contest by Webb himself," wrote the *Washington Post* political reporter Chris Cillizza on February 6. "I think Harris Miller (and his deep pockets) is the likely nominee. Miller isn't likely to beat

Allen, who remains extremely popular in the Commonwealth, but may do something more important for the Democratic Party: keep Allen occupied through November."

John J. Miller of the conservative *National Review* was similarly unimpressed, writing on March 20: "Democrats Harris Miller and James Webb will duke it out in a June primary to take on Republican senator and presidential wannabe George Allen. Miller probably will have a money advantage but may suffer from his background as a lobbyist, in a year when voters look ready to react against influence peddling; Webb is a recent convert to the party who may have troubling [sic] winning over Democratic loyalists. No matter who prevails, it will be tough for either man to defeat Allen. Likely Republican Retention."

While a few pundits acknowledged that Webb could make Allen sweat, the head-to-head matchup was dismissed as a long shot because Webb first had to beat Miller, who had begun digging in his heels for a tough contested primary. But Webb wasn't starting from scratch—he was supported by a draft movement already transitioning into a campaign force. As Webb advisor Steve Jarding told Feld and Wilcox, "With the netroots, there was an infrastructure"; the netroots "had some juice, had some experience."

The campaign immediately became a battle between the supposed Mark Warner–style pragmatic businessman Miller and Webb and his lifetime of national service. The potential weakness—and it was a big one—was that Webb had been a Republican. "The 60-year-old former Marine has a complicated résumé for die-hard Democratic voters to sort through," wrote the *Washington Post* in a March 8 story on the race. "Republican Capitol Hill staffer; Reagan administration official; supporter of Robb against Oliver L. North in the Senate campaign of 1994; supporter of Allen against Robb in the Senate campaign of 2000."

Rank-and-file primary voters harbored suspicions about Webb that were further reinforced when people found out that as navy secretary, Webb had opposed combat roles for women—a fact that became a key line of attack for the Miller campaign, attempting to undermine his opponent's party bona fides. "When we were fighting in the trenches to defeat George Bush and George Allen in 2000, you weren't just voting for them, you were endorsing them," Miller charged in a May 19 debate. Answering a later question, Miller pressed the attack, "When you welcome someone to the church, you don't necessarily invite them to be the choir director the next day."

Webb, for his part, spoke at length about his biography and record of service, but attacked Miller for giving contributions to Republican officials (including House Speaker Dennis Hastert) and pushing for job outsourcing while working as a lobbyist for the tech industry. At one point, he noted that Miller had been labeled the "AntiChrist of outsourcing," and at the end of the evening told Miller to "shut his mouth" so he could answer a question. (Ironically, the question was whether he would support Miller if Miller won the primary. Yes, he would.)

Without money, without a traditional organization, and without an experienced candidate, Webb's volunteer generals took charge, meshing old traditional field organizing with new tools and technology. Every time a Webb campaign appearance was scheduled, the *Raising Kaine* folks would drum up attention on their site, encouraging supporters to attend. After the event, they would report back with recaps, photos, and video, posting them on *Raising Kaine* and other blogs. The constant feeding of new information further ginned up buzz and excitement about Webb and his candidacy.

In the world of traditional politics, these so-called amateurs were considered small fry. While Miller may not have been a mesmerizing candidate, he had plenty of money and access to large establishment donors who could outspend Webb's cadre of grassroots volunteers and bloggers. While Webb workers scrounged up the ten thousand signatures to get their guy on the ballot, Miller acquired them at $0.75 a pop. While Webb volunteers literally created and printed out their own flyers to pass out, Miller had professional direct-mail people take care of his literature. While Webb didn't run a single television ad, Miller dumped over $1 million into television ads featuring images of Webb and Ronald Reagan.

But Webb's volunteers had advantages Miller's hired hands could never match. Their large numbers proved to Democratic voters that the Webb campaign was organized and energized. Webb volunteers depended on person-to-person contact to educate voters about his candidacy. They manned booths at fairs, participated in parades, and cleverly trailed Miller's campaign operation to pass out their own pro-Webb literature behind the paid Miller staffers. And they did this all at their own initiative, without permission or guidance from the campaign.

Inspired by the local Webb operation and the momentum that Webb was building on the ground, national Democrats enthusiastically began to hop on the bandwagon. On May 11, Senate Minority Leader Harry Reid and many of his Democratic colleagues in the Senate, including Dick Durbin of Illinois, Chris Dodd of Connecticut, Ken Salazar of Colorado, and Tim Johnson of South Dakota, announced their support of Webb. Former senators Tom Daschle of South Dakota and Max Cleland of Georgia followed suit. On June 8, Sen. Chuck Schumer of New York, the head of the Democratic Senatorial Campaign Committee (DSCC), took the controversial step of wading into the primary to pick sides—the sort of outside interference that normally raises hackles among party activists. But at least in this case, the DSCC was siding with the insurgents. The fallout was minimal—the cancellation of at least one DSCC fund-raiser by a big-money donor in Virginia and harsh words from some top state Democrats. "They've dug a hole that was unnecessary," Donald Beyer, the former lieutenant governor, told the *Washington Post* on June 13. "If Harris wins, they are going to look ridiculous. They will have irritated an awful lot of people."

Schumer, for his part, realized the emerging influence of the netroots. He reached out to some top bloggers, asking whether his involvement was warranted, signaling that he was more concerned about angering the party's netroots activists fueling Webb's campaign than he was about antagonizing a few big-money donors. This concern at top levels of the party about grassroots and netroots reaction was a testament to the power of activists like Feld and his fellows.

In the weeks leading up to the primary day, supporters canvassed, called, knocked on doors, blogged, and emailed in an effort to put Webb over the top. Tensions mounted, evidenced by the confrontational May 19 debate, as it became clear that the wealthy, establishment-chosen candidate might actually run the risk of losing to a draftee handpicked by dissatisfied—and self-directed—Democrats. These grassroots activists were no longer willing to suffer through a primary election with second-rate candidates ordained by the party establishment.

By Election Day on June 13, Miller had spent $1.7 million in the race, nearly three times Webb's $600,000. Yet that money, and all the advertising and mail and professional organization it bought, wasn't enough to overcome the efforts of the self-organizing generals who had identified, drafted, promoted, briefed, and campaigned for their candidate. Their word-of-mouth guerrilla operation garnered 53.5 percent of the vote for Webb to Miller's 46.5 percent, giving people-powered Democratic activists one of their three major primary victories in 2006.

At the end of the day, it was a story about people taking charge, being their own generals, and bucking the conventional wisdom of the politicos and the pundits. In today's world, there's no reason anyone should whine or complain that they are being shut out of the system. The tools are available to mount credible challenges to even the most entrenched power. Such efforts will always be lacking in resources, and will mostly face well-funded, establishment foes, but innovative tactics and smart use of money and technology can carry the day. Taking charge and rallying others to your cause can be a catalyst for change.

RAISE AN ARMY

In April 2000, Eli Pariser was all of nineteen years old and already a college graduate, employed as an IT worker at a Boston nonprofit, when he flirted with direct street action at a protest against the International Monetary Fund in Washington, D.C. After a few hours of dealing with cops, he had an epiphany. "All of a sudden, I realized that the scripted confrontation of attacking and antagonizing them wasn't going to get us anywhere," Pariser told *Mother Jones* magazine in a May 2003 interview. "It changed the way I was thinking, tactically."

That lesson was still on his mind when he woke up on September 12, 2001, and fired off an email to a bunch of friends, asking them to contact legislators and urge a nonmilitary response to the horrors of the previous day. He was spurred to action but didn't head for the streets. Little did he know what that solitary email would spawn.

Within days, he got hundreds of responses in his inbox. By September 14, he and a friend set the website 9-11peace.org on Pariser's server, calling for "moderation and restraint," and posted a petition that read, in part:

> "We implore the powers that be to use, wherever possible, international judicial institutions and international human rights law to bring to justice those responsible for the attacks, rather than the instruments of war, violence or destruction."

Pariser asked people to "sign" it, collecting their email addresses in the process. The email and the link to the website made their way around the world and back. What had begun as a small gesture of frustration had gone "viral," with thousands of similarly frustrated recipients happy to forward the petition to their email lists, exponentially spreading the email around the globe. Within a week, 120,000 people in 190 countries signed the petition. Pariser's server was about to crash.

Less than a month after 9/11, Pariser had half a million petition signers tucked in his server—three thousand pages' worth—which he printed and sent to the White House, to 10 Downing Street in London, to the United Nations, and to the NATO headquarters in Brussels. None of that seemed to have much of an effect, but the spontaneous project bred something much bigger.

Across the country in Berkeley, California, Wes Boyd and Joan Blades, the couple who had launched MoveOn.org in 1998 to get the nation beyond the Bill Clinton impeachment madness, watched Pariser's website traffic with interest. MoveOn had its own half a million email addresses, so Boyd contacted Pariser to see if they could join forces. "Eli was in the same place as we were when we got started," Boyd told *Mother Jones*. "We got in touch and said, 'Can we help?' " They merged that fall, effectively doubling their respective operations. Pariser was named executive director of MoveOn and Boyd, Blades, and Pariser went on to build one of the most effective progressive organizations on the political scene today.

Pariser's effort hadn't required much in the way of money or marketing. He used technology at his disposal, available in his small apartment. By tapping into a latent market need, he was able to set off a chain reaction. What's more, each one of those individuals signing and forwarding that petition also took it upon themselves to step up and lend voice and effort to the cause.

Bothering friends, family, and coworkers with what amounted to political spam took some courage, as did urging military restraint at a time when the country was eager to lash out in anger at the perpetrators of the 9/11 attacks. Yet change isn't generated by the timid and the temperate, but by the bold and passionate. Pariser did not develop a ten-point plan and implement it—he acted from his gut and from his deep convictions and found half a million allies online.

From that improbable beginning, MoveOn.org went on to become a political behemoth. In the 2003–2004 election cycle, the group raised a whopping $180 million from its members for political candidates. In the 2006 campaign cycle, its volunteers used "virtual phonebanking" software to make 7 million phone calls, organized seventy-five hundred house parties and six thousand in-district events, raised and spent $25 million targeting House races, and raised millions more for individual candidates. The money was a significant development for a movement that had difficulty raising the funds needed to beat back a dominant and well-funded conservative juggernaut. "In 2000 we raised almost $2 million in small contributions averaging $35," MoveOn's Joan Blades told *AlterNet* in a June 25, 2004, profile. "That may not seem like a lot of money to most people, but it was a revolution in fundraising for campaigns from average citizens. That is exactly where we want to be going as a democracy."

Today soliciting online donations is standard practice for progressive organizations, candidates, and the Democratic Party itself. But that was certainly not the case when MoveOn successfully pioneered the tactic.

If Eli Pariser, Joan Blades, and Wes Boyd brought people together for a common cause online, Gina Cooper did something equally innovative and significant—she took an online community of progressive bloggers seeking change and brought them face-to-face *offline*.

In late 2004, a few *Daily Kos* community members—led by a Unitarian minister with the screen name "Pastor Dan"—were busy hatching a plan to organize a large get-together for the community in a physical space. As gratifying as it was for Democratic activists to find each other on sites like *Daily Kos*, we craved something more—to meet in person and confirm that yes, we were indeed real people and not just electrons on a monitor. Community members were constantly organizing impromptu "meetups" around the country to socialize and organize, but this new effort aimed for something bigger, much bigger—a national get-together for the entire blogging community.

As the scope of the project grew, Pastor Dan was unable to juggle his day job as a minister with the demands of the expanding conference, so he begged off the project. In stepped Gina Cooper, a Memphis public school science teacher who was about to move to Northern California and who, being jobless in those days, had a little extra time on her hands. Raised by her sister as a southern Republican (she never knew her father and her mother died of lung cancer when she was ten), Cooper bucked not just her region's politics but her family's traditions to become a fierce progressive. She also thought big, and as her plans expanded far beyond the initial scope of the project, she was forced to postpone the conference from its original debut in 2005 and instead set her sight for Las Vegas from June 8–11, 2006.

Of course, dealing with a classroom full of surly teenagers didn't prepare her for planning a major blogger conference with hundreds of adults. Or maybe it did. She navigated the obstacles of blogger egos, selfish interest groups ("Where is the panel on *my* issue?"), a lack of supplies and funds, demanding conference hall labor unions, and an impossible-to-please audience. Registrations were open early but few signed up, with some people unsure it would be worth their while and others skeptical that the conference would even take place. I granted use of my "Kos" moniker to the conference, and it was dubbed "YearlyKos." The grander and more ambitious Cooper's plans became, the more I privately fretted that the whole thing would crash and burn, tarnishing my brand by association.

But I had always preached the importance of people stepping up and being allowed to prove themselves, so I suppressed those feelings of panic. I asked myself: What was the worst that could happen? An impossibly ambitious project would be stillborn and a few people would snicker at our failure. In other words, nothing of real consequence. Measured against the potential payoff, it was actually an easy call.

But those early months were tough, especially for Cooper. Without experience in conference management she had difficulty gaining traction. Money was hard to come by. And while the progressive movement was filled with people chattering about the need to "fund the progressive infrastructure," it seemed like all the money was going to the same old ineffective organizations that had already screwed things up, or new ones run by the same well-connected players. Donors consistently slammed metaphorical doors in her face. A few small grants—one from MoveOn, the other from Silicon Valley donors Deborah and Andy Rappaport— provided some seed money, as did the incessant hustling on *Daily Kos* via auctions and good ol'-fashioned begging. While the affiliation with *Daily Kos* gave the conference some credibility, it really wasn't much. At the time of conference planning, the site was best known for backing a bunch of Democratic candidates, most of whom, like Howard Dean, had lost. There was little reason for anyone to take us seriously.

But Cooper was undaunted. She was looking for a few good volunteers, and in Nolan Treadway she found a particularly rare one, a volunteer with relevant experience. Treadway worked at a hotel booking large conferences and was eager to get politically involved, especially after the demoralizing defeat of the 2004 elections. Treadway tried to join a local activist group, but didn't feel welcomed. "While I enjoyed the experience, I always felt like a bit of an outsider," he told me. "I'd never knocked on a door, I'd spent all of one afternoon on the phone for Kerry. Lots of these people had been with Howard Dean from the start and been to Iowa for him or to Nevada for Kerry. I had none of these skills to offer to the group." So a few months later, when he heard about the efforts to organize a conference, he finally had an opportunity to match his skills with a cause he believed in. In no time at all, he was charged with finding a venue for the conference.

With Treadway and dozens of other committed volunteers pitching in, things started moving. The conference received a solid boost on January 3, 2006, when Senate Minority Leader Harry Reid, the highest-ranking elected Democrat in the land, agreed to be the keynote speaker. It helped that the conference would be in Las Vegas and that Reid's home state is Nevada, but it was still a coup for the fledging organization desperate for credibility. Soon, other high-profile speakers came aboard, such as Virginia Gov. Mark Warner and U.S. Sen. Barbara Boxer of California.

With an increasingly impressive speakers list, registrations began to stream in, and with the registrations came a last-minute flood of sponsors. Yet the organizers often felt they were in over their heads. Even Treadway, with his experience booking conferences, found himself in unfamiliar territory: "I've often joked that from the moment that I signed the contract I was getting further away from things I knew how to do and closer to things I had no idea how to pull off."

In March 2006, with the conference three months away, Cooper and Treadway sat across from each other at a bar, apprehensive about their progress. "Is this really going to happen?" Treadway asked Cooper. "If we are going to pull the kill switch, now is the time." They didn't pull the switch, but simply considering the possibility seemed to have put them at peace.

I arrived in Las Vegas that June expecting our "conference" to be tucked away in a couple of meeting rooms past the vending machine and around the corner from the ice machines at a run-down, Howard Johnson–like hotel. Instead, Cooper and her army of volunteers had managed to stage a shockingly top-notch production, complete with one thousand attendees and 250 journalists from all over the world. Where I had once worried that the conference might damage my reputation, I was forced to spend the weekend redirecting praise from myself to those who had actually put it together ("What do you mean you had nothing to do with it? Your name is on it!").

The entire D.C. political press seemed to have descended on the conference, particularly the second day, after colleagues sent word back to their newsrooms that the conference had legitimate news value. Sure, many of their news reports mocked the hotel the penny-pinching conference had chosen as its locale, the aging Riviera Hotel and Casino on the outskirts of the Vegas Strip. Nonetheless, observers marveled at what a bunch of amateur volunteers had managed to pull off, and how the sessions, the speakers, the setups, and the schedule compared with the best of the professionally managed and run conventions.

Heartened by the success of that first convention, Cooper went on to dream even bigger for the next year. The 2007 YearlyKos convention took place at the cavernous McCormick Place in Chicago August 2–5. This time, attendance went up to fifteen hundred and was headlined by a Democratic presidential candidate forum that included all the top candidates, including Barack Obama, Hillary Clinton, John Edwards, Bill Richardson, and Chris Dodd.

In 2008, the conference outgrew its humble beginnings as a spin-off of the *Daily Kos* community and rebranded itself as Netroots Nation, to better represent the vibrant diversity of a progressive netroots that is far bigger than my site's little corner of it. They may not be grizzled veterans just yet, but the conference organizers have professionalized their operation, adding more paid staff, and learning from each conference as they continue building what is still quite the unlikely organization.

The examples of Eli Pariser and Gina Cooper illustrate the power of networks, of bringing people with various skills, initiative, and drive to build something larger than them. They also show that, with enough initiative and drive, we can become "professionals" overnight. Pariser didn't go to school to learn how to mobilize a million people to try and stop a war, and Cooper didn't have any special training to learn how to bring a thousand people at a convention to push for change, but both of them did just that, and did it extremely well. With that kind of stepping-up-to-the-plate mentality, and with the tools of new technologies, we can connect with like-minded people, we can join together and mobilize, we can set up conventions and strategize, and, most of all, we can build an army to effect change.

DON'T WAIT FOR AUTHORIZATION

Thomas Jefferson had no business writing the Declaration of Independence. He was an aristocratic planter and attorney by trade, with no professional background in writing. Neither should he have designed Monticello or founded the University of Virginia, invented the swivel chair or created the Library of Congress.

Charles Darwin was unqualified to put forth a theory of evolution that shook the world to its moral foundations. He was a medical school dropout who reluctantly took orders for the Anglican priesthood at his father's insistence; his enthusiasm as a self-taught naturalist was spurred by his devotion to attending competitive beetle races when he should have been in class.

Benjamin Franklin was an author and printer. By all rights, he was pathetically underqualified to found a nation, form America's first public libraries and fire departments, advance understanding of electricity, or invent lightning rods, bifocals, stoves, or odometers.

The world is often changed most radically by people who refuse to "know their place." So-called amateurs who refuse to rein in their curiosity or acknowledge areas of "expertise" have made specialized gatekeepers nervous, scornful, and defensive since time immemorial. Upstarts who deny that there are boundaries to knowledge and action, who defiantly meld interests and tear down walls, are a constant challenge to the status quo. But they are often considered by gatekeepers to be at their most dangerous when they refuse to acknowledge that "professionals" should handle whatever business is at hand: providing information, creating art, debating policy—or criticizing the gatekeepers themselves.

Yet we have always honored the polymath, the Renaissance man. Witness the glorification of Jefferson, Franklin, and Darwin. Or the celebration of the multitalented Winston Churchill: soldier, politician, Nobel Prize–winning historian, painter. Or Leonardo da Vinci, himself the prototype of the fabled "Renaissance man": painter, sculptor, inventor, anatomist, and architect.

Aside from the fact that they were born with natural gifts, there is a less obvious lesson to draw from their successes: They didn't sit around and wait for authorization to explore their talents and expand their horizons. They didn't wait to be properly accredited to venture into new fields. Rather, they let their interests and instincts guide their exploration.

But somewhere along the way, specialization became a characteristic of modernity. We are expected to master and focus on our profession, with anything outside that core dismissed as hobbies—mere trifles to pass time, rather than worthy of being taken seriously. Thus astronomy enthusiasts who discover new comets using their own equipment or publicly available data from NASA and the European Space Agency are referred to as "astronomy hobbyists." "Real" astronomers may do the same thing but get paid for it. But if *Merriam-Webster* defines "astronomer" as "a person who is skilled in astronomy or who makes observations of celestial phenomena," then why append "hobbyist" to their work?

Over the past few centuries, our society became enamored with the notion of professionalism as people used university degrees, professional certifications, and institutional power to establish new gates keeping out the "amateurs" and "hobbyists." Rather than celebrate the Renaissance man, the culture created zones of exclusion around professions, silos for specialists.

The most dramatic shift in our culture in recent years has been the rise of the amateur, particularly tied to new technology. Wikipedia, for example, is a user-maintained web encyclopedia, where anyone can edit or create entries on any subject. The encyclopedia uses the collective power of its massive community to produce and police the quality of the content rather than depending on a handful of "experts." According to its own website, in early 2008, Wikipedia had seventy-five thousand contributors working on 9 million articles in 250 languages.

Bloggers have taken the media world by storm, shoving aside self-described "experts" in the technology, political, sports, and entertainment realms. Amateurs are flooding video-sharing sites like YouTube with content. Unpaid musicians post their own original material on websites created for that purpose or on MySpace or Facebook pages.

And the public consumes all such content and seems to remain unencumbered—and unimpressed—by quaint notions of "credentials." Yet this notion is clearly defended by the traditional gatekeepers, especially in the political establishment and institutionalized media. The conservative movement, through its think tanks like the Heritage Foundation, has turned the notion of credentialing on its head: They simply declare a generalist an expert and disseminate the material of the new "specialist" far and wide.

During the height of the congressional and White House debates on public education spending in 2001, three Heritage Foundation staffers told 2.2 million newspaper readers that federal funding for low-income public schools was a failure and that Americans should use taxpayer-funded vouchers for private schools. At the same time, the published articles provided virtually no information that would enable the reader to judge the qualifications of the Heritage authors—Jennifer Garrett, Krista Kafer, and Stuart Butler—not one of whom, it turns out, had ever formally studied education.

Kafer's case is illustrative. During 2001, Kafer was the Heritage Foundation's most cited source on education. She was credited in forty-seven news items, more than twice as often as the next most cited source. On the Heritage Foundation web page, she is presented as a "senior policy analyst, education" with "expertise [in] school choice, education standards and testing, charter schools, [and] federal education programs." In the news media during 2001, she was identified most often as an "education analyst" (fourteen times), a "policy analyst" (nine times) or simply "of the Heritage Foundation" (nineteen times). According to her Heritage biography and an article in *Roll Call* (April 28, 1997), Kafer graduated from the University of Colorado with a BA in history in 1994. She then worked for the Colorado chapter of the National Right to Life Committee, as well as for Rep. Dave McIntosh (R-IN) and Rep. Bob Schaffer (R-CO), and Sen. Bob Dole's 1996 presidential campaign. According to the *Washington Post* (April 2, 2001), she joined the Heritage Foundation in the spring of 2001. It appears that Kafer has never formally studied or worked in the field of education.

Now, Heritage would argue that Kafer should be judged not by her credentials, but by her knowledge base and the value of her educational research. And they'd be right. Heritage proved that with the proper access to the media, a layperson can be taken seriously and have an impact on a national debate. So in a world where everyone has access to democratizing media, anyone can—and should—have a voice in important debates regardless of formal credentials. The important thing is whether they know what they are talking—or writing—about. It is their knowledge, their insights, their analyses, their talent that are important, not their background or specialized training.

This, of course, doesn't sit well with established "experts" who occupy their positions because of their credentials. The *PC Magazine* columnist John Dvorak, no Luddite, wrote this on November 2, 2004:

> "Nobody wants to admit it, but the Web's natural ability to remove normal interpersonal structures that prevent society from falling into chaos is not a benefit to anyone. Information revolution notwithstanding, the Internet will prove to be the undoing of society and civilization as we know it. It may not happen today, but it will happen sooner than we think.
>
> "Blogs are now the easiest way to remake oneself, as the tools for their creation are fantastic and easy to use. They have emboldened a lot of otherwise shy people. This is the New Media at work, creating false personas that are pumped up by other phonies. Under the right circumstances, virtual lynch mobs emerge like swarms of locusts—individual bugs may be easy to squish, but a swarm is dangerous. I think these online mobs, where one or two troublemakers rile up the frustrated, are just as dangerous."

Writing a column in the September 4, 2004, edition of the *Washington Post*, David Broder, gatekeeper for the gatekeepers, wept at the prospect of nonprofessionals entering his profession:

> "When the Internet opened the door to scores of 'journalists' who had no allegiance at all to the skeptical and self-disciplined ethic of professional news gathering, the bars were already down in many old-line media organizations. That is how it happened that old pros such as Dan Rather and former *New York Times* editor Howell Raines got caught up in this fevered atmosphere and let their standards slip."

Chris McCoskey, a sports columnist for the *Detroit News*, ranted about some "clever dude in his pajamas" in a column on November 3, 2007:

"Bloggers and personal, non-journalistic Web sites are starting to tick me off. Look, I appreciate and respect that in America, everybody has an opinion, especially on sports. And I respect everybody's right to share their thoughts with anybody who happens to own a computer via blogs.

"But people, let's not confuse what random fans and wanna-be pundits are tossing out there with legitimate reporting. The line is getting way too blurry now between Internet noise and actual journalism. It's actually getting to the point now where some (too many) of the bloggers are using cyberspace to discredit the legitimate media. [. . .]

"Journalism employs trained professionals. We actually have to go to school for this stuff. We take our jobs seriously. There are rules and standards that we are beholden to. There are ethics involved."

Entire books have been written about this bloggers/journalists conflict, like Andrew Keen's *The Cult of the Amateur: How Today's Internet Is Killing Our Culture and Assaulting Our Economy*. Zeroing in on bloggers, Keen writes:

"Unfortunately, the internet is bloated with the hot air of these amateur journalists. Despite the size of their readership, even the A-List bloggers have no formal journalistic training. And, in fact, much of the real news their blogs contain has been lifted from (or aggregated from) the very news organizations they aim to replace.

"It is not surprising then that these prominent bloggers have no professional training in the collection of news. After all, who needs a degree in journalism to post a hyperlink on a Web site? Markos Moulitsas Zuniga, for example, the founder of *Daily Kos*, a left-leaning site, came to political blogging via the technology industry and the military."

First, Keen needs to be corrected since he failed to do his journalistic homework: My biography on the *Daily Kos* website says this: "Moulitsas earned two bachelor degrees at Northern Illinois University (1992–96), with majors in Philosophy, Journalism, and Political Science and a minor in German." Furthermore, some simple research would have revealed that I was editor in chief of my campus newspaper, the *Northern Star*, at Northern Illinois University, that I was a stringer for the *Chicago Tribune* for three years, and that I had focused much of my work in law school on media law. He might have found that I was hired by the *Guardian* of London to help cover the 2005 elections in the UK, where I filed journalistic news reports from all over England. Keen would also have found a fairly lengthy list of journalism awards I've won over the years. (And no, that's not impressive. Journalists are second only to Hollywood in handing out meaningless awards by the bucketful.)

Second, I know from my own experience that "journalism" isn't something that is taught; it's something that is *done*. I learned more about journalism from covering school board meetings in rural Illinois for the *Chicago Tribune* than I ever did in a classroom. I know that a journalism degree, like most degrees, is worth little more than the paper it's printed on, as is the "code of ethics" published by the Society of Professional Journalists. Yet too many "professionals" are invested in their degrees and certifications and credentials and awards as a way to try and keep people *out* of what they perceive to be their private territory, struggling to preserve the illusion that only certain *kinds* of people are allowed to speak up—or to each other—in our culture.

Yet our society is ignoring the experts, with people not only adapting to this brave new communication world but actively embracing it—much to the consternation of a shrinking pool of dead-enders like the former "culture critic" at the *New Republic*, Lee Siegel. "I love the idea of the amateur—that's what popular culture is all about," he told *New York* magazine in a January 13, 2008, interview promoting his Luddite polemic *Against the Machine*. "But what the Internet's doing is professionalizing everyone's amateuristic impulses. Everybody wants to jump into the big time and be recognized and 'go viral.' They're not taking the time to just have fun. There's so much caution, so much derivation."

Hilariously, this is the same "critic" who used his June 29, 2006, column in *TNR* to lecture the masses on baseball caps for signifying "a lazily defiant casualness"—a signal that apparently infuriated him to the point of homicide: "When I see someone wearing a baseball cap in a movie theater, I want them to bring back the guillotine." Yet, he told his *New York* magazine interviewer that what ticked him off was online responses to the fact that he faked his identity online and trashed critics. "I react very badly when mediocrity throws a tantrum of entitlement. And that's what those people were doing." Savor that for a moment—the ego, the sense of self-entitlement, the notion that "mediocrity" should be muzzled. In times past, Siegel could use his perch at the *New Republic* to pass judgment on the masses and there was little they could do in return. But the culture doesn't care much anymore. Siegel and his ilk are just other voices in a discussion in which everyone has a say, and more important, where everyone is judged on the merit of what they are saying, not on their supposed "qualifications" or formal training.

Louis Bayard, reviewing Siegel's book on *Salon*, properly summarized Siegel's plight. "Siegel may have liberal credentials, but he is making, at bottom, a conservative argument: in favor of gatekeepers and cultural elites, against the cacophony of untrammeled opinion."

The Siegels of the world will always rant that their brilliance isn't properly respected; it seems the only true acknowledgment of their worth would be if listeners would shut up and stick to listening—and cede the entire floor to them, the credentialed experts. Unfortunately for them, that is unlikely. The content of what is said is more important than who is saying it. Respect and authority are no longer awarded based on academic degrees or the sanction of the existing gatekeepers. They can now be garnered the old-fashioned way—by working for it day in and day out and earning it through merit.

CULTIVATE YOUR ALLIES

Joshua Micah Marshall didn't set out to establish a new kind of integrated journalism when he founded *Talking Points Memo* (TPM) and began blogging about politics and current events in the midst of the post–Florida recount debacle in November 2000. But that's where his instincts, his talents, and his courage eventually led him. By 2008 he had clearly established a powerful new model that showed great promise as a dynamic integrative medium—built largely on Marshall's ability to plug into today's interconnected media world and use a national network of journalists *and* regular citizens to collect information, connect the dots, and report the truth.

A history graduate from Princeton University, Marshall began working on a Ph.D. in American history at Brown University before tiring of the staid academic atmosphere, according to a far-ranging profile of his blogging empire in the September/October 2007 edition of *Columbia Journalism Review*. He then followed a path oddly familiar to pioneers in online media, bouncing between technology gigs—Marshall designed some websites for law firms, for example—and doing the occasional freelance journalism (online law firm newsletters, spin-off articles on free speech). Eventually he landed an associate editor position with the *American Prospect*, but arcane ideological arguments among staff made the job untenable.

He moved to D.C. in 1999 as the *Prospect's* capital correspondent in an effort to salvage the relationship with the magazine through distance, but that didn't work, and in November 2000 he began writing *Talking Points Memo*. Five months later, he quit the magazine to devote himself to freelancing and building out *TPM*, which he initially intended to use as a sort of business card or digital billboard to advertise his skills to potential clients. Yet those freelancing jobs failed to provide enough of a living to make it all worth his while. "Why, when I was really only marginally able to support myself, was I spending all of this time doing something that couldn't make any money?" he reported asking himself in the *CJR* interview.

Yet he hit the mother lode when, in late 2002, he helped bring down Senate Majority Leader Trent Lott after the Mississippi Republican praised the 1948 segregationist presidential campaign of Sen. Strom Thurmond (see chapter 3), boosting *TPM* traffic from eight thousand to twenty thousand page views each day. The larger readership was happy to chip in a few bucks to support the site. The higher traffic also made the site a magnet for advertisers and the blog became a more lucrative enterprise. By the end of 2004, the site was generating $10,000 per month from advertising, according to *CJR*.

In 2005, readers chipped in $40,000 to help him launch his new community site, *TPM Cafe*, and hire his first full-time employee. Later in the year, another fund-raising drive netted $80,000, allowing him to hire two new reporters and to create another site for his growing stable of web properties—*TPM Muckraker*, which focuses on investigative journalism. Since then, Marshall also started the wonky, campaign-driven *TPM Election Central*. His network is among the largest political web-based operations in the United States.

In many ways, Marshall is a prototype of seat-of-the-pants flying in the unknown new information world. He has served as a creator of new networks that others plug into, and yet his style of pulling together the work of others also reaches out and plugs into networks that existed before *TPM* started—most notably, traditional journalistic enterprises.

Marshall's success has been largely driven by designing his sites to serve as an aggregator and analyzer of often obscure facts dug up by others; certainly he's worked sources and done original reporting himself, but he's the first to admit he sees his role in the new medium as something different than pure original investigative journalism. His readers send him tips, often culled from small-town newspapers, and he and his staff follow up, expand the story—and credit the original news source.

One of Marshall's most remarkable triumphs was his team's dogged insistence, after looking at local newspapers in Little Rock and San Diego, that there was an emerging pattern of partisan-inspired firings of U.S. Attorneys by Bush's Department of Justice. Marshall and his team were ridiculed by traditional media outlets like *Time* magazine, where Jay Carney, the magazine's Washington bureau chief, dismissed it as a left-wing conspiracy:

> "It all makes perfect conspiratorial sense!
> "Except for one thing: in this case some liberals are seeing broad partisan conspiracies where none likely exist."

Undaunted, Marshall and his investigative team lauded the local newspaper coverage, contacted locals, praised the reporters, and fed the story until—finally—the story broke into the mainstream and led to an investigation of the firings by Congress.

Marshall's team was so instrumental in forcing the story into the mainstream that *CJR* claimed *TPM* "was almost single-handedly responsible for bringing the story of the fired U.S. Attorneys to a boil. Not only were the major dailies slow to pick up on the controversy, but a Capitol Hill staffer says that the House Judiciary Committee itself would have missed the firings' significance if not for the barrage of reports from Talking Points." Their coverage of this story was a 2007 winner of the Polk Award for Legal Reporting—the first time a blogger had won this prestigious journalism award (in any category).

The *TPM* stable also tracked closely the bribery scandal surrounding Duke Cunningham in San Diego, reported by Dean Calbreath of the *San Diego Union-Tribune*, among others. In examining *TPM's* role in publicizing the wrongdoing, *CJR* had this to say:

> "Calbreath and his colleagues have worked for two years on the interlocking scandals involving the now-jailed U.S. Representative Randy 'Duke' Cunningham and his defense-contractor friends. *TPM* has often commented on the *Union-Tribune's* coverage of those stories, and Calbreath says that *TPM's* posts, even when they don't appear to break news, still push the story forward. The site 'provides reporters with sources that might not be at the top of our radar screen,' he says. 'Being based in San Diego, I'm not a big reader of *The Hill*, for instance. But by reading *TPM*, I can have easy access to [*The Hill's*] pertinent articles. The commentary at *TPM*, meanwhile, poses important questions that we might not have thought of on our own.'
>
> "The original local news reporters were rewarded by recognition in a national blog, and *TPM* was rewarded with goodwill and access to local expertise. Readers would often join in the newsgathering effort, sending their own reports and tips to help fuel or flesh out a story. The synergy created by the mutual aid and ac-

knowledgement process also extends to Marshall's hiring of little-known writers of promise, and supplying them with a salary and byline with which to make their name.

"'Within *TPM* lies the DNA of the future of journalism,' Justin Rood, a former *TPM* reporter who now works for ABC News, told *CJR*. 'In terms of its relationship with its audience, its ability to advance stories incrementally and to give credit to other news organizations, and its ability to get the story to readers—it's been able to foster a real spirit of collaboration.'"

This spirit of collaboration runs through all effective activism in the digital era, from Lowell Feld's discovery of James Webb and starting an online movement to draft him, to MoveOn's powerful email list and Eli Pariser's petition, to Gina Cooper's ability to attract volunteers to make her convention dream a reality.

And in large part, drawing in collaborators to reach a critical mass depends on the crucial ability to articulate a vision that is shared, and to create a narrative with a story that inspires, motivates, and lays out a path to change. Leaders—and all of us are potential leaders—need to master the art of storytelling as a necessary tool in building an effective collaborative movement.

CHAPTER 3

SET THE NARRATIVE

Effective leaders draw people into their cause by creating powerful stories, with clear distinctions between good and evil, hero and villain. Instead of bemoaning the fact that Americans love their entertainment culture, political activists need to borrow Hollywood's proven methods to structure gripping narratives and compelling communication strategies. Making politics and causes participatory, exciting, and fun is key to sustaining citizen involvement.

nside the GOP," wrote *Hotline* editor Chuck Todd in August 2005, "there's a sense that if you put Ronald Reagan and George W. Bush in a blender, the resulting concoction would be George Allen."

As a former governor of Virginia and its incumbent senator, Allen was seen—in 2005 and 2006—as a leading contender for the Republican nomination for president in 2008. The *Weekly Standard* reported on October 2, 2006:

> "Throughout 2005, a *National Journal* 'insiders poll' named him the frontrunner for the nomination. . . . That November, *National Review* editor Richard Lowry opined that Allen 'perhaps has a better chance of winning the nomination than any other Republican.' This sentiment carried over into the summer of 2006, when the *American Spectator*'s David Holman wrote that 'a familiarity with George Allen explains his presidential contender status: notable biography, solid political record, and affable demeanor.' "

In other words, James Webb, fresh off his netroots-fueled Democratic primary victory over Harris Miller (see chapter 2) in June 2006, wasn't facing just your average, run-of-the-mill incumbent senator, a breed already tough to defeat given that more than 90 percent of incumbents win reelection. Webb, who had never been an elected official before, was going head-to-head with a Republican heavyweight who was busy scoping out a presidential run.

Allen was a strong campaigner with an enviable history of dramatic electoral wins under his belt. In the Virginia governor's race in 1993, he had overcome a twenty-nine-point deficit in the polls and a $1.5 million fund-raising disadvantage to defeat his Democratic opponent by a healthy seventeen points. In 2000, Allen was the only Republican in the country to unseat an incumbent Democratic senator, defeating Sen. Chuck Robb. Then he took his winning ways national, taking the helm of the National Republican Senatorial Committee and leading his party to a four-seat pickup in 2004. Making matters more difficult for Webb was the fact that Virginians had voted for George Bush 54 percent to 46 percent in 2004.

So confident was Allen of his presidential destiny that he spent inordinate amounts of time in New Hampshire and Iowa rather than tending to his reelection effort. Even as Webb was battling Miller in the Democratic primary, the *Washington Post* political columnist Chris Cillizza delivered the conventional wisdom in a March 8, 2006, online chat with readers:

> "Can either [Webb or Miller] make a general election against Allen competitive? In theory, yes. But, neither Webb nor Miller have any experience as statewide candidates while Allen is a proven vote-getter and begins the race with a massive cash advantage. I think the practical effect of Webb and Miller running is to keep Allen from maintaining an active national schedule as he contemplates a bid for president in 2008. At the moment an Allen loss seems extremely unlikely."

Progressive bloggers who helped push Webb to victory over Miller in the June primary were energized from that improbable win and had begun casting about for a narrative that would gain traction against the formidable incumbent.

At first, they jumped on Allen's out-of-state travels, as his presidential ambitions generated some good ammunition. During a visit to Iowa in 2006, he claimed to the assembled crowd, "I just wanted to make it clear to all of you all that I wanted to be born in Iowa." The midwestern crowds loved the pander, but it didn't play so well back home when his constituents caught wind of it. On another Iowa campaign swing, in Cedar Falls, Allen declared, "I made more decisions in half a day as governor than you

can make in a whole week in the Senate." While at a breakfast in Daven-
port, Allen lamented how the Senate was "too slow for me." The *New York Times* reporter Sheryl Gay Stolberg picked up on the Iowa swing and wrote on March 26, 2006, that Allen was "bored with life in the Senate," and quoted fellow Republican U.S. senator John Warner from Virginia issuing a warning, "George has got to pay attention." Bloggers ran with that story, helpfully offering to "forcefully retire" Allen so he could fulfill his lifelong dream of being an Iowan.

But that narrative—of a senator wanting to be president—didn't get much traction. People liked Allen, who racked up approval ratings of 63 percent in a September 2005 *Washington Post* poll. To defeat him, a more substantive narrative was needed than "he pandered to Iowans."

And then rather suddenly, a powerful story line gelled around the issue of bigotry and Allen's shady history on racial issues. On September 10, 2000, the *Richmond Times-Dispatch* had reported:

> "U.S. Senate candidate George Allen wears his conservative
> heart on the sleeve of his cowboy shirt and makes no bones about
> his commitment to law and order. Visitors to his old law office
> near downtown Charlottesville used to see a grim and graphic
> reminder of his view of criminals. Dangling from a ficus tree in
> the corner was a noose, a reminder that the Republican politician
> saw some justification in frontier justice."

There were other clues to Allen's views on race. At home, he had prominently displayed a Confederate flag. As a state legislator in the '80s, he'd opposed a state holiday in honor of the Reverend Martin Luther King Jr. As governor, he had decreed April as "Confederate Heritage Month" without even a passing condemnation of slavery. And when the city of Richmond commemorated the tennis star and local hero Arthur Ashe Jr., who was black, by erecting a statue on an avenue reserved for statues of Confederate war heroes, Confederate-flag-waving protesters disrupted the statue's dedication ceremony. Allen was conspicuous in his absence.

Then came the "macaca" incident. It was August 11, 2006, less than three months from Election Day, and Allen was campaigning in Breaks,

Virginia, when he decided to have some fun with a Webb volunteer who had been shadowing him for five days with a video camera, an Indian-American named S. R. Sidarth. With Sidarth's camera running, Allen addressed his all-white audience, "My friends, we're gonna run this campaign on positive, constructive ideas, and it's important that we motivate and inspire people for something." Then he turned to Sidarth's camera, pointed at him, grinning, and said:

> "This fellow over here, with the yellow shirt, macaca or whatever his name is, he's with my opponent, he's following us around everywhere. And it's just great, we're going places all over Virginia and he's having it on film and it's great to have you here and you show it to your [sic] opponent because he's never been there and probably will never come. [. . .] His [sic] opponent right now is actually with a bunch of Hollywood movie moguls. We care about fact, not fiction. So let's give a welcome to macaca here. Welcome to America and the real world of Virginia!"

The audience cheered and applauded Allen's bullying taunts, all of it captured on film by Sidarth. The fallout soon began.

Initially, the Allen campaign reacted to questions about the "macaca" remark by saying he meant to say "mohawk" — as in the hairstyle — though Sidarth didn't have one. Then he claimed he'd meant to call Sidarth "caca," which made even less sense. Then he insisted he'd made up the word. "Macaca," it turns out, is a genus of monkey found in countries ranging from northern Africa to Japan. It was also used as a slur by francophone Europeans against Africans. And lo and behold, it just so happened that Allen's grandmother was French Tunisian. In effect, Allen had called a young brown kid a "monkey" on camera for the world to see.

Sidarth had lived his entire life in Virginia, a possibility that clearly never crossed the minds of Allen or his audience members despite the growing sophistication of booming Northern Virginia. The Webb campaign jumped on the macaca slur, but used it to suggest to cosmopolitan Northern Virginians that Allen didn't consider them "real Virginians."

That narrative, however, was a very regional one, designed to generate votes in an area of the state rich with potential Democratic votes. But online, bloggers focused on the race aspect. Here was filmed proof of the racist Allen that they'd always suspected existed, the one who proudly displayed Confederate flags and opposed the MLK holiday.

The video became a YouTube sensation and ultimately made national news. Meanwhile, Allen was refusing to apologize as his campaign struggled to keep from being derailed by the controversy.

Two weeks later, as the macaca frenzy began showing signs of playing out, the *Nation* gave the story a needed boost by publishing a 1996 photo of Allen with several members of the Council of Conservative Citizens. The CCC was a white separatist organization born from the White Citizens Council during the civil rights era, an overt counterpart to the more secretive KKK. The group was often referred to as the "uptown Klan" or "a white-collar Klan" and the initials "CCC" were no coincidence. According to the *Nation*, even the Reagan speechwriter Peggy Noonan "declared that anyone involved with the CCC 'does not deserve to be in a leadership position in America.' "

Lowel Feld, by then working as the netroots coordinator for the Webb campaign, responded to the *Nation* piece by asking on his blog, "Is anybody out there still seriously arguing that George Allen isn't an outright racist?"

In late August, Mike Stark, a University of Virginia law student, a blogger, and an activist, confronted Allen at a campaign event at the school:

STARK: ". . . given what's been in the news, I think some of us at the law school have some other questions on our mind. Have you ever used the word 'nigger'?"

ALLEN: "Oh listen . . ."

STARK: "Have you?"

ALLEN: "No."

STARK: "You never have in your life?"

ALLEN: "No."

Allen's unequivocal denial came back to haunt him when *Salon* published allegations on September 24 from former colleagues and college classmates of Allen that suggested he had lied to Stark. A former football teammate of Allen's, Dr. Ken Shelton, claimed that Allen frequently used the "N" word, and came forward with one particularly hairy story taking place not long after the movie *The Godfather* was released in 1972, with its famous scene of vengeance where the severed head of a horse is placed in an enemy's bed:

> "Shelton said he also remembers a disturbing deer hunting trip with Allen on land that was owned by the family of Billy Lanahan, a wide receiver on the team. After they had killed a deer, Shelton said he remembers Allen asking Lanahan where the local black residents lived. Shelton said Allen then drove the three of them to that neighborhood with the severed head of the deer. 'He proceeded to take the doe's head and stuff it into a mailbox,' Shelton said."

Each discovery reinforced the narrative — George Allen is a racist — and further worked on establishing a conventional wisdom to that effect. At a September 18 debate in Tysons Corner, a local journalist asked Allen whether his Tunisian mother was Jewish. Allen went into a rage, attacking the questioner. "To be getting into what religion my mother is, I don't think it's relevant," he blustered. In a way, Allen was right, and he might've scored some points had he stopped there. But he didn't. He pressed his attack on the journalist, mocking her question, and then demanding she refrain from "making aspersions."

This was a stunning admission. To Allen, suggesting his mother was Jewish was "making aspersions." His violent reaction to the notion that he might have Jewish blood was frightening. After the debate, he admitted that perhaps he was part Jewish, but that he "still had a ham sandwich for lunch" and that his mother "made great pork chops." It was as if he feared that his friends at the CCC would turn their backs on him if they knew the truth about his heritage.

By the end of September, the narrative had become conventional wisdom: Sen. George Allen was a racist. Bloggers had set the framework by planting the seeds of the narrative, then stood back and let Allen's own behavior flesh it out, enthusiastically promoting each new revelation online. Allen's favorability numbers kept plummeting, and by Election Night the race was so tight that it was one of the last two Senate races called that night. When the last votes were counted, James Webb had done the impossible, beating Allen 49.6 percent to 49.2 percent, a difference of about nine thousand votes out of 2.3 million.

All stories, even fictional stories, have heroes and villains, and the best of them feature strong, memorable, and seemingly unbeatable villains — be it Darth Vader, Hannibal Lecter, or the Wicked Witch of the West. Indeed, you can't even begin to consider the hero until you have a villain. After all, there's no need to seek a savior if all's well in the world. As the film critic Roger Ebert once said, "Each film is only as good as its villain. Since the heroes and the gimmicks tend to repeat from film to film, only a great villain can transform a good try into a triumph." The filmmaker Alfred Hitchcock was even more direct: "The more successful the villain, the more successful the picture."

TARGET YOUR VILLAIN

It was the beginning of the 2004 Christmas season, so Fox News blowhard Bill O'Reilly needed a villain to boost his sagging holiday season ratings, when his 3 million viewers began to lose interest in news-related programs in favor of holiday shopping, parties, sports, and travel. O'Reilly hit upon the perfect enemy at the perfect time of year: secularists. And not just any secularists, but secularists so evil they wanted to destroy Christmas. Thus was born the now-annual "War on Christmas."

Or, to be more precise, reborn. O'Reilly was following in a long and hallowed holiday tradition of ultraconservatives using the "War on Christmas" stunt to scapegoat the villain du jour. The newly founded John Birch Society in the late 1950s had used exactly the same shtick against "Reds" to get a frenzied public relations boost and swell its anemic ranks, according to Michelle Goldberg, who did an overview of the history of the "War on Christmas" for *Salon* in November 2005:

> "In 1959, the recently formed John Birch Society issued an urgent alert: Christmas was under attack. In a JBS pamphlet titled 'There Goes Christmas?!' a writer named Hubert Kregeloh warned, 'One of the techniques now being applied by the Reds to weaken the pillar of religion in our country is the drive to take Christ out of Christmas—to denude the event of its religious meaning.' The central front in this perfidious assault was American department stores, where the 'Godless UN' was scheming to replace religious decorations with internationalist celebrations of universal brotherhood. [. . .]
>
> "The pamphlet called on all Americans to fight back by informing department stores that those with improper ornamentation wouldn't be getting their business."

But the Birchers weren't even the first to use this trick. *News Hounds* website reported on December 15, 2004, that Henry Ford's anti-Semitic 1921 tract "The International Jew" claimed that there was an international Jewish conspiracy to destroy Christmas:

> "And it has become pretty general. Last Christmas most people had a hard time finding Christmas cards that indicated in any way that Christmas commemorated Someone's Birth. Easter they will have the same difficulty in finding Easter cards that contain any suggestion that Easter commemorates a certain event. There will be rabbits and eggs and spring flowers, but a hint of the Resurrection will be hard to find. Now, all this begins with the designers of the cards."

Ah, yes. The card designers. And the Jews. Or the Communists. Or the UN. For O'Reilly, this decade's villains are the secular progressives, an army of them out to destroy everyone's holiday through lawsuits and changing social norms, by agitating against public displays of religious imagery and by eliminating the word "Christmas" from the holiday lexicon. Originally fueled by a decision by the New York public schools to eliminate displays of nativity scenes (frowned on by courts for blurring the distinction between church and state), O'Reilly vowed to keep track as the injustices kept piling up. In 2005, Target stores stopped using the word "Christmas" in their advertising in favor of the more inclusive "Happy Holidays." To the barricades! Soon, the American Family Association organized a boycott and sent a petition to the company with 700,000 signatures. Target backed off, as did Wal-Mart after a nearly identical "outrage." Other retailers were targeted, like Best Buy (which caved) and Gap, Inc. (which did not).

The fronts in this "War on Christmas," and the insidious secularist forces on the offensive, multiplied. A frenzy was set off after Lowe's home improvement stores supposedly began calling their Christmas trees "family trees." In reality, the reference was from a single catalog the company claimed was a proofing error, and a visit to the company's website turned up pages of "Christmas" items (including "Christmas trees").

O'Reilly knew that the enemy didn't have to actually exist to rally the troops, whip up interest, and — incidentally, of course — stoke his ratings. Conservatives suddenly had a reason to tune in every night for a cup of wassail outrage as the villainous secularists waged an imaginary "war" against Christmas.

The conservative icon Ronald Reagan was a master at not letting a few facts get in the way of a good villain to stoke his base into action. Making arguments against gun control, Reagan once explained, "In England, if a criminal carried a gun, even though he didn't use it, he was not tried for burglary or theft or whatever he was doing. He was tried for first degree murder and hung if he was found guilty."

When the White House spokesman Larry Speakes was informed that the story was simply not true, he replied, "Well, it's a good story, though. It made the point, didn't it?" The story was so false it made *Washington Monthly*'s "The Mendacity Index," which listed Reagan as telling the story for the first time in April 1982 . . . and then retelling it to the *New York Times* four years later.

O'Reilly and Reagan understood the value of a good villain, especially to get their base motivated. The problem was they simply *manufactured* them to suit their political cause du jour. Unlike the elites, ordinary people like us don't have the luxury of making stuff up. Luckily for us, we don't have to—there are plenty of real villains around.

Sen. Joe Lieberman was the bane of all progressives—a wolf in sheep's clothing. A Democrat, he had done more to foster disharmony about Iraq in his party's ranks than anyone else. As the go-to voice whenever a media outlet needed a Democrat to criticize other Democrats, Lieberman built a high-profile, nationwide media persona on the principle of dividing his supposed party.

The media loved him as much, if not more, than Republicans did. That may be because he provided a regular source of controversy for them—constantly berating his fellow Democrats, which is "sexy" from a traditional journalism perspective. A Republican berates a Democrat? Ho hum. Big deal. But a *Democrat* berating a Democrat was gold, spurring countless "Democrats divided" stories. Savvy conservatives (and wrong-headed liberals) could find no better way to needle progressives than to helpfully suggest Democrats would be more palatable if only they were more like Saint Joe. His quotes dissing his party are legion. Even when aiming for the White House in 2003, he spoke on August 4 at the National Press Club of all places and said this about his fellow candidates:

> "Some Democrats, on the contrary, still prefer the old, big government solutions to our problems. But, my friends, with rec- ord deficits, a stalled economy and Social Security in danger, we can't afford that. I share the anger of my fellow Democrats with George Bush and the wrong direction he has taken this nation. But the answer to his outdated, extremist ideology is not to be found in the outdated extremes of our own."

On February 10, 2005, he explained to the *Hill* newspaper why he thought Democrats had lost the 2004 elections: "Democrats became, to many voters in the country, the antiwar party and, of course, the culturally, morally permissive party. And that's not where a majority of the American people are, and that's why they voted the way they did in this election."

But no Lieberman admonition encapsulated the degree of separation between the Connecticut senator and his party—and infuriated rank-and-file members—more than his reproachful warning from a December 6, 2005, speech to the Center for Strategic and Budgetary Assessment: "It is time for Democrats who distrust President Bush to acknowledge that he will be commander-in-chief for three more critical years, and that in matters of war we undermine presidential credibility at our nation's peril."

In other words, Democrats ought to shut up and stand behind Bush in all "matters of war." Connecticut Democrats, sick of Lieberman's sanctimonious camera-grabbing routines, set out to find a candidate to challenge him in the Democratic primary in 2006. It would prove a tough task. As a three-term senator, Lieberman had money and connections to spare, and as Al Gore's vice presidential running mate in 2000, he could claim gravitas. Efforts to draft any of the state's top elected Democrats failed, as all of them feared repercussions from the Democratic Party establishment and saw such a race as career suicide. Several names were bandied about, and a college professor even jumped in the race, but no one with a credible shot was available. That is when Greenwich multimillionaire Ned Lamont threw his hat into the ring.

Lamont was an affable, if slightly awkward, politician. A true blue blood, his great-grandfather was a founding partner and CEO of J. P. Morgan, part of the moneyed American aristocracy. He had the desire, credibility, and—perhaps most important of all—the money to make at least a remotely credible challenge to Lieberman.

Throughout 2005 and into 2006 Lieberman took heavy incoming from Connecticut grassroots activists. The narrative was a simple one— Lieberman enabled the grossly unpopular George Bush and his agenda. The clarity of this message in Lieberman's case was aided by its ability to be boiled down to a single image, one of the hallmarks of a striking and powerful story line. In George Allen's case, it was the frozen video image of him pointing at Sidarth and calling him "macaca." And for Lieberman, his electoral fate was sealed with a kiss. Literally. The iconic image captured on camera showed President George W. Bush grabbing Lieberman's head in both hands and planting a kiss on his cheek after the 2005 State of the Union address.

The photograph of "The Kiss" made its way onto hundreds of blog posts and thousands of campaign buttons. Most ingeniously, grassroots bloggers and local activists created a brilliant prop for street theater antics—a huge papier-mâché float of the kiss, mounted on a pickup truck—that trailed Lieberman from one campaign appearance to another.

Lamont ended up beating Lieberman 52 percent to 48 percent in the primary, an amazing feat for a man with no prior political experience who took on a three-term incumbent senator in his own party.

In hindsight, however, the narrative created about Lieberman in the primary came back to haunt Lamont. Lieberman left the Democratic Party and successfully ran against Lamont as an independent in the general election. The Republican candidate, Alan Schlesinger, ran a feeble campaign and the Republican National Senatorial Committee indicated, though not explicitly, that it was supporting Lieberman. While Democrats mostly stuck by Lamont, Connecticut Republicans overwhelmingly voted for Lieberman. To them, kiss or no kiss, being George W. Bush's strongest friend in Congress was a *positive*. Lieberman won the election with 50 percent of the vote, Lamont receiving 40 percent and Schlesinger getting 10 percent.

In some ways, defeating Lieberman in the primary was enough to meet one of the most important goals of the challenge: movement progressives were able to boot Lieberman out of the Democratic Party and eliminate an irritable source of internal disunity. From that point on, Lieberman's criticisms would have to be hurled from the outside, lessening their newsworthiness to the traditional media. And that happened because activists were able to develop his identity as a villain—in this case, as a traitor to the cause.

CRAFT YOUR HERO

But one clear lesson to draw from the Lieberman-Lamont fight is that Lieberman eventually succeeded partly because of the inability of Lamont and his supporters to develop a strong positive narrative about him.

This story had a great villain, but a gripping, sympathetic hero never materialized. Lamont was genuine in his politics and desire to provide a progressive—and antiwar—voice in the Senate, but his was not an easy personal history to work with. He was wealthy and had always been wealthy, living in the richest part of Connecticut, far removed geographically and demographically from the working-class parts of his state. Despite his upper-class background, Lamont did have an authentic commitment to alleviating problems of the middle and working classes. Long before considering running for public office, he'd routinely donated his time to teach entrepreneurial skills to some of the state's poorest public school students. While the pro-Lamont story leaned heavily on this admirable volunteerism, it was not meshed into a broader story line about Lamont—it didn't really address what motivated Lamont, what his deep convictions were, and why he wanted to be in the Senate, other than the fact he believed he was better than Lieberman.

Had Lamont's character and convictions been developed and articulated the way James Webb's were, he might have beaten Lieberman.

Webb's personal story resonated well among voters—he was a classic American patriot. A 1968 graduate of the U.S. Naval Academy, an infantry officer, and a highly decorated Vietnam combat veteran, Webb had spent a lifetime serving his country. And in a nation of immigrants, he came from a long line of Scottish Americans who had fought in every single one of America's wars. His wasn't pedigree of the royal sort; it was pedigree of the kind that matters, the kind earned.

Enriching that simple story line were other positive traits. Webb was a talented best-selling author with a sharp intellect, yet spoke to voters in a simple, direct, and blunt style that separated him from the usual politician. He had been a Republican in a state still full of them, and could explain with conviction why he had left the GOP for the Democratic Party. He loathed public speaking, reluctantly attended events swarming with politicians, like fairs and parades, and drove Democratic Party officials bonkers with his refusal to spend half his day calling potential donors ("dialing for dollars").

Voters sensed that he was a man of his word and knew that what they saw is what they would get. The surface oddities—the anti–Iraq war former naval secretary, the reluctant campaigner, the U.S. Marine turned award-winning novelist—combined to create a complicated persona that made voters want to learn more about him.

His central narrative—a straight-talking patriot who wants to serve his country—sidelined whatever flaws he had. This posed a big problem for Sen. George Allen and his Republican allies. In a moment of desperation, Allen's campaign threw a Hail Mary pass to that portal of last resort for all sleaze, the *Drudge Report*. Twelve days before the election, on October 26, the *Drudge Report* had a screaming headline:

ALLEN'S REVENGE: EXPOSES UNDERAGE
SEX SCENES IN OPPONENT'S NOVELS

> Sen. George Allen, R-VA, unleashed a press release late Thursday that exposed his rival's fiction writing, which includes graphic underage sex scenes.

The press release was followed by examples of supposedly offending passages from Webb's novels. One came from Webb's 1981 novel, *A Sense of Honor*: "You wouldn't have believed it, Swede. She just dropped her britches and lifted up her skirt and pissed like a man. Didn't lose a drop, either. Not a drop." Another was from Webb's 2001 bestseller, *Lost Soldiers*, a book about a former marine back in Vietnam twenty-five years after the end of the war:

> "A shirtless man walked toward them along a mud pathway. His muscles were young and hard, but his face was devastated with wrinkles. His eyes were so red that they appeared to be burned by fire. A naked boy ran happily toward him from a little plot of dirt. The man grabbed his young son in his arms, turned him upside down, and put the boy's penis in his mouth."

Or this passage from Webb's 1991 novel, *Something to Die For*, which explored how political power struggles in Washington, D.C., impact U.S. forces fighting in the Third World:

"Fogarty . . . watch[ed] a naked young stripper do the splits over a banana. She stood back up, her face smiling proudly and her round breasts glistening from a spotlight in the dim bar, and left the banana on the bar, cut in four equal sections by the muscles of her vagina."

Then there was the passage from Webb's 1983 book, *A Country Such as This*, a tale tracking three 1951 U.S. Naval Academy graduates, as they deal with war, career, and marriages—a book rereleased by the U.S. Naval Academy's publishing arm eighteen years after its initial publication, for the benefit of its cadets:

"[He] could see Jawbone and Ashley Asthmatic [two guards at a Vietnamese prison camp] napping together in the grass. They faced inward, their arms entwined. It looked like they were masturbating each other. It didn't surprise him. It was common to see men holding hands, embracing, playing with each other. Some of them [the guards] had wanted him. He could tell in those evanescent moments between his *bao cao* bow, the obligatory deference when a guard entered his cell, and the first word or blow that followed it. Quick, grinding voices, turgid with repressed passion. An exploratory reaching of the hand near his groin."

It was clear from reading the passages that none of them was simply gratuitous sex. But that didn't stop Allen from fuming in his press release:

"Why does Jim Webb refuse to portray women in a respectful, positive light, whether in his non-fiction concerning their role in the military, or in his provocative novels? How can women trust him to represent their views in the Senate when chauvinistic attitudes and sexually exploitive references run throughout his fiction and non-fiction writings? Most Virginians and Americans would find [such passages] shocking, especially coming from the pen of someone who seeks the privilege of serving in the United States Senate, one of the highest offices in the land."

The right-wing apparatus was predictably "shocked" and faithfully picked up the drumbeat. The attack jumped quickly from press release, to the *Drudge Report*, to Rush Limbaugh, to the rest of conservative-dominated AM talk radio, and to Fox News. Conservative surrogates fanned out across the cable news networks to "debate" the charges, expressing extreme disapproval at the horror of Webb's perverted mind, and helpfully suggesting he drop out of the race.

But the attack backfired. Webb and his defenders noted that Webb was simply describing scenes he had seen while serving in Vietnam, scenes drawn from a soldier's experiences. Even Republican senator John Mc-Cain had written a blurb for one of the jacket covers.

Webb responded without a hint of regret about what he had written. Speaking at a rally three days after the *Drudge Report* outbreak, Webb told supporters:

> "I have lived in the real world, and I have reported the real world in my writings. I started working when I was twelve years old, and I fought in a brutal war. I saw its ugliness while George Allen was hanging out at a dude ranch . . . I was reporting from the slums of Bangkok when George Allen was schlepping around in his limo. . . . I have written about what I have seen, and that is the duty of a writer, to help people understand the world around us, with all its beauty and all of its flaws."

Sacrifice, duty, and a commitment to the truth. Worse for Allen's campaign, it turned out Webb's book *Fields of Fire* was on the official reading list of the commandant of the U.S. Marines. What had been designed as an election-eve stunt to puncture the positive Webb narrative with questions about his moral character ended up reinforcing the Democrat's positive traits instead—a task made easier because the Webb narrative as a faithful public servant was already as solid a piece of conventional wisdom as Allen's burgeoning reputation as a bigot and racist.

It was a lesson in the advantages of developing a strong, positive protagonist who can withstand harsh attacks on his or her character.

Think back to Al Gore in 2000 and try and recall his run for office. What comes to mind? The impressions that stick the most are probably that he was wooden, lifeless, had no personality. While those traits took a toll on Gore, no line of attack hurt him more than the claim that he was an "exaggerator." Designed to pierce Gore's ethical Boy Scout image— arguably his crucial strength—the exaggerator line of attack was hammered hard by Republicans as they worked to establish that narrative. Their efforts met with great success. The story about how Gore supposedly "invented the internet" was a typical Republican dirty trick, as Eric Boehlert pointed out in a November 26, 2001, *Rolling Stone* article:

> "In 1999, candidate Gore was taping an interview with CNN's Wolf Blitzer in which he said, 'During my service in the United States Congress, I took the initiative in creating the Internet.' He was no doubt referring to his landmark 'information superhighway' speeches, as well as his well-known support of high-tech research that stretched back into the 1980s. (For the record, Vinton Cerf, often called "the father of the Internet," not to mention futurist Newt Gingrich, have both publicly vouched for Gore's role in helping to shepherd the Internet to life.)
>
> "So who coined the phrase 'invented the Internet' and attached it to Gore? His Republican opponents, who faxed out a press release suggesting Gore had claimed to have done exactly that."

It was a narrative that the press was eager to promote, and Republicans fed it with one Gore "exaggeration" after another—that Gore claimed he and his wife were the inspirations for Erich Segal's tragic couple in *Love Story*, that his grandmother was paying more for the same medication that she gave her dog, and that Gore claimed to have exposed the Love Canal toxic waste dump. Before long, Gore looked little different from the ethically compromised Bill Clinton he was hoping to succeed in the White House. "The Republicans did a very good job pushing that stuff, and the press reveled in it," Tony Coelho, Gore's former campaign manager, told Boehlert. "They wanted to bring down 'Prince Albert.' "

Of course, it didn't help that Gore and his allies were completely un-successful at articulating a clear positive narrative about him, which made him more vulnerable to attacks from the Bush campaign. When they began to tag him as an "exaggerator," that charge began to stick, partly because Gore had not been inoculated from such charges by the develop-ment of a positive story that voters could easily grasp. Gore had failed to define himself; the Republicans did it for him.

Often, the GOP didn't even have to prompt the press to create Gore exaggerations—reporters did it all on their own. During a September cam-paign stop, Gore told a crowd of union workers that his mother used to sing him to sleep at night using "Look for the Union Label" as a lullaby. The press started digging and discovered the story was a fraud and "must be labeled untrue," as USA Today's political columnist Walter Shapiro reported. The TV jingle was written in 1975, when Gore was twenty-seven years old. The story was quickly picked up by cable TV's talkers and print columnists as another "bizarre fabrication."

The only problem was that Gore told the tale as a joke, confirmed by the video of the event.

Meanwhile, Bush and his handlers successfully crafted a narrative about him in both his presidential campaigns. In 2000, Bush's reputation as "a uniter, not a divider" proved remarkably resilient. At a time when the country was supposedly riven by divisions from the Bill Clinton impeach-ment saga, Bush would "heal" the country and bring everyone together for the common good. And he was a "compassionate conservative," different from the Grinches people had come to dislike in Newt Gingrich's Repub-lican Congress. Bush was especially appealing to Catholic Reagan Demo-crats who believed the Left had gone too far in the 1960s and 1970s, but who also thought that Reagan and Bush had taken things too far away from caring for the least among us.

Four years later, after proving that division and disunity served his agenda better, Bush was remade as the "war president," the tough guy who could "keep America safe" and win its overseas entanglements. No more compassion, no more uniting. But it was still a clear and simple character profile easily understood by voters—Bush would be the resolute hero who would protect us from scary terrorists. John Kerry, on the other hand, was never able to provide a positive narrative for his candidacy other than saying, in so many words, "I am not Bush!"

Today, all I remember about Gore's campaign was the *Saturday Night Live* debate skit of Gore screaming "Lockbox!" as an answer to every question. As for Kerry, I'm not sure there's anything I remember. As Kerry's and Gore's cases illustrate, failure to fully develop your hero can severely diminish chances of success, a lesson that for some reason Democrats have had more trouble grasping than Republicans.

EXPLOIT THEIR WEAKNESSES

The most arresting narratives revolve around a well-defined hero and villain fighting it out over something uniquely important to the time and place. When it comes to activism, this usually means that core respected values need to be at stake in order to grab attention and spur action.

In the case of George Allen, activists tried out several story lines in attacking him. Questionable ethics attracted little attention. Absent a major ethical lapse, the only thing such charges elicit is a yawn and the observation, "Obviously he's corrupt . . . he's a politician!" Efforts to mock Allen's pandering in Iowa never gained traction for the same reason: It's understood that politics breeds pandering and that almost all politicians do it.

But the issue of racial prejudice proved to be different, striking as it did straight at values all Americans cherish—fairness, opportunity, and tolerance. The macaca moment, in addition to exposing Allen's ugly bigotry, also provided voters with a trait they despised, even in a politician— bullying. Pointing his finger at the young brown Indian-American kid, sporting a mean smile while his all-white supporters cheered in the background as he "welcomed" Sidarth to the "real Virginia" was not a pretty picture. All people could see was a bigoted bully playing to the assembled racist good ol' boys. Like a punch to the gut, the incident hit hard, provoking instinctive revulsion. Fleshed out by Allen's other racist-leaning indicators—an obsession with Confederate flags, the use of the "N" word, placing a severed doe's head in a black family's mailbox—it made for a profile that no self-respecting Virginian wanted to support.

In Virginia, race was a surprisingly salient issue. It's a state with a legacy of trying to distance itself from the backwaters of racial prejudice, and Allen's rhetoric truly threatened to link the state back to that distasteful past. In addition, Northern Virginia was experiencing dizzying growth with an influx of diverse residents from all over the world streaming in for its booming high-tech, high-wage jobs and employment in the burgeoning federal bureaucracy. Virginia's very character had shifted in a way Allen failed to take into account, and he was ill-prepared to deal with the new face of his state. In Virginia, circa 2006, "tolerance" was a value that its growing pool of sophisticated voters expected from its elected leaders.

Tolerance, in other words, had become a core respected value in Virginia, and Allen's violation of it doomed him.

Four years earlier and deeper in the South, another Republican committed political suicide by violating the same value. A thirty-year career in politics went up in flames in two weeks.

On December 5, 2002, Senate Majority Leader Trent Lott, of Mississippi, spoke at the one hundredth birthday party of former senator Strom Thurmond, who had run for president of the United States in 1948. In his remarks, Lott said: "I want to say this about my state: When Strom Thurmond ran for president, we voted for him. We're proud of it. And if the rest of the country had followed our lead, we wouldn't have had all these problems over the years, either."

There was a big problem with Lott's remarks that day. Thurmond, of South Carolina, had run for president on the State's Rights Democratic Party (the Dixiecrats), a *segregationist* splinter group of Democrats. While the statements failed to make a ripple in the traditional media, bloggers immediately pounced on it.

"Of course, Thurmond ran as the presidential candidate on the 'States-Rights Democrat' or 'Dixiecrat' ticket—a candidacy that was based exclusively and explicitly upon the preservation of legalized segregation and opposition to voting rights and civil rights for blacks," wrote Joshua Micah Marshall of *Talking Points Memo* the next day. "There's a sort of agreement in Washington these days—with Thurmond's retirement and hundredth birthday—to sort of forget about all that unpleasantness."

That same day, Duncan Black, posting under his pseudonym of Atrios at *Eschaton*, dug up the Dixiecrat platform, and quoted from the section opposing repeal of the poll tax:

> "The negro is a native of tropical climate where fruits and nuts are plentiful and where clothing is not required for protection against the weather . . . The essentials of society in the jungle are few and do not include the production, transportation and marketing of goods. [Thus] his racial constitution has been fashioned to exclude any idea of voluntary cooperation on his part."

Another *Atrios* post on December 7 pointed out that "Trent Lott's home state led the nation in black victims of lynching from 1882–1930, both in terms of the absolute numbers and per capita of the black population. And through 1962 as well."

CNN interviewed Lott that same day, neglecting to ask him about the Thurmond remarks. But the *Washington Post* did, and reported on the response:

> "Lott's office played down the significance of the senator's remarks. Spokesman Ron Bonjean issued a two-sentence statement: 'Senator Lott's remarks were intended to pay tribute to a remarkable man who led a remarkable life. To read anything more into these comments is wrong.'
>
> "Bonjean declined to explain what Lott meant when he said the country would not have had 'all these problems' if the rest of the nation had followed Mississippi's lead and elected Thurmond in 1948."

The story clearly was alive and had reared its head in the traditional media. On December 9, Lott was asked on CNN about his comments and issued an apology. "A poor choice of words conveyed to some the impression that I embraced the discarded policies of the past," Lott said. "Nothing could be further from the truth, and I apologize to anyone who was offended by my statement."

Marshall's journalistic instincts had told him he was on to something big and he was on the trail, digging up stuff. That same day, he posted a quote from an interview that Lott gave to *Southern Partisan* magazine in 1994, proudly displaying his admiration for Jefferson Davis, the president of the Confederate States:

> "More and more of The South's sons, Jefferson Davis' descendants, direct or indirect, are becoming involved with the Republican party. The platform we had in Dallas, the 1984 Republican platform, all the ideas we supported there—from tax policy, to foreign policy; from individual rights, to neighborhood security— are things that Jefferson Davis and his people believed in."

As with George Allen, the narrative around blatant racism cemented quickly: Trent Lott was a racist who longed for the days of the Confederacy. Once clearly defined, the key was to keep feeding that story. Marshall was relentless in his pursuit, and the next day, December 10, he found evidence that Lott's remarks, far from being a simple "poor choice of words," as he'd been claiming, were regularly incorporated into routine stump speeches. Campaigning in Mississippi in 1980 with Ronald Reagan, along with Strom Thurmond, Lott had said, "You know, if we had elected this man thirty years ago, we wouldn't be in the mess we are today." Claims that Lott's statements on Thurmond's hundredth birthday had been an inadvertent slip of the tongue or poor word construction rang hollow, and the story was once again fueled—this time with the addition of lying on top of bigotry.

And so it continued. On December 11, Marshall published a 1983 court ruling against the conservative Bob Jones University in Greenville, South Carolina, which had fought the loss of its tax-exempt status because it practiced racial discrimination in its admissions. The decision noted that Trent Lott had filed an amicus brief in support of the university's discriminatory practices.

The next day, December 12, Lott issued a second apology, this one to friendly conservative radio host Sean Hannity:

> "I wanted to honor Strom Thurmond, the man, who was turning one hundred years old. He certainly has been a legend in the Senate both in terms of his service and the length of his service. It was certainly not intended to endorse his segregationist policies that he might have been advocating or was advocating fifty-four years ago. But obviously, I am sorry for my words, they were poorly chosen and insensitive and I regret the way it has been interpreted."

In that interview, Lott also denied knowing anything about the Council of Conservative Citizens—the same KKK front group George Allen would later deny any association with—despite the fact that Lott had spoken at the group's meeting a few years earlier. It got worse five days later, when the *Washington Post* dug up Lott issuing an endorsement of the CCC in one of the group's newsletters, saying they "[stood] for the right principles and the right philosophy." Later it turned out that Lott had also led the charge to maintain race discrimination at his college fraternity.

Each "drip, drip" that emerged further fueled the story and, fighting for his political life, Lott offered up a third apology on December 13, holding a news conference in his hometown of Pascagoula, Mississippi:

> "Segregation is a stain on our nation's soul. There's no other way to describe it. It represents one of the lowest moments in our nation's history and we can never forget that. [. . .]
>
> "I apologize for opening old wounds and hurting so many Americans. I take full responsibility for my remarks and only hope that people will find in their heart to forgive me for this grievous mistake. Not only have I seen the destruction wrought by the racist and immoral policies of the past, I will do everything in my power to ensure that we never go back to that kind of society again.
>
> "In the days and months to come, I will dedicate myself

to undo the hurt I have caused and will do all that I can to contribute to a society where every American has an opportunity to
succeed."

At this point the narrative shifted from new revelations to the drama of
his struggles simply to retain his leadership office. On December 15, the
Washington Post reported that Lott had sought help from the prominent
black Republicans Condoleezza Rice and Colin Powell, and had been
rebuffed by both. The next day, there was yet another apology, the
fourth, this one on Black Entertainment Television. On December 19,
former president Bill Clinton upped the ante in a remarkable way, as reported by CNN:

> "Former President Clinton said Wednesday it is 'pretty hypo-
> critical' of Republicans to criticize incoming Senate Majority
> Leader Trent Lott for stating publicly what he said the GOP does
> 'on the back roads every day.'
>   " 'How do they think they got a majority in the South anyway?'
> Clinton told CNN outside a business luncheon he was attending.
> 'I think what they are really upset about is that he made public
> their strategy.' "

Clinton's comments were ingenious in a way, because he connected
Lott to the entire Republican Party and its electoral strategy in the South.
This left the party bigwigs with two choices: They could either back Lott's
continued Senate leadership, thereby acknowledging Clinton's charges,
or they could dump Lott in hopes of saving the party from being dragged
down with Lott.

Lott resigned as Senate majority leader the next day.

The Thurmond-Lott debacle would have been a blip, a one-day story,
without the pickup from bloggers like Duncan Black and Josh Marshall,
but even their efforts would have been for naught had they not generated
new revelations and information to keep the story alive. It was a fourteen-
day process, and at any point an absence of new fuel for two to three days
could have killed the story and spared Lott's hide. Instead, the steady drip

of new revelations allowed it to build critical mass, transfer from the blog world to the traditional media, and eventually led to his downfall. *Time* magazine acknowledged their role in a December 16 wrap-up story:

> "If Lott didn't see the storm coming, it was in part because it was so slow in building. The papers did not make note of his comments until days after he had made them. But the stillness was broken by the hum of Internet 'bloggers' who were posting their outrage and compiling rap sheets of Lott's earlier comments."

Ultimately, the Lott story resonated with the public because it undermined cherished values and revealed a deep character flaw, a major weakness. Racism in a person, or racial discrimination as a policy, is deeply offensive to most Americans, and when it involves a public figure, it becomes a matter of societal shame.

REINFORCE THE NARRATIVE

Riding and driving the news-cycle is key to reinforcing the narrative, as illustrated by Rudy Giuliani's presidential campaign.

Ben Smith of *Politico* delivered a bombshell in late November 2007: former New York City mayor Giuliani, a front-runner for the GOP presidential nomination at the time, had billed obscure city agencies for police security details for himself and his mistress as they spent weekends in the Hamptons over three summers between 1999 and 2001. The bookkeeping subterfuge was apparently necessary to throw off nosy reporters, who were told that he was teaching his son how to play golf when instead he was cheating on his second wife, soon to be replaced by the mistress in question, Judith Nathan.

While the information would undoubtedly end up as campaign fodder for his more moralistic GOP primary foes, the big question was whether the story would gain momentum or whether it would stall. If it was the latter, the damage would be relatively minimal.

Giuliani moved immediately to try to nip the story in the bud, claiming his personal life off-limits and attacking the "liberal press" for their "hit job." However, that attempt at media intimidation had zero effect, as Giuliani suffered a week's worth of constant revelations in his taxpayer-supported adultery scandal (or "Sex on the City," as it was dubbed on *Daily Kos*). The city's tab for his indiscretions ballooned as a full accounting was made, to nearly half a million dollars, while current and former mayors and city bureaucrats rejected Giuliani's claims that such account gimmickry was standard practice.

When papers reported that Nathan had received taxpayer-supported police protection, then police commissioner Bernard Kerik (later indicted on sixteen counts for tax fraud, conspiracy, and making false statements) claimed Nathan's protection was warranted because of an unspecified threat to her safety after the affair became public. However, further investigation proved she'd received such protection months before the affair became public knowledge. Diana Taylor, the girlfriend of Mayor Michael Bloomberg (Giuliani's successor), gleefully pointed out to the *New York Daily News* on December 1, 2007, that she didn't need a security detail. "I don't have security in Bogota or Nairobi or Moscow when I travel there on business, why would I need security in the safest city in the world?" she asked.

By the time the story petered out two weeks later, voters knew that police had been assigned to protect Nathan's family even when she wasn't around, and that New York's Finest were expected to run her errands and walk her dog. The details dribbled out day by day, and the story became indelibly etched into public consciousness by the steady stream of revelations. Giuliani never recovered. His national poll numbers cratered, from a first-place high in *Rasmussen Reports'* mid-November survey of 27 percent to 14 percent in January 2008, fourth in the field.

Given our news-cycle-driven media world, one of the ways a story stays alive after it is initially reported as breaking news is through the addition of new elements as the days go by. Sometimes, these new elements can be simply new characters.

Randy "Duke" Cunningham, a San Diego–area Republican congressman with eight terms under his belt, pled guilty in November 2005 to charges of conspiracy to commit bribery, fraud, and tax evasion, with a complex money trail documented in court and newspaper accounts that involved $2.4 million in bribes received. On March 3, 2006, Cunningham was sentenced to eight years and four months in prison and ordered to pay back $1.8 million in restitution. But it wasn't the arcane kickback schemes to defense contractors and the convoluted real estate deals that Cunningham participated in that kept the nation's attention. It was the lurid minor details and the ragtag crew of con men introduced to the public on a daily basis that fed the story.

There was Mitchell Wade, head of the defense contract firm MZM, which reaped tens of millions of dollars in contracts Cunningham steered his way. Wade not only bought the congressman's house for more than it was worth in a back-scratch move, he gave Cunningham a yacht—the *Duke-Stir*. Tales of Cunningham cavorting naked with hookers in the yacht's hot tub, filled with polluted water from the Potomac River, made headlines for days. The women testified to the naked Cunningham feeding them grapes while he lounged in the rank water.

Joining Cunningham in his *Duke-Stir* hot tub adventures was Brent Wilkes, another Cunningham briber and defense contractor. Wilkes didn't just party with his favorite congressman aboard the yacht; tales of poker parties at the Watergate with hookers, liquor, and limos emerged, attended by the former CIA executive director Kyle "Dusty" Foggo and other operatives with such vivid names as Brant "Nine Fingers" Brasset.

Resembling sensational roles cast by Hollywood producers, unforgettable characters continued to crawl out of the woodwork as the story progressed: Thomas T. Kontogiannis, a Long Island real estate developer who traded in boats and bribes with Cunningham. Kontogiannis's nephew, John T. Michael, owner of a mortgage company, who made shady loans on Cunningham's San Diego land deals; real estate agent Elizabeth Todd, who'd never made a sale before engaging in wildly inflated multimillion-dollar deals for Cunningham.

By the time the disgraced Cunningham resigned in tears, with his wife stone-faced at his side for the last time (she filed for divorce immediately afterward), the combination of mawkish repentance, sordid personal details, and an ensemble cast straight out of a Humphrey Bogart film, the complicated money trail ended up not mattering nearly as much to voters as the real-life soap opera.

Not for the last time, gripping narrative trumped dry accounting details in holding the public's interest, and the steady stream of new and colorful characters fed the serialization of a story for weeks and months on end.

Each individual bit of news and information that emerges needs to be evaluated through the prism of how it fits in and reinforces a larger narrative. Often the connection doesn't have to be direct or obvious. The photo of George Allen with the Council of Conservative Citizens leadership became a cornerstone of an evolving narrative, one that bore some unintentionally ironic undertones. When New York mayor Rudy Giuliani campaigned with Allen, Allen proudly told the crowd, "You can tell a lot about people by the folks they stand with." Blogging the remarks, I retorted, "You sure can," then reposted the photo. What should have been a plus for Allen's campaign became yet another opportunity to reinforce the narrative: Allen was racist.

Bill O'Reilly and his fellow Christmas warriors have been able to build on the "War on Christmas" story line by continuously reinforcing it year after year. Every year since the early 1990s, Michigan lit a "Holiday Tree" in front of the state Capitol. Christmas survived fine in Michigan with a Holiday Tree for fifteen years, until it became the latest outrage in the "War on Christmas" in 2005. A year later, it once again was a "Christmas Tree," but by then, no Christmas warrior cared or noticed. The incident had served its purpose and the "War on Christmas" brigade had long since moved on to the next outrage, methodically feeding the "war" narrative.

AIM FOR THE GUT, NOT THE BRAIN

There's a reason why "feed the children" commercials feature heart-wrenching images of starving children—flies crawling across their faces, eyes encrusted, bellies bloated—rather than spreadsheets about child poverty rates in Africa or Latin America. Emotional connection moves us.

Statistics do not. Unlike "facts," we process values at the gut level, not by using reason.

For years, Apple tried to compete with the PC world by arguing specs — megahertzes and gigabytes and so on. Apple's market share was steadily eroding, and the company was widely assumed to be in its last throes. Co-founder Steve Jobs, ousted in 1985, triumphantly returned to the company in 1996. Almost immediately he set out to revamp the company's product line, slashing programs and products, and launched a new generation of projects designed to give the company a veneer of "lifestyle cool."

As geeks looked on, laughing at what they saw as inferior products with little native applications to make them worthwhile to mass audiences, Jobs spearheaded a new marketing campaign. Titled "Think Different," it merely portrayed innovative historical figures with a tiny Apple logo in a corner (while launching a thousand arguments about whether the slogan was grammatically correct). Not only did the ads omit product information, they omitted product altogether. Viewers instead saw black-and-white pictures of such icons as Muhammad Ali, César Chávez, John Lennon, Albert Einstein, Mahatma Gandhi, Jane Goodall, Pablo Picasso, and Amelia Earhart. The ad campaign was clearly aiming to identify the computer company with some of history's most creative and innovative public figures.

Over the next ten years, Apple introduced new products, starting with Mac OSX and iMac, and then branching out into other consumer products, such as the iPod, the iTunes digital music software, and the iPhone. By 2007, fully recovered and enjoying Microsoft-level domination of market segments like digital music players, Apple continued to eschew technical data and instead marketed a lifestyle, not just a product, understanding that you don't become a cultural icon by communicating to the brain.

Steve Chazin, a former Apple marketing executive and the author of an e-book titled *Marketing Apple: 5 Secrets of the World's Best Marketing Machine*, says Apple understands that it needs to sell more than the product's features:

> "Look carefully at Apple's iPod commercials. You'll see lots of happy, energetic people dancing in silhouette against a colorful

and ever-changing background. Notice the distinctive white head-phones flowing in unison to the owner's movements. What you don't see is a focus on iPod.

"The reason is simple. Apple isn't selling you an MP3 player. They are inviting you to experience the Apple lifestyle and to become part of the iPod community. Use any other MP3 player and you'll hear good music. Use an iPod and you'll feel good. You'll fit in."

This approach stands in sharp contrast to Microsoft's marketing—from commercials to packaging. A clever YouTube parody captured differing marketing dynamics perfectly, taking the original Apple iPod's spartan packaging and wallpapering it with Microsoft's trademark clutter—bulleted tech specs, marketing copy, and extraneous images, stickers, and icons, all in a bunch of colors. By the end, it turns into a Microsoft product, giving you a whole lot of details and information about product specs, and stripping it of all emotional appeal. It would fail just as Microsoft's own entry in the digital music space—the Zune—has failed.

ClickZ columnist and marketing consultant Bryan Eisenberg says Apple sells emotional content. On January 4, 2008, he wrote:

> "Simply put, Apple understands people. It knows that people make emotional decisions, then use intellect to justify those decisions. Dancing shadow people with iPods aren't an intellectual argument for buying an iPod, they're raw emotional appeal. At the heart of every successful Apple product, you'll find a deep understanding of what moves people emotionally at many different levels."

What's true in the fast-paced, highly competitive world of technology marketing should be considered doubly true in any area where persuasion is the goal. In Eisenberg's telling words, you need that "deep understanding of what moves people" and you need to be able to hang it together with a compelling story.

Words and images matter a whole lot. Conservative activists realized this early on, and have been avid practitioners of the art of "framing" for more than a decade. One of the top framers in contemporary politics, Frank Luntz, defines his work on his firm's website as follows:

> "We find the EXACT words and phrases to help you succeed —
> the messages that will frame the debate and generate support for
> your side of the issue. The words your customers use and the
> words that speak to them. This is about more than identifying the
> strongest language and talking points — it's about figuring out how
> to reframe the debate. [. . .]
> "Which images and visuals will have the greatest impact? Which
> facts and figures can change opinions? And which individual words
> have the ability to put your position on the linguistic high ground?
> We'll uncover the language that matters. We'll show you the *words
> that work* and the best way to use them — guaranteed."

Thus, for Luntz, "oil drilling," with its connotations of being invasive, dirty, and destructive to the environment, becomes "energy exploration," which recalls a pioneering spirit. "Global warming" becomes "climate change," as though industrialization's destructive impact on global weather patterns is nothing more than the changing of the seasons. The inheritance tax, which affects only 2 percent of the wealthiest Americans, becomes the "death tax," creating the perception that it affects everyone and must be avoided.

The person most responsible for bringing the art of framing to the Democratic side is George Lakoff, a professor of linguistics at UC Berkeley, and the author of the definitive progressive tome on framing, *Don't Think of an Elephant.* In the July 17, 2005, issue of the *New York Times* magazine, Matt Bai explained:

> "According to Lakoff, Republicans are skilled at using loaded
> language, along with constant repetition, to play into the frames
> in our unconscious minds. Take one of his favorite examples, the

phrase 'tax relief.' It presumes, Lakoff points out, that we are being
oppressed by taxes and that we need to be liberated from them. It
fits into a familiar frame of persecution, and when such a phrase,
repeated over time, enters the everyday lexicon, it biases the debate in favor of conservatives. If Democrats start to talk about their
own 'tax relief' plan, Lakoff says, they have conceded the point
that taxes are somehow an unfair burden rather than making the
case that they are an investment in the common good. The argument is lost before it begins."

In April 2004, the antiwar wing of the Democratic Party was getting
antsy. Its hero in the Democratic primaries that year, Howard Dean, had
flamed out. Presumptive nominee John Kerry and the party establishment
shuffled uncomfortably when the topic of Iraq was brought up. Sensing
blood in the water, George Bush went in for a rhetorical kill: "We're not
going to cut and run from the people who long for freedom." It was a good
phrase for Republicans, as William Safire noted in a May 2 piece in the
New York Times magazine:

> "The phrase . . . is always pejorative. Nobody, not even those
> who urge leaders to 'bring our troops home,' will say, 'I think we
> ought to cut and run.' It is a phrase imputing cowardice, going
> beyond an honorable surrender, synonymous with bug out (prob-
> ably coined in World War II but popularized in the Korean con-
> flict); both are said in derogation of a policy to be opposed with
> the most severe repugnance."

Nevertheless, Kerry fell headlong into the trap, responding a week
later, "I don't believe in a cut-and-run philosophy." In other words, he was
using the enemy's language to discuss the issue, thereby *reinforcing their
frame*. Republicans had successfully painted Democrats as "cut and run-
ners," a disparaging phrase, and even the party's own standard-bearer had
adopted the language when discussing his position on Iraq. It defined the
"frame" in which the Iraq debate was conducted. Rather than a debate
over the safety of our troops, it became one of retreat and surrender.

In 2006, as the two parties geared up for that November's elections, the phrase made a comeback. Dana Milbank of the *Washington Post*, in a column on June 21, 2006, noted the excessive use of the phrase by Senate Majority Leader Bill Frist:

> "Not quite six minutes after the Senate chaplain prayed yesterday for God to use senators 'as agents of your grace,' Majority Leader Bill Frist (R-Tenn.) started the sloganeering. 'If we break our promise and cut and run, as some would have us do, the implications could be catastrophic,' he said. In case anybody missed that, he also said 'we can't cut and run' twice on CBS News and issued a follow-up press release titled: 'FRIST DENOUNCES DEMOCRATS' PLAN TO CUT AND RUN.'"

However, by midyear, Bush's chief political advisor, Karl Rove, urged his fellow Republicans to change tack and begin using the phrase "stay the course," which was meant to be a more positive contrast of the Republican position to the negative "cut and run" frame used against Democrats. It was an unmitigated disaster, and became a favorite line of attack for Democrats in a rare display of rhetorical jujitsu, as described by Peter Baker in the October 24, 2006, edition of the *Washington Post*:

> "But the White House is cutting and running from 'stay the course.' A phrase meant to connote steely resolve instead has become a symbol for being out of touch and rigid in the face of a war that seems to grow worse by the week, Republican strategists say. Democrats have now turned 'stay the course' into an attack line in campaign commercials, and the Bush team is busy explaining that 'stay the course' does not actually mean stay the course."

The Republicans got too clever for their own good and dove headfirst into a buzz saw, proving that framing isn't the full prescription for political victory. But "cut and run" had a good, long season and proved wildly successful in implicating Democrats in 2004 as a party of surrender and defeat.

OWN THE STORY

Every story has an ending, and the good ones invest the listeners, readers, or viewers in how everything is resolved. There is a universal desire for happy endings, and even when a good story doesn't provide one, we still *yearn* and *root* for them.

So we've talked about the importance of crafting good stories in order to vest people in the causes we care about. But there's a big difference between traditional stories and the stories we craft—our stories have yet to end. And so as we engage the audience, we give them a chance to help write that happy ending. It's an empowering effect, giving the audience the emotional investment in the story, and then offering them an active and engaged role in shaping its conclusion.

Gina Cooper and her volunteers wanted a conference in which bloggers would finally meet each other face-to-face. In Virginia, Webb's ragtag insurgents wanted nothing more than to see their guy replace George Allen in the United States Senate. In Connecticut, Democratic activists wanted to prevent Lieberman from further undermining their party in the media, and so on.

It was the summer of 2007, and the Republican presidential field for the most part was a menagerie of unappealing misfits, unable to capture the fancy of Republican voters, let alone the public at large. But one candidate, the quixotic Texas congressman and libertarian Ron Paul, was building an army of disciples thousands strong.

Still, they were getting little respect. Paul's fund-raising was anemic, he polled in the low single digits when he registered in surveys at all, and there were concerted efforts by party establishment regulars to exclude him from Republican debates and right-leaning forums across the internet. At the end of the third-quarter fund-raising period, in late September, however, a major Paul campaign fund-raising drive netted $1.2 million in a week and slightly more than $5 million for the entire three-month quarter, an incredible amount for a fringe candidate espousing such fringe ideas as a return to the gold standard, allowing guns in schools, an end to birthright citizenship, and the elimination of the "do not call" registry. The candidate and his ideas could claim virtually no mainstream support.

Things quickly changed after that third-quarter financial reporting period. Inspired by Paul's message and hungering to see their candidate gain wider recognition, Paul supporters set out to do what the official campaign itself seemed incapable of doing—raising the kind of funds that would force the political and media worlds to take their candidate seriously. So on November 5, without any guidance or sanction from the Paul campaign, supporters set off what they called a "money bomb," raising $4.3 million in one twenty-four-hour period. On December 16, they followed up with a $6.4 million one-day haul. Both days broke online fund-raising records, and led to a $19 million fourth-quarter haul, eclipsing the entire GOP field and approaching amounts raised by superstar Democratic fund-raising champs Barack Obama and Hillary Clinton. It was suddenly harder to dismiss Paul as an irrelevant candidate.

In addition to the money, Paul's thousands of supporters fanned out across the nation to plaster their neighborhoods with self-printed posters, flyers, and stickers, while building the most extensive web presence of any candidate in any party in the race. These supporters had a goal for their candidate—the White House—and getting there without the support of either the political or media establishments would require them building a mass movement and raising the money necessary to cover the enormous expenses of modern campaigns.

Clearly, Paul's overall shortage of money and organization—no matter how energized by his supporters—was never going to be enough to appeal to the Republican base. But by building a movement based on Paul's decidedly odd vision for America and forcing the political world to take notice, his supporters increased the chances of the Texas congressman remaining an important and influential fixture on the American political scene for years to come.

Unlike a traditional story, the public narratives we build have no tidy, wrapped-up ending. A loss one day, like Ron Paul's quick fade out of the 2008 Republican presidential contest, does not preclude resurgence in later years. Sometimes a defeat, like Barry Goldwater's 1964 blowout loss, is just a step toward ultimate victory, as the Arizona Republican spurred a nationwide grassroots revolt that ultimately lay claim to the United States government (see chapter 7).

Given an enemy to fight and a hero to root for, ordinary people can move beyond cheering from the sidelines to becoming part of the story with a personal stake in the ending. Whether they canvass, or phone bank, or rally their friends, or write letters to the editor, or raise money, or do any of the countless different things that can effect change, their actions will ultimately determine how the story ends. And if the investment in the story is deep enough, and the happy ending inspiring enough, people will move mountains to make that happen.

CHAPTER 4

REINVENT THE STREET PROTEST

To many observers, if politics isn't in the streets, it's not happening. This misconception is a leftover from the 1960s, when protesters were making the most of their new visual medium, television. Today's new tools allow an exciting hybrid of technological and digital advocacy matched with real-life demonstrations, and much of the most effective current organizing is taking place under the radar before it goes public and visible.

April 4, 2004, was Palm Sunday, but for some of the American troops in Baghdad, it turned out to be more of a Black Sunday. Casey Sheehan, a twenty-four-year-old from Vacaville, California, had just returned from being an altar server at mass before volunteering to head out as part of a "quick reaction force" to rescue a pinned-down unit. It turned out to be an ambush in Sadr City and Casey and seven others were killed under a barrage of rocket-propelled grenades. Casey had joined the army when he was twenty and had been in Iraq two weeks when he died.

Deeply religious, he had considered enlisting as a chaplain's aide before entering as a mechanic. While he planned to become an elementary school teacher once he was finished, Casey reenlisted during the war in Iraq in solidarity with his friends, knowing full well his unit would be deployed.

His mother, Cindy Sheehan, memorialized poignantly, "Casey is a hero who belongs to history now, but I wish he were a living breathing coward."

In June, a couple of months after Casey's death, Sheehan (and other parents who had lost children in Iraq) met with President George W. Bush. While Sheehan initially reported that the meeting went well, as time passed, her shock turned into anger as she learned how the Bush administration had manufactured evidence about Iraq's weapons of mass destruction and its ties to al-Qaeda, and as she learned more about the reality on the ground for American troops. Still in grief, she began expressing her anger in media interviews and on *AlterNet* as well as *Daily Kos,* where she occupied not a high-profile slot on the site's main content section, but appeared as a diarist—one of tens of thousands on the site. But her words stood out from the crowd. Her narrative was powerful and her cause was righteous. And soon, Sheehan would do more than just write about her grief.

In January 2005 she was a founding member of the Gold Star Families for Peace, made up of parents who had lost sons and daughters in Iraq. By the summer of 2005, Sheehan had become more and more agitated about the war—and about her meeting with Bush, as she told *Uruknet.info* on July 5:

> "His mouth kept moving, but there was nothing in his eyes or anything else about him that showed me he really cared or had any real compassion at all. This is a human being totally disconnected from humanity and reality. His eyes were empty, hollow shells and he was acting like I should be proud to just be in his presence when it was my son who died for his illegal war! It was one of the most disgusting experiences I ever had and it took me almost a year to even talk about it."

Then, when she watched Bush give a speech on August 3, her anger boiled over, especially when she heard the president say the following:

> "Our men and women who have lost their lives in Iraq and Afghanistan and in this war on terror have died in a noble cause, in a selfless cause. Their families can know that American citizens pray for them. And the families can know that we will honor their loved one's sacrifice by completing the mission, by laying the foundations for peace for generations to come."

That day, Sheehan decided she had to act. Early the next morning, she posted a diary on *Daily Kos*, saying after she heard those "hurtful and asinine statements," she and the Gold Star Families for Peace had decided to go to Crawford, Texas, where Bush was vacationing that week, to ask him, among other things, this question: "We would like for him to explain this 'noble cause' to us and ask him why Jenna and Barbara are not in harm's way, if the cause is so noble."

Those words spread online like wildfire while Sheehan set out that same morning in her Veterans for Peace bus with forty cars in tow. By the time she arrived in Crawford two days later, she was already an internet celebrity and had piqued the interest of the White House press corps, bored senseless in the Texas heat. Had Sheehan come to Crawford as part of a major organized protest march, it would have been a less interesting—and less broadly covered—"protest march" story. Had she tried to meet with Bush at the White House, it would've been a nonstarter. Down in Crawford, she simply walked with some supporters toward the vacationing president's ranch, asking to meet him. When asked by the scrum of reporters, who nearly outnumbered her fifty or so supporters, why she was there, she answered: "I want to ask the president: Why did my son die? He said my son died in a 'noble cause,' and I want to ask him what that noble cause is."

That plaintive cry from a grieving mother brought home the tragic reality of a war previously too abstract and distant for most Americans. This was not a story about people protesting foreign policy decisions or American imperialism or abortion funding or tax breaks for the rich. This was a mother wanting to confront the man who sent her son to his death.

Bush tried to defuse the situation by sending two high-ranking staffers—National Security Advisor Stephen Hadley and White House Deputy Chief of Staff Joe Hagin—to meet with Sheehan the day she arrived in Crawford. They sat on cheap $7 lawn chairs and had a chat with her, basically telling her that there was no way in hell she'd meet the president. She decided to stay put anyway.

On August 12, her decision paid off. Bush, en route to a Republican National Committee fund-raiser scheduled to raise $2 million, had to drive in his motorcade within one hundred feet of the protesters. Sheehan stood on the side of the road, holding a sign that read, "Why do you make time for donors and not for me?" highlighting the fact that Bush would be munching on crab cakes and hobnobbing with fat cats while a grieving mother sat in the Texas heat waiting for answers about her dead son.

The vigil kept making news, ironically, because of hostile pro-war individuals. On August 14, one of Bush's neighbors, Larry Mattlage, fired a shotgun near the camp. "I'm getting ready for dove season, and if y'all are going to stay here, I'll practice," he was captured saying on CNN, demanding that the protesters go home. Asked to explain his comment, Mattlage responded ominously, "Figure it out for yourself." Another evening, a Waco resident plowed his pickup truck through a field of crosses (and stars and crescents) representing each of the then nearly one thousand fallen soldiers in Iraq that protesters had erected next to their camp. The driver was eventually arrested for criminal mischief. A distant cousin of Larry Mattlage, Fred Mattlage, actually lent his land to the protesters, allowing them to set up shop even closer to the Bush ranch. Pro-war groups began to stage counterprotests, further giving the media reason to cover the "conflict" generated by Sheehan's efforts, helping spread the word.

The vigil lasted three weeks until September 1, when the protest began to fizzle out. An increasingly motley crew of spotlight-hogging personalities began arriving at Camp Casey, attempting to steal a bit of the limelight (see chapter 6). Meanwhile, the devastating Hurricane Katrina had landed on the Gulf Coast on August 29, rightfully dominating media coverage. The next day, Sheehan announced plans to close shop.

Sheehan didn't mind the fact that Bush chose not to meet with her. She told the Associated Press on August 30, "I am very, very, very grateful he did not meet with me, because we have sparked and galvanized the peace movement. If he'd met with me, then I would have gone home, and it would have ended there."

"Peace movement" or not, antiwar sentiment spread across the country that summer. In late July, a *USA Today*/Gallup poll found that 53 percent of Americans thought going to war was the right thing, while 46 percent thought it was "a mistake." By mid-August, the numbers were down to 44 percent positive, and 54 percent thinking it was a mistake. By mid-September, helped by the Katrina disaster, the numbers slipped further to 39 percent to 59 percent, respectively. No doubt "Camp Casey" had played its part in bringing those numbers down, a stark contrast to those ineffective antiwar protests in February 2003. Seeing hundreds and then thousands of names on a list of dead was too abstract for people to fully grasp. Seeing the devastating results of just one of those deaths made it real. America had seen, in an uncomfortably vivid close-up, the true cost of the war.

The whole Camp Casey experience was successful, at least early on, for several reasons. The protest was unlike any other protest, so it had novelty going for it. It was not another planned, organized, nationwide march where the only issue is how many people show up. Here, it didn't matter how many people there were—that wasn't the story at all. It featured a simple narrative of an individual human tragedy at its core. And it had the element of drama: Would the president meet Cindy Sheehan or wouldn't he? Had Bush met with her on that first day, the protest would've been over.

ADAPT AND INNOVATE

Georgiy Gongadze was a well-known Ukrainian journalist with a history of violating censorship decrees, a trait that got him fired from various television and radio gigs. Working as a journalist in President Leonid Kuchma's Ukraine was no easy task, unless you worked for the larger mass-media outlets which were owned by Kuchma's allies and toed the official line. So Gongadze tried a different route. In April 2000, seeking freedom of expression and less government harassment, he cofounded *Ukrainian Pravda* (truth) on the web, focusing on politics and media and taking a critical approach in covering Kuchma's government. The internet was still a nascent medium in much of the world and it was accessible only by a small sliver of the Ukrainian population, too insignificant to merit much attention from government censors.

On September 16, 2000, Gongadze mysteriously disappeared shortly after he came in possession of documents proving corruption inside Kuchma's inner circle. On November 3, his body was found in a forest outside Kiev, decapitated and doused in acid. Forensic analysis determined that the acid bath and decapitation had occurred while Gongadze was still alive.

Shortly thereafter, the opposition politician Oleksandr Moroz dramat-

ically took the floor of Parliament to charge Kuchma with direct involvement in the crime. "The professionally organized disappearance, a
slow-moving investigation, disregard for the most essential elements of
investigation and incoherent comments by police officials suggest that the
case was put together," he declared. Then he released tapes of Kuchma's
conversations secretly recorded by his bodyguard, which Moroz believed
implicated Kuchma's government in Gongadze's murder.

Gongadze's murder and subsequent revelations sparked a broad grassroots effort to rid Ukraine of the Kuchma regime. Writing in *Foreign Affairs* (March/April 2005), Adrian Karatnycky said: "In 2001, a significant
anti-Kuchma movement had flourished in Ukraine, prompted in part by
the president's 'tapegate.' Although these mass protests eventually dissipated amid violence instigated by agents provocateurs, they represented a
kind of dry run for the next revolution."

The leaders of those protests kept organizing, many of them online,
where they continued to build the infrastructure for their final showdown.
Until the murder, the vast majority of Ukrainians had never heard of the
internet. And though most Ukrainians still did not have access to it, the internet became a serious alternative to the official propaganda machine
used by some of the most influential in Ukrainian society—journalists,
students, opposition organizers, human rights lawyers, and entrepreneurs.

In 2004, new presidential elections pitted Kuchma's chosen successor,
Victor Yanukovych, against the opposition leader Victor Yushenko. With
Kuchma still serving as president, there was a virtual media blackout of
Yushenko, but his tireless campaigning was drawing huge support for elec-
tions scheduled for October 31, 2004. On September 6, less than two
months before the polls, Yushenko was poisoned with the toxic chemical
TCDD, a harmful dioxin that is a by-product of herbicides like Agent
Orange. Rushed to Vienna after the attack, his life was barely saved but
the poison had radically disfigured the handsome politician's face.

In that highly charged atmosphere, the internet became a chief way to
undermine the official state propaganda, while giving people a safe outlet
to get involved in the race. Humor was a key weapon. In late September,
as Yanukovych traveled through a heavily pro-Yushenko region, he was

pelted with something, collapsed to the ground in dramatic fashion, and was immediately hauled away by bodyguards. Security forces confiscated all videotapes of the incident from the crowd, while the official state media announced that Yanukovych had been viciously hit with a video camera battery. Unfortunately, one video recording survived and made its way on to Channel 5, the sole opposition television station that barely reached 3 percent of the country. Slow-motion replays of the videotape (later on YouTube) showed that it wasn't a camera battery that hit Yanukovych — it was an egg! The "egg incident" became an instant hit. An online game called The Boorish Egg allowed players to fight pro-Yanukovych thugs by throwing eggs at them. Ukrainian websites hosted all manners of jokes, puns, and skits, all based on the egg incident. It was this creativity that helped many Ukrainians join the political conversation, while jokes created online kept protesters upbeat during the many nights of protest of the coming "Orange Revolution."

Joshua Goldstein in "The Role of Digital Networked Technologies in the Ukrainian Orange Revolution," a research paper for Harvard's Berkman Center for Internet and Society, notes how critical these actions were:

> "The ability to diffuse tension through humor and satire was crucial to the success of the Orange Revolution. As Henry Jenkins points out [in his 2006 book *Convergence Culture: Where Old and New Media Collide*], some of these things may look more like play than civic engagement, 'yet these forms of popular culture also have political effects, representing hybrid spaces where we can lower the political stakes (and change the politics of language) enough so that we can master skills we need to be participants in the democratic process. The Internet vastly accelerated this cultural tool, by making more channels of subversion available to opinion makers and other leaders.' Every joke and pun created by this community of activists and directed at Yanukovych further drew attention to the vastly different information environments and political futures that the two candidates represented."

None of the candidates received 50 percent of the vote on October 31, 2004. While there were reports of voter irregularities, a second election was held November 21 between the top two vote getters—Yanukovych and Yushenko. When the runoff election votes were counted, Yanukovych was declared the winner and all hell broke loose. With more than ten thousand election monitors nationwide, the nonpartisan Committee of Voters of Ukraine announced that it was "the biggest election fraud in Ukraine's history." Karatnycky wrote, "According to the group, 85,000 local government officials helped perpetrate the fraud, and at least 2.8 million ballots were rigged in favor of Yanukovych." Netroots groups like *Maidan* ("public square"), organized online, also had more than five hundred members monitoring the election, while using its message boards to gather and collect reports of fraud from readers and activists. For example, a student's cell phone recorded a university professor in Kiev illegally instructing his students to vote for Yanukovych. Surprisingly, the nation's intelligence agency (which had been blamed for the Yushenko poisoning) provided the opposition with much of its evidence of voter fraud, using wiretap intercepts of high-ranking government officials.

International and internal pressure forced a second do-over runoff election, and once again, the government used massive fraud to swing 2.8 million votes in favor of Yanukovych, sparking the Orange Revolution— the sprouting of tent cities all around the country by orange-wearing pro-Yushenko supporters, gathering peacefully by the hundreds of thousands, chanting, "*Razom nas bahato! Nas ne podolaty!*"—"Together we are many! We cannot be defeated!" Eventually, the country's Supreme Court had little choice but to order a third runoff vote (this one free and fair), which Yushenko handily won. "We are free. The old era is over. We are a new country now," he declared, officially bringing an end to the Orange Revolution.

The Orange Revolution wasn't the first set of protests that the Kuchma regime had faced. But it's the first that actually worked. It's important to note that the seeds of the Orange Revolution were planted years before the first protester hit the streets, with the creation of alternate news operations online (even with their tiny audiences). For instance, *Maidan* focused its efforts on networking with other pro-democracy organizations in Eastern

Europe and became one of Ukraine's main election monitoring organizations. They also engaged in activist training, networking, and offered a data repository.

Meanwhile, another group called *Pora* ("It's Time") emerged as a direct response to the censorship of the mass media, inspired and trained by the Serbian Otpor movement, which had helped bring down the Serbian strongman Slobodan Milosevic in 2000. Its website stated: "Under conditions of far-reaching censorship and absence of independent media, the main idea of PORA was the creation of alternative 'mass media,' in which volunteers deliver election-related information 'from hand to hand' directly to people throughout Ukraine." With internet penetration at only 8.5 percent of the population, *Pora* aimed to get vital but censored information from that tiny minority out to the masses. Through online forums, its volunteers generated an estimated 40 million copies of thirty-seven different materials—flyers, leaflets, stickers, brochures—to ensure their message would receive a mass airing. Meanwhile, cell phones allowed them to coordinate their efforts, as Goldstein writes:

> "By September 2004, *Pora* had created a series of stable political networks throughout the country, including 150 mobile groups responsible for spreading information and coordinating election monitoring, with 72 regional centers and over 30,000 registered participants. Mobile phones played an important role for this mobile fleet of activists. Pora's post-election report states, 'a system of immediate dissemination of information by SMS was put in place and proved to be important.' Some groups provided the phones themselves, while others provided SIM cards, and most provided airtime."

Pora's network provided new revelations of government wrongdoing and electoral fraud, feeding the story, reinforcing the narrative, and ensuring its protesters remained motivated and committed to their ultimate goal. Each new demonstration was reported via SMS message, posted online, then broadcast by opposition leaders to the cheering masses in speeches and via their own media outlets, adding momentum to the effort and necessary morale boosts as protesters camped out for eleven days in frigid winter weather.

The Orange Revolution was successful because of its media landscape, the undemocratic regime's inability to recognize the internet as a real threat, the adoption of democratizing media online and off (from the web to cell phone SMS messaging), obvious fraud, and the groundwork laid by reformer groups and journalists. Ultimately, what the Ukrainian experience showed was that with determined activists making creative use of both online and offline technologies, people can be mobilized to bring about regime change. The specific avenues open for such organization and mobilization will vary from place to place, so the real challenge is to adapt and innovate ways to organize and mobilize people.

SPEAK WITH ONE VOICE

The traditional protest march inevitably devolves into a hodgepodge of conflicting interests and causes, each using the march as a vehicle to try and bring attention to their pet issue. In a fragmented media environment, cutting through the noise requires a clear and simple message. Otherwise, the reaction you get will be, well, like *The Daily Show*'s Jon Stewart:

STEWART: On Saturday, a 100,000-strong peace march descended on Washington seeking to crystallize America's dissatisfaction with the war into one single idea.

CLIP OF YOUNG MALE SPEAKER: Peace!

STEWART: Okay.

CLIP OF MALE SPEAKER: Justice!

STEWART: (pause) Fine.

CLIP OF MALE SPEAKER: Environmental protection!

STEWART: (pause, confused look on face)

CLIP OF MALE SPEAKER: No racism!

STEWART: (dumbfounded, speaking in Valley Girl–like voice) Dude! I didn't hike from Oberlin for this!

On December 16, 2005, the Republican-controlled U.S. House passed HR 4437, a draconian bill that would classify not only undocumented immigrants as felons, but also anyone who helped them enter or remain in the United States—in essence criminalizing families for helping out their kin. The bill, sponsored by Wisconsin Republican James Sensenbrenner, would "[subject] an individual who knowingly aids or conspires to allow, procure, or permit a removed alien to reenter the United States to criminal penalty, the same imprisonment term as applies to the alien so aided, or both." It passed 239–182—an odd Christmas present for an estimated 11 million people in the United States.

The Senate, on the other hand, took a different approach. Prodded by President Bush, the Republican-controlled Senate debated an immigration reform bill granting undocumented immigrants a "path to citizenship," so long as they paid a fine, learned English, had proof of gainful employment, and hadn't run afoul of the law. For the virulently anti-immigrant House, such efforts were unacceptable regardless of the impossibility of forcibly expelling 11 million people from the country. Years of rising anti-immigrant rhetoric and scapegoating of immigrant communities (and particularly those from south of the border) boiled over into the mass media. And in a culture where the family unit is particularly central to their lives, it was the proverbial straw that broke the camel's back.

One of the first indications of the reaction in the Latino community came on February 14, 2006, when 1,000 demonstrators rallied at the Independence Mall in Philadelphia. Three weeks later, a modest 20,000 rallied in Washington, D.C. Then came a surprisingly big march—100,000 strong—in Chicago. Then, the week of March 23, the protests exploded nationwide: 30,000 marched in Milwaukee, 20,000 in Phoenix, while 80,000 immigrants refused to show up for work in Georgia. Then,

on March 25, half a million marched in Los Angeles, an impressive number even for an area with a high Latino population. What followed in April
was more impressive—not in the numbers as much as in the inland, non-
border locations: 50,000 in Denver; 7,000 in Columbus, Ohio; 5,000 in
Detroit; 9,000 in Nashville; 500,000 in Dallas; 40,000 in St. Paul; 6,000
in Des Moines; 50,000 in Atlanta; 75,000 in Ft. Meyers, Florida; 3,000 in
Grand Junction; 20,000 in Indianapolis; 10,000 in Lexington, Kentucky;
100,000 in Phoenix; 25,000 in Seattle. You could almost feel the shock in
lily-white Utah as 15,000 Latinos took to the streets in Salt Lake City, or
when 3,000 marched in the small farming community of Garden City,
Kansas. In Boise, Idaho, the 5,000 who took to the streets may have been
the largest public demonstration in the state's history. One shocked
anti-immigrant group in Idaho hilariously pleaded for an "American"
response:

> "Distressed and dismayed at the protest for amnesty? Close
> Our Borders Committee has reserved the park at the above times.
> The hope is to have as many people as possible show up with their
> own old-fashioned AMERICAN snacks, picnics, barbeque grills,
> any variety of games—from jump ropes and hula-hoops to horse-
> shoes or Frisbees etc. A celebration of American culture would be
> great on the illegal aliens protest-day."

All power flows through media, and these protests demonstrated that
in several ways. First, the Anglo-American media was mostly clueless about
what was brewing in the Latino community, and so was taken by surprise
when the marches erupted. As spontaneous as the demonstrations appeared, they were, in fact, preceded by a lot of buzz and organizing work
in the Latino community. Spanish-language television, and more important, Spanish-language radio, provided much of the spark for the protests
and also laid down the ground rules, such as insisting that only American
flags be flown. Invisible to Anglo America, these ethnic media outlets
spent weeks laying the groundwork. This was explained by Félix Gutiér-
rez, a journalism professor at the University of Southern California in Los

Angeles, in an interview with Jeffrey Brown on PBS's *NewsHour* program on April 11, 2006:

> JEFFREY BROWN: Paint a picture for us, Professor Gutiérrez. Paint a picture of Spanish-language media today. How—how diverse, in terms of voices, in terms of politics, in terms of ownership?

> FÉLIX GUTIÉRREZ: Well, it's—it's a growing medium. . . . [H]ere in Los Angeles, we have sixteen radio stations, about six TV stations, two daily newspapers all in Spanish. And this is part of a nationwide trend. It's big business. It's not mom-and-pop local operations, but Univision, Telemundo. Telemundo is part of NBC. We have the big newspaper chains, like Hearst, Tribune, Belo, Knight Ridder, all doing things in Spanish, one way or another. [. . .]

> JEFFREY BROWN: Now, Professor Gutiérrez, there has been a lot of mulling lately about how the mainstream media really picked up on all this quite late in the game, raising the question about whether it is missing a lot of what's going on in this country. What do you think about that?

> FÉLIX GUTIÉRREZ: You can't be well informed if you pay attention to the so-called mainstream media, the general circulation dailies, network TV, for instance. People just have more choice. . . . And if the general-audience media had been paying more attention to the Latino media the week before the demonstration here in Los Angeles, where we had half a million people, they would not have been surprised at what turned out on Saturday. That was a consistent message, and, as we counseled earlier, that people should show up, they should demonstrate their rights, and that they should do so in a peaceful way, which is part of our First Amendment rights in this country.

The Los Angeles efforts even drew people from the faraway Central Valley. "Lots of people started calling the station asking for information about the march, so we decided to do something about it," said DJ Diana Miramontes of KLOG 98.7 FM in Merced, California, in a Spanish-language report for New America Media on March 27, 2006. "We interviewed an activist who could explain HR 4437 and shared information about the march. Calls flooded in, including someone offering a free bus." Merced is 273 miles from Los Angeles, and like much of that region has a huge population of immigrant farmworkers. Stations hundreds of miles away gave tips to its listeners planning on trekking to the protest. A report from the Univision affiliate in Fresno, California—about 220 miles away from Los Angeles—helpfully suggested listeners check their cars' oil and antifreeze levels before embarking.

The Saturday edition of *La Opinion*, the largest Spanish-language daily in the United States (circulation: 125,000), screamed "*A Las Calles!*"—"To the Streets!"—at the top of its page, with photos from various pro-immigrant protests from around the country filling the broadsheet, plus a map of the protest route. Spanish-language television, such as the stations Univision, Telemundo, and TV Azteca, urged their viewers to take to the streets.

Besides print, radio, and TV, cell phones (and the internet, to a much lesser extent) were critical to the massive participation of young immigrants. Some schools kept students from walking out and joining many of the protests, as students learned about the protests by shooting text messages to each other. "It's a very, very potent form of communication," University of Houston communications professor Garth Jowett told KPRC Local 2 in Houston on March 29, 2006. "In a matter of minutes, literally, they can get a crowd to assemble someplace within half an hour, of tens of thousands of people, simply by everybody text messaging five people."

While all the organizing took place through Spanish-language media and cell phones as well, the marches were a nationwide success because of their single, unified message. They were not protesting and giving speeches about a bunch of different issues. When the first few marches generated controversy over the flying of Mexican and other Latin American flags, the word went out—only Americans flags were to be displayed at the marches. The narrative was set: America was a nation of immigrants.

Signs proclaimed "We are America." Spokespersons reinforced that message: "We come to this country not to take from America, but to make America strong. And we do not deserve to be treated the way we have been treated." Demonstrators were asked to bring their children, which lessened the chance of violence, since the children would serve as restraint for both the demonstrators and the police. But more important, it would reinforce the notion that anti-immigration efforts were fundamentally antifamily. Demonstrators wore white to symbolize solidarity, offering great visuals for the cameras.

The message was so clear, so universally intuitive, that every participant easily adopted it. As one seventeen-year-old marcher said: "My parents are immigrants. We Mexicans are not here to fight against Americans. We're here to become Americans." Spanish-language radio DJ Pedro Biaggi explained to Jeffrey Brown on the PBS *NewsHour* on April 11, "[I]t doesn't get any more complicated than just delivering the pure and simple message of where we're going and why we're going there."

The Senate passed its immigration reform bill without the draconian House language on May 25, 2006 (S.2611), but House Republicans quickly declared the bill dead on arrival. As a *New York Times* editorial said on May 27:

> "The Senate has given the cause of immigration reform a lot of momentum, which it will need since it is now heading for a brick wall: the House of Representatives. The House Judiciary Committee chairman, James Sensenbrenner Jr., in the role of head brick, called the Senate bill 'a nonstarter' the morning after it passed.
>
> "Discussing the odds of reconciling the House and Senate legislation into one bill, Mr. Sensenbrenner struck a tone of deathly pessimism. The chambers had once been miles apart, but now they were 'moons apart or oceans apart,' he said, grasping for words to convey the vastness of his gloom, and the ferocity of his bargaining stance."

With the House unable to come to an agreement with the Senate, the legislation—both the Senate *and* House versions—died with the expiration of the 109th Congress.

While the Senate's immigration reform bill with its "path to citizenship" would've been a step forward for the immigrant community, the defeat of the mean-spirited House bill was a huge milestone. The "debate" had previously been a one-sided affair, with their targets—undocumented immigrants—too afraid of deportation to assert themselves politically. It was easier to lay low and pray that they wouldn't get rounded up by the authorities. Yet suddenly, seemingly out of nowhere, brown people had risen with one voice, in some of the least expected corners of the country. As one community organizer said, "We decided not to be invisible anymore." It was a wake-up call for the media and the broader public, and even community activists watched in wonder as the seemingly leaderless demonstrations spontaneously arose.

The protests were novel and unexpected, they had a clear, sympathetic and media-friendly message, they provided great visuals, and they even tapped into a hot-button national issue of immigration laws. Momentum built from the first demonstrations in February through the end of April. Millions marched, and the nation was transfixed.

If those marches were an example of how to conduct street protests with a clear unified message and theme, the May Day marches that followed soon after showed how *not* to do it.

The organizers of the traditional May Day marches on May 1, celebrating International Workers' Day, announced that they would further the cause promoted by the immigration rights groups. And while the intentions may have been good, the execution was a disaster. I watched the marchers begin to line up in San Francisco that morning, and along with the brown immigrant protesters were the usual suspects—hippie retreads demanding legalization of marijuana, the tired "Stop Imperialism!" zealots, the predictable "Free Mumia!" signs, the inevitable "Free Palestine!" crowd, even a few "Free Tibet!" proponents. Any unity of message or purpose was lost. As a planned march, there was nothing novel or interesting about the effort. There were no new story lines or narratives for the media to run with. And there's nothing more boring and stale than writing a story that's essentially "a bunch of people marched and chanted stuff."

It was a lost opportunity. Had all these groups surrendered their pet causes for one day, they could have reinforced the original narrative by showing how pro-immigration efforts had spread beyond the brown community and become a more multiethnic, multinational phenomenon. Instead, a bunch of selfish people hijacked the effort, so it completely dissipated. The spontaneity, the uniqueness, the dramatic stories from the original protests had disappeared. The story was dead.

To be fair, perhaps there was nowhere else for the protests to go. The original organizers had responded quickly, almost organically, to a sense of frustration. In a perfect world, the protests would've evolved into a lobbying operation, pressuring lawmakers to pass friendly legislation, finding the best stories (divided families, hard workers struggling to achieve the American dream, and so on) to package and market to traditional media outlets, hence continuing to build popular sympathy and support for comprehensive immigration reform.

Then again, something far more fundamental than mere street action was spurred by the three-month campaign. Many Latinos, previously afraid of asserting themselves, had suddenly found their voice and realized that real change required participation in the political process. Protesters had marched with signs that read "Today we march, tomorrow we vote," and they made good on their promise. Part of the increased voter turnout in the 2006 elections was prompted by hostile actions against Latinos, wrote Gabriela Lemus, an AFL-CIO executive: "Cities like Hazelton, Pa., passed ordinances that racially-profiled Latinos and demanded that English be the only language spoken. Minutemen became the vanguard of vigilantism against immigrants, but also harassed Hispanic voters in places like Tucson, Ariz. Congressional campaigns ran attack ads designed to motivate the anti-immigrant base. All of these efforts backfired. Instead of a massive uprising against immigrants at the polls, we witnessed a tide of Hispanic voters casting their ballots."

It was quite a tide. While the Latino vote in the 2002 midterm elections was 5.3 percent of total voter turnout, that number spiked to 8 per-

cent in the 2006 midterm elections—a 37 percent jump. The numbers
were even more dramatic in 2008, according to a study by the NDN Hispanic Strategy Center: Latino turnout in the presidential primaries was
three times higher than in the 2004 primaries, increasing their percentage
of the overall vote from 9 percent in 2004 to 13 percent in 2008—a 44
percent increase in just four years. If the message was "We Are America,"
there was no better way to drive it home than to cast that ballot on Election Day.

BUILD A WAVE

While we as a nation like to pretend that racial tensions are a thing of the
past, the small town of Jena, Louisiana (population 2,971 in 2000), was a
rude reminder that we in fact have a long way to go.

On August 31, 2006, at an assembly at Jena High School, Kenneth
Purvis, a black student (in a school with a 90 percent white student body),
asked the vice principal whether he could sit under the shade of a large
oak tree in the center of the school courtyard, in what was traditionally the
"white" side of the Jena High School square. (Black students normally sat
on bleachers near the school's auditorium.) The vice principal told Purvis
he could sit wherever he wanted. The next morning, that tree was adorned
with two nooses. "The noose, in the context of Louisiana, is a symbol of a
technique of racial intimidation," later explained Professor Anita L. Allen,
of the University of Pennsylvania's law school, to the BBC on October 25,
2007. "Up until the 1940s, African-Americans were ritualistically hung
from nooses in trees, killed and tortured—and this memory persists."

Three students were fingered for the action. State and federal law en-
forcement officials (including an FBI agent) determined no crime was
committed; had the nooses been hung by adults, it could've been treated
as a federal hate crime. Regardless, on September 7, the school's principal
recommended the three students be expelled from the school. However,
at the insistence of Superintendent Roy Breithaupt, the school board over-
ruled that recommendation and opted instead for a two-week, in-school
suspension and some Saturday detentions. Breithaupt saw the actions

merely as a "boys will be boys" thing. "Adolescents play pranks. I don't think it was a threat against anybody," Breithaupt told reporters. As for the temporary suspension, he defended the board's actions, saying, "To say that these students were simply 'slapped on the wrist' is a grave misconception of what punishment actually took place."

The school authorities' casual response angered the community's African-American population, as did the school board's refusal to let them address the board on the matter.

That set off a series of racially charged fights at the school, precipitating at least one "lockdown" on September 8, and disciplinary referrals of black students spiked sharply. The local white-owned newsweekly, the *Jena Times*, blamed black parents for overreacting. At a September 18 school board meeting where African-American parents were given a mere five minutes, Tracey Bowen said, "Everyone says that we went overboard but I don't believe we went overboard with this. Right is right—no matter what color you are." With school disciplinary incidents on the rise, on a particularly volatile day in late September, LaSalle Parish district attorney Reed Walters was urgently asked to address the school's student body. Flanked by police, he told students: "Look, I can be your best friend or your worst enemy. With the stroke of a pen I can make your life miserable." Walters said later that he was responding to some white girls who were talking or playing with their cell phones during his remarks, and that he also added "so I want you to call me before you do something stupid" to the end of the threat. Black students said Walters was looking right at them.

Two months later, on November 30, the school was burned down, and the teens later charged with arson were a racially diverse group apparently trying to destroy their poor grade records. Nevertheless, the burning raised tensions back up again with rampant speculations that it was race-related.

On December 1, students were having a party at the Jena Fair Barn when six black students, including sixteen-year-old Robert Bailey Jr., attempted to enter looking for a friend. The party was being hosted by a woman for her daughter and her mostly white friends. Minding the front door, the woman told the six that it was a private party and they could not come inside, but she went in to find the friend. As they waited, a white man, Justin Sloan, came out with a group of his friends and started a fight, punching Bailey in the face, knocking him to the ground. Bailey didn't fight back, and everyone scattered. Sloan was later charged and convicted of simple battery.

The next day, Bailey and two friends, Theodore Shaw and Ryan Simmons, both seventeen, were exiting the Gotta-Go, a local convenience store, when they ran into Matt Windham, who they said was in Sloan's group the night before. Seeing Bailey with two others, Windham turned tail and ran toward his truck to get his shotgun. Bailey gave chase, and seeing Windham pull out the shotgun, wrestled it away from him. Witnesses on the scene, saw only Bailey chasing after Windham and taking his shotgun away. And based in large part on those eyewitnesses, the three students were charged with assault, second-degree robbery, conspiracy to commit second-degree robbery, and theft of a firearm.

Tensions were at an all-time high, and teachers at Jena High School begged the administration to postpone classes until things could simmer down. But the administration ignored the warnings and promptly resumed classes as scheduled that Monday, December 4. Things were chaotic at the school. Makeshift classrooms filled the hallways and the school gym because of the fire damage to several classrooms, while the place reeked of smoke. Conditions were ripe for what happened next.

Eyewitness accounts vary (in large part because pending legal proceedings made everyone clam up), but apparently student Justin Barker, seventeen, a friend of the students who admitted hanging the nooses, taunted Bailey during lunch at the school's gymnasium for getting his "ass whipped" at the Fair Barn party. One of Bailey's friends, Mychal Bell, sixteen, exchanged a few harsh words before Barker gave Bell the finger and moved on. Moments later, the bell rang to mark the end of the lunch period, and students began moving en masse toward the gym's doors. Seeing Barker pass near them, Bell allegedly said, "There's the white motherfucker who was running his mouth," and threw the first punch. His friends, including Bailey and Shaw, as well as Carwin Jones, eighteen, and Jesse Rae Beard, fourteen, allegedly piled on, kicking and stomping Barker as he lay on the ground until he was rendered unconscious. He spent three hours in an emergency room with injuries to his hand, face, and ears. One of his eyes was swollen shut. After he was released, Barker attended a school party that evening.

That beating incident became the genesis of the eventual "Jena 6" who were charged: Bell, Bailey, Shaw, Jones, Beard, and Purvis (who was accused of being in the melee but likely wasn't). Minister Alan Bean, the executive director of Friends of Justice and an early champion for the six students, explained to me the ways the incident could be—and was— interpreted. "When your buddy starts something, given the dictates of street morality, you've got to show you've got his back," Bean said. "The intensity of the assault can be explained by either (a) the fact that the Jena 6 are heartless and sadistic street thugs, [District Attorney] Reed Walters' position, or (b) that this was the final act in a steadily intensifying series of violent encounters between two groups of kids that can be traced back to the official mishandling of the noose incident, my position."

Still, given that Walters was the district attorney and not Bean, Walters's view prevailed. But Walters upped the ante by charging the students with attempted second-degree murder and conspiracy to commit second-degree murder. All were charged as adults except for Beard, and bails set so high—between $70,000 and $138,000—that they sat in jails for months because their families could not afford to bail them out. In a timeline of the Jena 6 case written for outside media, Bean wrote:

> "Mr. Walters' decision to increase the charges of defendants involved in the alleged fight at the school to attempted second-degree murder and conspiracy to attempt second-degree murder [has] transformed a routine school fight into a premeditated gangland hit perpetrated by street thugs intent on murder. This bizarre escalation of charges is impossible to justify on even the most extreme and pro-prosecution interpretation of the meager facts at hand."

The town's long-marginalized African-American community was incensed, outraged at the outsized charges and the double standards. How, they asked, could the youths be charged with "attempted murder" when the target was well enough to attend a party that same evening? And why were the original noose-hanging white students given a simple suspension, and even Sloan, who beat Bailey, charged only with simple battery? The black community saw the attempted murder charges of the Jena 6 as patently unjust and racially discriminatory.

The first trial, of Mychal Bell, only made matters worse. On the opening day, June 26, 2007, Walters reduced the charges to aggravated second-degree battery and conspiracy to commit aggravated second-degree battery—which requires the use of a "dangerous weapon." The weapon? The tennis shoes Bell was wearing. ("According to this reasoning, every fight participant is guilty of aggravated assault unless he shows up naked," raged a furious Bean on his blog.) The only adult who witnessed the attack couldn't place Bell at the scene. Other eyewitnesses offered conflicting accounts of whether Bell was involved or not. Bell's lawyer, an African-American public defender, didn't oppose Walters's decision to charge the sixteen-year-old as an adult, didn't call any witnesses or offer any evidence, nor did he challenge the selection of the all-white jury that voted to convict.

About the same time, a new phenomenon was taking shape below the radar, driven by the sense of injustice evident in the Jena 6 charges. Watching all of it, and furiously writing about it, was the self-styled "Afrosphere"— black bloggers who were outraged by the racial discrimination they saw and how it was being accepted by the traditional media.

For example, in a timeline compiled to assist outside media in getting the "facts" of the story, the *Jena Times* repeatedly put its own spin and bias on events. Consider this entry:

> "September 9–November 30, 2006: Despite the media promoting racial tension, there were no such reports of any violence or destruction during this time period. Disruptions at school were only those of typical disruptions, nothing related to any racial divide, thus, putting to rest any speculation that there was true racial tensions [sic] in town."

Clearly, such attempts were aimed at covering over the ugliness beneath the surface—both events of the past and the present. This was, after all, a town that had voted for former KKK Grand Wizard and self-styled "white nationalist" David Duke when he ran for governor in 1991, and little seemed to have changed since then, according to Eddie Thompson, a white Pentecostal preacher writing on the *AuthorsDen* website on December 15, 2006:

> "I've lived here most of my life, and the one thing I can state with absolutely no fear of contradiction is that LaSalle Parish is awash in racism—true racism. Here in the piney woods of central Louisiana, where some gentle, old, Christian, white women still call graying black men 'boy' and some angry, young, Christian, black teens attack pizza delivery trucks that would dare enter their neighborhood, racism and bigotry are such a part of life that most of the citizens do not even recognize it."

The black bloggers took up the cause of the Jena 6 with a passion. Originally alerted to the story by Bean, whose timeline of the Jena 6 story was distributed to national journalists like Howard Witt of the *Chicago Tribune*, Tom Mangold of the BBC, and Wade Goodwyn of NPR, as well as bloggers like Jordan Flaherty and Bill Quigley, these citizen journalists began their own investigations into the story. "It is interesting that the early bloggers on this story were white, but that the Jena 6 never really resonated with white readers," said Bean. "Only when the black bloggers got hold of the story did it really take off."

On July 17, Color of Change, an email list of activists modeled after MoveOn, blasted the story to its then 100,000 members, and the story was adopted by the wider Afrosphere. They provided blow-by-blow coverage of Bell's trial proceedings, they raised money for the youths' legal defense, and as anger over the trial arose, the Afrosphere began organizing a September 20, 2007, protest in Jena meant to coincide with Bell's sentencing. Black bloggers issued a press release asking "that the mainstream traditional media step forward and discharge their duty to provide coverage of this vitally important event to their viewers and readers and act as 'the fourth institution' of governmental 'checks and balances' that constitutional framers intended the press to be."

Because of their dogged persistence, the story burst out of the Af-rosphere, gaining traction in a wider arena. Rappers like Ice Cube and Mos Def spread the word in the hip-hop community. Black radio DJs, especially Steve Harvey and Michael Baisden, gave the story heavy airplay. Journalists like the *Chicago Tribune*'s Witt followed the story in print. CNN's Paula Zahn provided the earliest television coverage. The fact that the protest now included most of the nation's most prominent African-Americans, like Jesse Jackson, Al Sharpton, Martin Luther King III—suddenly *following* the lead of a new, younger generation of African-American activists and hip-hop stars—pushed the story onto the national stage.

As Witt, of the *Chicago Tribune*, wrote on September 18, 2007, two days before the protest:

> "As formidable as it is amorphous, this new African-American blogosphere, which scarcely even existed a year ago, now com-prises hundreds of interlinked blogs and tens of the thousands of followers who within a matter of a few weeks collected 220,000 petition signatures—and more than $130,000 in donations for legal fees—in support of six black Jena teenagers who are being prosecuted on felony battery charges for beating a white student.
>
> "'Ten years ago this couldn't have happened,' said Sharpton, who said he first heard about the Jena case on the Internet. 'You didn't have the Internet and you didn't have black blogs and you didn't have national radio shows. Now we can talk to all of black America every day. We've been able to form our own underground railroad of information, and when everybody else looks up, it's already done.'
>
> "Hotels are booked up for miles around Jena, the Louisiana State Police are drawing officers from across the state to help con-trol the crowds, and schools and many businesses in the town of 3,000 will close Thursday in anticipation of 10,000 or more dem-onstrators who are expected, organizers predicted."

As it turned out, 15,000–20,000 protesters marched in Jena on Septem-ber 20. With Jesse Jackson and Al Sharpton in the lead, it seemed like yet another Operation Push or Rainbow Coalition effort, a recurring image from decades past. The reality was different. "As I remarked in my story about black bloggers on the eve of the Jena demonstration, the big-name civil rights leaders like Rev. Jesse Jackson and Rev. Al Sharpton were following the bloggers to Jena, not leading them," Witt, of the *Chicago Tribune*, told the *Dallas South* blog in an interview on October 11, 2007. "Were it not for black blogs and black talk radio, tens of thousands of ordinary black Americans would never have climbed aboard buses for a 20-hour trip to such a remote little Louisiana town."

Eventually, the Jena 6 saw their charges reduced to a more rational and defensible level. Bell's initial conviction as an adult was vacated by a Louisiana appeals court that remanded it back to juvenile court, and the case was eventually settled for reduced charges after much legal wrangling.

One clear conclusion to be drawn from the Jena 6 experience is how activist gatekeepers—those who once decided what would be protested, and where and how that protest would take place—are no longer necessary. As with the media, activism is being democratized. Similar to the Spanish-language media that pushed the immigration story protests, the black bloggers and activists, along with an assist from black radio DJs, were crucial in busting the story out in the open, beyond Jena, and beyond Louisiana. As the *Washington Post* columnist Eugene Robinson wrote on the day after the protest, September 21, 2007:

> "We still might not know about what was happening in Jena if the case hadn't been noticed by bloggers, who sounded the alarm. And I'm quite sure there would have been no busloads of protesters descending on Jena if the cause hadn't been taken up by a radio personality [Michael Baisden] best known for R-rated banter about sex and relationships [and] other black radio hosts."

The broader victory was in bringing renewed attention to an issue many Americans thought the nation had successfully dealt with. That was accomplished not by simply marching in the streets and hoping the traditional media showed up to cover it, but by working for months to carefully craft the narrative, publicize the story, push it into ever larger media outlets—from Alan Bean's first efforts, to rare and isolated traditional media coverage like Witt's in the *Chicago Tribune*, to the Afrosphere, to the broader blogosphere, to black radio, to major news outlets like the *Washington Post*.

It was a wave, gradually building size and speed until, having reached a critical mass, it crested—crashing onto the national consciousness.

CHAPTER 5

FEED THE BACKLASH

When your enemies begin to notice you—and attack you—you have arrived. Instead of avoiding confrontation with gatekeepers and opponents, embrace it and feed it. Stoking the flames of controversy brings visibility to your issues, raises your profile and effectiveness, and begins a cycle of ever-increasing attention that you can use to your advantage.

itting atop the media food chain, with the highest-rated cable television news show, Bill O'Reilly rakes in $9 million a year, mostly because he produces forty-three minutes a night of vitriolic shouting, cutting off microphones, interrupting guests, bullying liberals, and pure Id Gone Wild, officially known as *The O'Reilly Factor* on Fox News.

And it was from that lofty perch that O'Reilly had taken aim at his latest target—Shawn Hornbeck, the fifteen-year-old boy in Missouri who'd been kidnapped and sexually assaulted for four years by a forty-one-year-old homicidal deviant before being freed in January 2007. On his "Impact" segment shortly after Hornbeck's reunion with his parents—and the release of a fellow thirteen-year-old held with him—O'Reilly questioned why the boy hadn't attempted escape during his years of captivity. The bombastic host's answer? "The situation here for this kid looks to me to be a lot more fun than what he had under his old parents. He didn't have to go to school. He could run around and do whatever he wanted. . . . There was an element here that this kid liked about his circumstances."

Here is a glimpse of those envious circumstances that O'Reilly thought Shawn "liked," as reported by the Associated Press on October 9, 2007:

> "After Shawn was abducted at gunpoint while riding his bike in rural Washington County, Devlin took the then-11-year-old to his apartment in suburban St. Louis, where he repeatedly sexually assaulted the boy. Days later, Devlin took Shawn back to rural Washington County in his pickup truck, apparently intent on killing him.

"He said he pulled Shawn from his truck and began to strangle him. Shawn resisted.

" 'I attempted to kill (Shawn) and he talked me out of it,' Devlin said. Devlin stopped the choking, but then sexually assaulted the boy again. Prosecutors said it was at that point that Shawn told Devlin he would do whatever was asked of him in order to stay alive.

'This boy made this contract, this deal with the devil, only to survive,' Washington County Prosecutor John Rupp said."

When San Francisco moved to limit access of armed forces recruiters to high school students in the city, O'Reilly said, "And if al-Qaeda comes in here and blows you up, we're not going to do anything about it. We're going to say, look, every other place in America is off-limits to you, except San Francisco. You want to blow up the Coit Tower? Go ahead."

Staying true to his shameless shtick, he later denied the above statement made on his own show. O'Reilly is a master of the manufactured outrage, such as the trumped-up crusade against a mythical "War on Christmas" (see chapter 3). In the same vein, he's egged his viewers on to help him rain bile on such un-American entities as the San Diego Padres baseball team, excoriated for allowing gays into the park when children might be present:

"It is almost unbelievable, but the San Diego Padres scheduled a promotion for gays on the same day the team gave away hats to kids. So thousands of gay adults showed up and commingled with straight families. . . . Ten years ago, this never would have happened in America. . . . And now, you better check your local listings if you go anywhere."

In O'Reilly's world, you can enforce rules that keep gays—or children in "straight families"—away from the ballpark.

And as already evidenced by his discussion of Hornbeck, no tragedy is beneath his exploitation when he feels the need to score cheap political points, from bashing immigrants when an undocumented drunk driver killed two girls in Virginia Beach, to barking "Cut the mic!" when the son of a Port Authority worker killed on 9/11 expressed reservations on his show about the war in Afghanistan. In the latter case, even silencing him wasn't enough; an outraged O'Reilly summoned Fox News Security to haul him off the set.

But there *is* an upside to O'Reilly. His opponents can *use* him to garner national attention for their cause — or for their book. One of the first to benefit from O'Reilly's blustering pomposity was the comedian and author Al Franken. In 2003, Franken authored *Lies and the Lying Liars Who Tell Them: A Fair and Balanced Look at the Right*, an examination of the corruption and falsehoods perpetuated by right-wing personalities, such as Ann Coulter and Rush Limbaugh. O'Reilly was featured prominently in the book — in fact, he graced the cover — slated for release by Dutton Books, an imprint of Penguin, that September.[1]

During a booksellers' luncheon in June broadcast live by CSPAN, Franken sat on a panel with O'Reilly, who also had an upcoming release to hawk. In his allotted opening time, Franken laid out some of the material from his book, pointing out that O'Reilly claimed winning a prestigious Peabody Award for his TV work when, in fact, he'd never received one. This set O'Reilly off. He called Franken "Vicious, and that's with a capital V, a person who's blinded by ideology," as reported on June 2, 2003, by Fox News. As O'Reilly tried to make his case that he'd confused the names of two awards (Polk, Peabody), Franken attempted to speak and was cut off in trademark fashion by O'Reilly: "Shut up! You had your thirty-five minutes! Shut up! We're supposed to be on here for fifteen minutes and this idiot goes thirty-five," O'Reilly barked. Franken gently reminded him, "This isn't your show, Bill," and the crowd roared.

The CSPAN fracas must have gotten under O'Reilly's skin. On August 12, a month before the release of Franken's book, Fox News filed suit against Franken and his publisher, Penguin Group, to stop them from using the phrase "fair and balanced" in the book's title and from using an unflattering picture of O'Reilly on the cover. The lawsuit called Franken a "C-level political commentator" who "appears to be shrill and unstable"

---

[1]Full disclosure: this book is published by Celebra, also a Penguin imprint.

and charged that "[Franken's] intent is clear—to exploit Fox News' trademark, confuse the public as to the origins of the book and, accordingly, boost sales of the book."

Of course, it was Fox's *lawsuit* that truly boosted sales of the book. Newspapers nationwide carried stories about the lawsuit. Hundreds of bloggers across the web slapped the phrase "Fair and Balanced" at the top of their sites and invited Fox's legal department to sue them as well. If only they'd been so lucky! Penguin, taking advantage of the free publicity, moved up publication of the book from September 22 to August 21 and upped its print run. On August 22, U.S. District Court Judge Denny Chin rejected Fox's demand for an injunction against publishing the book, ruling that the suit was "wholly without merit, both factually and legally" and concluding that Fox was "trying to undermine the First Amendment." Franken mined comedy gold from the suit: "When I read 'intoxicated or deranged' and 'shrill and unstable' in their complaint, I thought for a moment I was a Fox commentator," he remarked; and "Usually when you say someone was literally laughed out of court, you mean they were figuratively laughed out of court, but Fox was literally laughed out of court."

Fox withdrew the lawsuit, sniffing, "It's time to return Al Franken to the obscurity that he's normally accustomed to." Too late. The book, which had been at #489 on Amazon's list before the lawsuit was filed, quickly shot up to #1. Three weeks later, 300,000 copies of the book had been sold and *Lying Liars* was the #1 *New York Times* bestseller. Thus, Franken might have only been half joking when he claimed to be "disappointed" at the lawsuit's withdrawal. "I was hoping they'd keep it going for a few more news cycles," he told Paula Zahn of CNN on August 25, 2003.

Franken's gain from batting around O'Reilly was not lost on Keith Olbermann. A former sportscaster turned political commentator, Olbermann had begun broadcasting *Countdown* in early 2003—competing directly with *The O'Reilly Factor* in the 8:00 p.m. time slot, but with a far smaller audience. Olbermann astutely noted his rival's thin skin and set out to needle him into publicly acknowledging *Countdown*.

Olbermann began his campaign innocuously, with a new feature on his show called "Worst Person in the World." Every night, he would feature three nominees, a "worse" (bronze) and "worser" (silver), capping it off with the "worst" person (gold). He'd kicked off the segment in the summer of 2005, and by November, O'Reilly had been named "worst person in the world" fifteen times.

Finally, on November 29, O'Reilly put up an enemies list on his website titled "A Message from Bill: Media Operations that Traffic in Defamation," with the statement: "These are the worst offenders. In the months to come, we expect to add more names to this list. We recommend that you do not patronize these operations and that advertisers do the same. They are dishonest and not worth your time and money." The list included the *New York Daily News*, the *St. Petersburg Times*—and MSNBC.

Upping the pressure, Olbermann handed out all *three* of the nightly awards to O'Reilly on November 30. He wanted more than a mention on a website and he continued his taunts.

Finally, on December 22, he drew blood, with O'Reilly charging his red flag at long last: "Speaking of disasters," O'Reilly told his audience, "our competitor at MSNBC is a notorious smear merchant. So far this month, December, the *Factor's* third rerun at four in the morning has beaten MSNBC's original eight o'clock program more than fifty percent of the time. Unbelievable."

Olbermann immediately pounced back. "It is curious, isn't it, that he brands me a smear merchant yet instead of trying to refute just one of the hateful things we've quoted him as saying or doing, he instead turns to the ratings? That's probably because the only things we've smeared O'Reilly with have been his own quotes. To borrow another phrase, when you're as guilty as he is, change the subject." Bloggers lapped it up and promoted the brewing feud and—by extension—Olbermann's show. As the conflict escalated, it became part of an ongoing soap opera, a narrative of the highest order. The public had a top-notch villain in O'Reilly and a sympathetic, smart, and attractive hero in Olbermann. And the desired outcome? O'Reilly had made this a battle about ratings, and there was no better way to slay this villain than to deny him his obvious greatest joy in life—the top ratings.

And as Olbermann told the Associated Press in a January 8, 2006, article, "He's writing this material for me. I'm thinking of sending him a check. Day after day he just gets weirder and weirder and weirder."

It got even weirder in February 2006. O'Reilly lashed back with a "petition" to MSNBC's chairman demanding the network replace Olbermann:

> "We, the undersigned, are becoming increasingly concerned about the well-being of MSNBC and, in particular, note the continuing ratings failure of the program currently airing weeknights on that network at 8:00 PM EST.
>
> "It is now apparent to everyone that a grave injustice has been done to the previous host for that time slot, Phil Donahue, whose ratings, at the time of his show's cancellation three years ago, were demonstrably stronger than those of the current host.
>
> "Therefore, in an effort to rescue MSNBC from the ratings basement and to restore the honor and dignity of Mr. Donahue, who was ignobly removed as host three years ago, we ask that you immediately bring Phil Donahue's show back at 8:00 PM EST before any more damage is done."

The problem with the petition—aside from the fact that it allowed Olbermann to gleefully sign it himself on the air—was that the premise was wrong. Rather than being a "continuing ratings failure," *Countdown* was experiencing the strongest ratings on the cable news network. In fact, in March 2006 the show scored a rare ratings victory for MSNBC by taking the number-two ranking for its time slot. O'Reilly still led by a sizeable margin, but Olbermann's show kept climbing, with a 28 percent increase in ratings over March 2005, and a dramatic 63 percent increase in the coveted twenty-five-to-fifty-four age group, the demographic most valued by advertisers. Olbermann couldn't believe his luck, and kept up his provocations: "The median age of viewers of this program is 58.7. The median age of viewers of Mr. O'Reilly's program is 68.6. So if you want to be concerned about 'well-being,' Bill, be concerned about the odds of your viewers living into next week."

O'Reilly was being pushed to the brink, and his typical bluster was reaching a fever pitch. A caller to O'Reilly's radio show was threatened with a visit from Fox security after he playfully mentioned Olbermann's name. "You know, we have his—we have your phone numbers, by the way, so if you're listening, Mike, we have your phone number. And we're going to turn it over to Fox security, and you'll be getting a little visit," O'Reilly ranted.

All of this was proving a treasure trove for Olbermann. "Bill thinks he has his own police," he observed. Then, he needled his rival on that sorest of all topics—ratings—readily returning to the topic of O'Reilly's graying audience. In June, when O'Reilly claimed that MSNBC had lower ratings as a network than six years prior, Olbermann could hardly contain his glee:

> "Bill, boy. Bill-O! Hey! Over here. Back in reality-based reality. The latest ratings have come out. From a year ago to right now, MSNBC's ratings are up 12 percent overall, 13 percent among viewers 25 to 54, and at the hour you and I are on head to head, we're up 37 percent and you're down 20 percent and—I know, I'm sorry, too many numbers in there. [. . .] Listen Slappy, FOX's ratings are lower than they were five years ago. Bill-O, 267,000 of your viewers have vanished since last June. Call FOX security, they're missing! [. . .]"

By July, a *New York Times* feature on the feud suggested Fox News and O'Reilly seemed to have finally realized that they were Olbermann's pro bono PR firm:

> "Every time Mr. O'Reilly took umbrage at the slams, it seemed to add a bounce to Mr. Olbermann's ratings—one reason, perhaps, that Mr. O'Reilly's reactions seem to have tailed off more recently. Nobody at Fox News wants Mr. Olbermann to get any more of a draft from Mr. O'Reilly's popularity."

The fact that the feud itself had crossed over from cable news and blogs to the nation's highest-profile newspaper was in itself validation of Olbermann's strategy of feeding the backlash.

Most important, as Olbermann told the *New York Times*: "You don't punch down. If you're in my position, you punch upwards." And as he expanded on the notion to CBS: "Every time [O'Reilly] opens his mouth, I get more viewers." His job was to keep O'Reilly opening his mouth, and he executed brilliantly. O'Reilly's backlash was Olbermann's gain.

EMBRACE THE ATTACKS

The journalist Jeremy Scahill wrote an article for the *Nation* on May 8, 2006, about Blackwater Worldwide, the security contractor, and opened it with a description of a tragic incident involving four Blackwater employees in Iraq:

> "It is one of the most infamous incidents of the war in Iraq: On March 31, 2004, four private American security contractors get lost and end up driving through the center of Falluja, a hotbed of Sunni resistance to the US occupation. Shortly after entering the city, they get stuck in traffic, and their small convoy is ambushed. Several armed men approach the two vehicles and open fire from behind, repeatedly shooting the men at point-blank range. Within moments, their bodies are dragged from the vehicles and a crowd descends on them, tearing them to pieces. Eventually, their corpses are chopped and burned. The remains of two of the men are strung up on a bridge over the Euphrates River and left to dangle. The gruesome image is soon beamed across the globe."

One of the places that image and story was beamed was into my living room in Berkeley, California, where the sensational and grizzly details dominated the news of the day. On that morning of April 1, sleep-deprived and cranky from having a four-month-old son at home keeping me up at night, I read about the incident and saw the image.

Then I stumbled across the overlooked news that five U.S. soldiers had been killed near Falluja as well that same day. Having served my country in uniform, having worn combat boots, my loyalties have always been with my brothers and sisters in arms. As is always the case when reading about casualties from Iraq, I got angry. And I got angrier as I realized that the Blackwater mercenaries were front-page news *everywhere*, while the hero soldiers who had given their lives for their country, not for cash, were relegated to the back pages when mentioned at all. I couldn't believe it.

I had no intention of writing about the attacks. I knew I was too angry, tired, and cranky to do so lucidly anyway. But as I was scanning the diaries posted on *Daily Kos*, I saw one on the Blackwater deaths. Without giving it a lot of thought, writing straight from the gut, I went into that diary's comments and posted this:

> "Every death should be on the front page. Let the people see what war is like. This isn't an Xbox game. There are real repercussions to Bush's folly. That said, I feel nothing over the death of mercenaries. They aren't in Iraq because of orders, or because they are there trying to help the people make Iraq a better place. They are there to wage war for profit. Screw them."

Immediately, *Daily Kos* users began to upbraid me for the callousness of the remark. Comments that were responding to my initial comment claimed: "That is the most disgusting comment I have ever seen on this blog," and "regardless of what they were doing there, they were HUMAN BEINGS," and "screw them?! I hope this is an April Fools' comment." A full-blown diary, not just a comment on my comment, went up an hour later, titled "kos—over the line!" and it contained the succinct critique, "hey kos—WRONG. That attitude is BULLSHIT." Most of the *Daily Kos* community seemed to agree, so the next day I clarified my initial reaction:

> "There's been much ado about my indifference to the mercenary deaths in Falluja a couple days ago. I wrote in some diary comments somewhere that 'I felt nothing' and 'Screw them.'
>
> "My language was harsh, and, in reality, not true. Fact is, I did feel something. That's why I was so angry.
>
> "I was angry that five soldiers—the real heroes in my mind— were killed the same day and got far lower billing in the newscasts.

I was angry that 51 American soldiers paid the ultimate price for Bush's folly in Iraq in March alone. I was angry that these mercenaries make more in a day than our brave men and women in uniform make in an entire month. I was angry that the US is funding private armies, paying them $30,000 per soldier, per month, while the Bush administration tries to cut our soldiers' hazard pay. I was angry that these mercenaries would leave their wives and children behind to enter a war zone on their own volition [. . .]

"So not only was I wrong to say I felt nothing over their deaths, I was lying. I felt way too much. Nobody deserves to die. But in the greater scheme of things, there are a lot of greater tragedies going on in Iraq (51 last month, plus countless civilians and Iraqi police). That those tragedies are essentially ignored these days is, ultimately, the greatest tragedy of all."

By then, the right-wing hordes had latched on to my comments. They smelled liberal blogger blood in the water. James Taranto, in the *Wall Street Journal* column "Best of the Web," covered the initial remark and my clarifying one on the same day—April 2—that I made it. He quoted and linked to a conservative expatriate blogger in Shanghai, Michael Friedman, who wrote: "So much for the left's great blogging hope . . . When you sleep with pigs you shouldn't be surprised if you wake up covered with muck and smelling like shit, and these politicians are all sleeping with a pig. Smell anything?"

The controversy caused some *Daily Kos* advertisers to cancel. Democratic Rep. Martin Frost of Texas was the first, pulling his ad the same day I made the clarification comment, going so far as to create a form letter that was sent to people complaining to the campaign about supporting *Daily Kos*:

"Thank you for contacting us.
"As a former Army Reserves member, spouse of an Army General on active duty and an American, Martin finds these words extremely irresponsible and highly offensive. As soon as this post-

ing was brought to our attention we immediately severed any tie to the website. [. . .]

"The views expressed by that website in no way reflect Martin's positions and as stated earlier his advertising has been pulled. Congressman Frost supported the President's efforts to remove Saddam Hussein and his murderous regime and stands 100% behind our troops who are fighting terrorism both abroad and right here at home.

"There is no place for these disgusting remarks in this nation's discussion on foreign policy."

Two more advertisers followed suit in the next couple of days—Democratic congressional candidate Joe Donnelly in Indiana and an environmental organization called Environment 2004 (long since defunct)—and another Democratic congressional candidate, Jane Mitakides of Ohio, pulled her ad the following Monday.

Emboldened by those early victories, the conservative bloggers expanded their campaign to demand that other liberal sites de-link from *Daily Kos*, a tactic that in theory would starve the site of traffic and lead to a drop-off in advertising revenue. Here, they were rebuffed by most liberal bloggers, and I had hopes the controversy would die out over the weekend.

Those hopes were dashed pretty spectacularly when the John Kerry presidential campaign decided to make a big show on Saturday of pulling its link to *Daily Kos* from the campaign's website, posting on its campaign blog, "In light of the unacceptable statement about the death of Americans made by *Daily Kos*, we have removed the link to this blog from our website."

Great, I thought. The Kerry campaign's high-profile denunciation was a gift from heaven to my tormentors, not only giving the story legs for several more days but guaranteeing the issue would cross over into traditional media, as in fact, it did. Not only the *Wall Street Journal*, but other prominent conservative media operations like the *Weekly Standard* joined the fray. Even the British publication the *Spectator* decided to get a few licks in on April 10, calling me "the epitome of the post-9/11 re-primitivised political activist. By 're-primitivised,' I mean the armchair insurgent's version of that Fallujah carnival." The right wing, so adept at creating villains, had decided I was the next in line.

Months later, the media columnist Adam L. Penenberg would remark in the July 7 edition of *Wired*, "Now, the fact that a blog could be de-linked from a presidential candidate's official website (and actually had advertising to lose) is noteworthy—it shows that blogs have indeed arrived as a force to be reckoned with." From the distance of a few months, the events could be seen as acknowledging the growing role of blogs in the media and political landscape.

At the time, though, I'd never experienced such direct assault, and I was more than a little bewildered, feeling at times like the whole world was crashing down around me. People were saying horrible things about me on blogs, on the radio, in newspapers and magazines. I worried about whether my friends would abandon me, whether my family would be embarrassed, whether everything I'd worked so hard to build would come crumbling down. And yes, a handful of progressive bloggers I'd always considered allies did indeed abandon me or join the witch hunt—and that hurt more than losing advertisers or John Kerry's vow of disassociation.

Yet there was a bright side to this. For one, I discovered who my real friends and allies were. Additionally, it identified those activists who had the good strategic sense to understand the implications of what the conservative blogger frenzy could mean to future organizing on the left. The blogger Jerome Armstrong, who would later coauthor *Crashing the Gate* with me, pointed out the political ramifications in an April 4 posting on *MyDD*:

> "What Kerry's blog has done is bend to the will of the radical fringe right of the blogosphere. The rightwing blogosphere is right this moment undergoing a coordinated email campaign to every part of the Democratic establishment, beating them into a submissive dismissal of *Daily Kos*, because of one offhand comment made, which Kos had already retracted. First the advertisers, then John Kerry. What's next, the DSCC, the DNC and the DCCC

blogroll? You think the wingnuts will be satisfied then? No, they'll just go after the next link, and the next blogger."

One advertiser that wasn't beaten into "submissive dismissal of *Daily Kos*" was the Minnesota House Democratic Caucus, which not only refused to bail on the site, but issued a defiant statement of support on April 7: "This intimidation isn't going to work. And, yes, that's exactly what it is: intimidation, standard-issue Republican fare. We don't agree with Kos' mercenary death comments but we respect and support his right to express himself, just as we respect and support Mr. Friedman's right to disagree. We do, however, recognize the attack on the advertisers for what it is: another Republican intimidation tactic."

The advertiser-boycott effort truly died on April 11 when Brad Carson, a Democratic senatorial candidate in heavily conservative Oklahoma, publicly refused demands to pull his link to *Daily Kos* from his campaign blog. If the right wing failed with Carson, given the particulars of his race and region, they were almost certainly doomed to fail elsewhere.

Ultimately, I received an invaluable firsthand lesson about high-profile activism—the more I was attacked over my "screw them" comments, the more I was thrust into the national spotlight. Sure, I had to answer the inevitable question about my comments, but I was doing it on *Nightline* and other high-profile shows, like *Q&A* with Brian Lamb:

LAMB: As you know, the most controversial thing you've done is make a comment about four mercenaries that died at Fallujah. I've got the quote here.

"I feel nothing over the death of the mercenaries. They are there to wage war for profit. Screw them."

And a lot of people went crazy over that comment. Why did you say it? Do you regret saying it? And how much criticism did you get on it?

MOULITSAS: I regret the way it was phrased. It was not very politically correct. But the sentiment behind it was very appropriate, and I still stand by it.

I mean, the whole context of this was the four mercenaries that

were killed in Fallujah. That exact same day five [soldiers] were also
killed, but they were nowhere in the news.

And I wore combat boots. Like I said, unlike most of my critics—
the vast majority of my critics—I actually wore combat boots. To me,
my first and foremost concern is for our men and women in Iraq and
in the Gulf region and in Afghanistan.

Media outlets started calling me up, treating me as a source for political stories. Book agents were emailing me interested in representing me.
In short, I was suddenly on the media radar. And I realized that the more
my political opponents attacked me, the more they credentialed me as
someone who should be taken seriously. Traffic to my site skyrocketed,
from about 4.5 million page views in March 2004 to 5.8 million the following month—a 29 percent increase in a single month and a record for
the site despite an otherwise slow news period that falls between the primaries and the earnest start of the general election. "The 'screw them'
remark is how I first heard of you and *Daily Kos*," wrote Barb Morrill, now
a *Daily Kos* contributing editor. "I was a regular on the Kerry blog and
there was a big discussion when the Kerry campaign pulled your link, so
I came over to check it out."

As I gained a ton of readers, every advertiser I lost was replaced with
new ones within days. Because I gave no refunds to the fleeing advertisers,
I ended up making double revenue for those ad slots. That April wasn't
just my best traffic month until that point, it also ended up being my most
financially lucrative one, an unexpected windfall I directed toward beef-
ing up my site's infrastructure.

Oddly enough, Dean Barnett of the conservative *Weekly Standard*
probably offered in retrospect one of the best evaluations of the import of
the entire incident in an article, "Taking Kos Seriously," published nearly
a year after the "screw them" remark:

> "While politicians distanced themselves from the site, Kos's
> fans stayed put. . . . And since the eyeballs remained, politicians
> soon returned. Political advertisers who had left were replaced in

short order by other office seekers. At first it seemed the entire affair might ruin Kos; in the end it was, as he put it in an interview
with the *New York Times*, nothing more than a 'blip.'"

The right wing thought it was destroying me, but instead all the hul-
labaloo conservative bloggers created simply drew curious readers who
had never visited the site before—and provided me with the financial
resources to manage the extra growth the attention generated. Even now,
four years after the comment was made, right-wing bloggers, the Republican Party, and conservative pundits continue to reference the "screw
them" remark, still clueless as to how instrumental their obsession with
the phrase was in building *Daily Kos* into what it is today. More important,
U.S. military anger at Blackwater has subsequently confirmed my sentiments born out of kinship with my brothers and sisters in arms. And even
today, seeing how these war-profiteering companies put our American
troops at risk with their reckless behavior and unjustified killings of Iraqi
civilians, I have nothing but contempt for their operations.

Screw them.

★   ★   ★

The fact is that when the whole controversy started, I had no idea it would
mushroom into a major "scandal." Many issues first gain traction fairly low
on smaller media outlets and blogs, only getting the attention of larger and
more important entities after they have been test-driven in smaller markets. In all cases, not just that of the mercenary comments, *Daily Kos* was
initially criticized by small-time bloggers, and only gradually did the site
work its way up the ladder to bigger and better enemies. The incongruity
between a larger media outlet beating up on a relatively small blog—
punching down, as Olbermann said—often can look ridiculous, while
elevating the notoriety of the person or group being punched, so to
speak.

For example, on January 14, 2005, the conservative magazine the
American Spectator dedicated a whole column to attacking *Daily Kos*,

saying the site was "the closest thing we in the blogosphere have to the *New York Times*, both in volume of readership and absurdity of content," while simultaneously claiming the site's influence "never extended beyond the 'Bush is Hitler' crowd." The obvious question: Why write about it then?

As noted above, the larger and more respected *Weekly Standard* showed a healthy respect for the site in "Taking Kos Seriously," in which the author, Dean Barnett, wrote, "Many in the conservative blogosphere have been quick to label Kos a 'moon bat' because of his unforgiving left-wing politics and his strident tone. . . . However, [this] obscures the vital fact that Moulitsas leads an influential movement, a movement whose influence is likely to grow even larger."

On that front, I received a generous helping hand from no less than the Republican National Committee. In August 2006, a lengthy six-page press release from the RNC was blasted to the group's entire media list, with a screaming headline: "WHO IS MARKOS MOULITSAS ZUNIGA? A Partisan 'Nutroot' Who Turned His Hate-Filled Blog *Daily Kos* Into A Leadership Post In The Democrat Party." And what exactly was the "news hook" for the tirade? I took a vacation.

> "*Daily Kos* Blogger Markos Moulitsas Zuniga Back From 'Relaxing' Vacation: Moulitsas Just Got Back From Summer Vacation: 'I got back from El Salvador really early this morning, so I'm still catching up on the last week's news.' (The *Daily Kos* Website, www.dailykos.com, Accessed 8/22/06) Moulitsas: 'I'm still playing catchup after my very relaxing, very nice vacation.' (*Daily Kos* Website, www.dailykos.com, Accessed 8/22/06)"

Fresh off attacking me for my dastardly vacation, the RNC press release tore into me for not being on welfare:

> "MOULITSAS IS A FAT CAT LIBERAL BLOGGER FOR HIRE Moulitsas Makes An 'Excellent Living': '[Moulitsas Achieved] Enough Success With Kos That He Says He Is Able To Live In Costly Berkeley, Calif., Entirely Off Its Ad Revenue . . . '

(Daniel Terdiman, 'A Blog For Baseball Fans Builds A League Of Sites,' The *New York Times*, 4/18/05) Moulitsas: 'I make an excellent living. Absolutely.' (ABC's '*Nightline*,' 7/24/06)"

All in all, the press release was 2,785 words long, full of citations for things like calling Bush a "moron" and Vice President Dick Cheney "evil," and weird statements like "Two-Thirds Of Democrat Leadership Fled To YearlyKos Convention" (how does one "flee" *to* a convention?). The release also highlighted the site's efforts on behalf of "defeatocrat" candidates like James Webb, Jon Tester, and Sherrod Brown, all of whom went on to win their races that November.

The primary consequence of that ludicrous press release was to very clearly telegraph to the entire national political press corps that the Republican Party considered *Daily Kos*, and me, a threat.

Who else proved eager to step up and give *Daily Kos* a boost? Bill O'Reilly, of course. What set him off were four comments—among the millions posted by diarists and readers—that had used harsh words against the pope and Israel. "[A] vicious far-left website called the *DailyKos* [is] one of the worst examples of hatred America has to offer," he ranted on July 16, 2007. He escalated the rhetoric the next day: "[T]his is hate of the worst order. It's like the Ku Klux Klan. It's like the Nazi party. There's no difference here." On July 23, in what had become a jihad, O'Reilly spat, "It's kind of like Al Capone," and also compared me to Mussolini. On July 30, he lost his top when Joe Lieberman's pal, Lanny Davis—no friend to *Daily Kos*—nonetheless pushed back against O'Reilly's over-the-top rhetoric.

DAVIS: I would not advise a candidate to stay away from a group [like the *Daily Kos*] unless you can generalize accurately about the entire group.

O'REILLY: It's a hate group! It's a hate group!

DAVIS: I don't accept the fact that the entire site is filled with hate. But I do agree—

O'REILLY: Hey, look. There was some good stuff on the Nazi site. You know, give to the kids. Give to the Aryan kids. Come on. It's a hate site. You know it.

Meanwhile, Republican campaigns tried unsuccessfully to make an association with *Daily Kos* a winning issue. In Montana, *Daily Kos* played a role in drafting Jon Tester into the Democratic primary for the U.S. Senate and ultimately unseating the entrenched Republican incumbent Conrad Burns in the 2006 general election. "By continuing to accept Kos' support, using his blog to raise money, and even linking to it from his own site, Jon Tester has assumed responsibility for comments like this. Jon Tester should remove the link to '*Daily Kos*' from his site and repudiate Kos' hate-filled politics," demanded the National Republican Senatorial Committee (NRSC) on July 31, 2006. A Burns television ad on "who supports Jon Tester" noted: ". . . And took nearly $100,000 from a group that mocked American deaths." The incumbent senator George Allen's campaign in Virginia issued its own press release on October 16, 2006:

> "Jim Webb has proudly accepted over $130,000 in tainted money from a controversial liberal website that is helping him and other Democrats raise money.
>
> "'Jim Webb has proven he will do anything for liberal Democratic money—even that of a fringe liberal blogger who gloats about the deaths of American contractors in Iraq,' said Allen Campaign Manager Dick Wadhams.
>
> "'Jim Webb continues to reveal just how far left he will go to finance his campaign,' Wadhams said. 'Even if it means selling out to extremists like *Daily Kos*.'"

Despite their failure to gain anything from such attacks in 2006, Republicans continued building up *Daily Kos* credibility—and traffic—in

2007. "How is Boulder liberal Mark Udall spending his district working period?" a November 29, 2007, NRSC press release asked, after mentioning a fund-raiser I was helping publicize for Udall in San Francisco. "Sipping Pouilly Fuisse in San Francisco with the angriest of liberals. How does that help Colorado?"

By then, I had ridden all that criticism to a slot as an "occasional columnist" in *Newsweek* magazine for the 2008 election cycle. To balance me out, *Newsweek* brought in Karl Rove, President Bush's legendary right-hand man and chief strategist and confidant. On November 9, Rove attended a conference about politics and the web. Specifically citing "liberal blogs such as DailyKos.com," he declared, "The Web has given angry and vitriolic people more of a voice in public discourse. People in the past who have been on the nutty fringe of political life, who were more or less voiceless, have now been given an inexpensive and easily accessible soapbox, a blog."

The notion may seem absurd and counterintuitive, but inviting attacks suggests you're a force to be reckoned with. And when your enemy takes you up on the invitation, it is evidence that your efforts are drawing blood.

Right-wing media figures have built entire careers on the simple precept of feeding the backlash. Rush Limbaugh's smashmouth style of talk radio invited a flood of criticism that he rode to prominence. The author and columnist Ann Coulter strains to top her ridiculous, over-the-top statements knowing that each one of them, inevitably widely reported, will propel her current book (and there's *always* a book being promoted when she pulls her shtick) ever higher on the bestseller lists. Liberals fall for it every single time, protesting her campus speeches, blogging her latest outrages furiously, and playing into her traps. The joke is on her opponents—just as the joke was on mine.

Mastering the art of feeding the backlash has a necessary corollary. Don't slip up and feed the backlash of your opponent. Liberals need to learn to stop taking the bait every time the sensationalist right-wing attack dogs spew extremist foolishness. The Coulters and Limbaughs of the world owe their success—as I do—to the inability of their detractors to ignore them.

KNOW WHEN TO IGNORE AN ATTACK

Keith Olbermann responds to every single Bill O'Reilly attack, and for the longest time O'Reilly responded in kind. Now who got the better end of the deal? Olbermann used his attacks on O'Reilly to build his own credibility, ratings, and influence, while O'Reilly used his attacks on Olbermann to . . . build Olbermann's credibility, ratings, and influence.

If you're getting hit from above, by all means hit back. Hard. And often. If you're less known, you might invite further attention, and in the worst case, you remind observers that those above you fear you. But if you attack those below you, especially those below you in terms of name recognition, you're helping elevate their status, something you always want to deny your enemies. Furthermore, you risk looking like a bully. But obviously, it's not always simple and formulaic. There are times when you may find yourself in a situation where gauging the sincerity of your attacker may affect whether you should respond or not.

When I faced incoming fire over my comments about the Blackwater mercenaries, one of the lines of attack from my conservative critics was that I apologize for my remarks. The response I posted wasn't an apology. It was never meant to be. What I wrote was an *explanation*. I also knew that no apology, even if paired with thirty lashes, would have been enough to satisfy the enemies of *Daily Kos*. They were seeking to discredit me, paint me into a corner as an America-hating fringe character, and any apology would've been met with further demands. They were insatiable, and I refused to go through the motions of trying to satisfy them.

Sometimes calls for apologies are simply ploys to keep the dialogue going, and to feed a desire to see an opponent utterly debased and humiliated. Obviously, it's best not to give in to these kinds of demands.

When progressive bloggers began going after Sen. Trent Lott's effusive praise of Strom Thurmond's segregationist past (see chapter 3), an apology would not have been acceptable in light of Lott's long history of racist politics. So each of his apologies, rather than help calm the waters, only fanned the efforts to tar and feather him. It's debatable whether Lott could have survived had he shut his mouth after his first apology, but there's no doubt that his repeated efforts to appease only hastened his downfall.

There are, of course, times when you may be asked to respond to legitimate concerns or questions, and in that case it's better to respond quickly and honestly. If the intentions are sincere, it pays to be humble, gracious, and open. But when the goal is to harm or destroy, be careful about giving an inch.

Discerning when to respond to an attack and when to ignore it is one of the most difficult challenges an activist can face, and there are no guarantees of success with either strategy. Rules like "Don't punch down" can help, and figuring out when a critic is sincere—or able to be satisfied—is certainly valuable. But the truth is, there are some backlashes that don't help build a reputation, but destroy it, as Trent Lott found out. In such circumstances, the best bet may be to starve a story of oxygen and try to survive to fight another day. Often, if there's no news "hook" upon which to build a narrative without new information, the story will die from neglect.

In late 2007, Senate Minority Leader Mitch McConnell spoke about American troops in Iraq and said, "Nobody is happy about losing lives, but remember these are not draftees, these are full-time professional soldiers." This was the kind of "disrespect the troops" story that Republicans had foisted upon hapless Democrats and then feasted on for the better part of a decade. There was no other way to interpret this than, "They signed up for this, so they asked for it." Immediately, bloggers rose up in anger. McConnell's Democratic opponent for the U.S. Senate seat in Kentucky, the Iraq war veteran Lt. Col. Andrew Horne, demanded an apology. McConnell's office refused to respond or engage. His silence meant that in a matter of days, the story had lost all impetus and was soon dropped and forgotten by a fickle and easily distracted media.

Of course, it's not always as simple as "ignore the bad news." There are times when ignoring a story will render it impotent, and other times when doing so will let the story fester and grow. Again, this is one of the most difficult decisions to make, and choosing the wrong tactic can prove fatal in some circumstances. John Kerry found that out the hard way.

On May 4, 2004, a group of Vietnam veterans held a press conference

at the National Press Club in Washington, D.C., to announce the formation of a group called Swift Boat Veterans for Truth (SBVT). Like Kerry,
the presumptive Democratic presidential nominee at the time, each of the
veterans had served on a "swift boat," a small, fast patrol boat used for
counterinsurgency operations on the coasts and rivers of Southeast Asia.
These veterans were no allies of Kerry, however. SBVT declared that its
purpose was to "discuss Kerry's war crimes charges, Kerry's record, and to
request that Kerry authorize the Department of Defense to release the
originals and the complete files relating to his military service and medical
military records."

The close ties between SBVT and George W. Bush's Texas supporters
were evident from its debut. The press conference was organized by longtime Republican flack Merrie Spaeth. As Joe Conason reported the same
day on *Salon*, Spaeth had worked in the Reagan administration's press
operation and had coached Kenneth Starr before his congressional testimony on the Whitewater case. Ted Olsen, George W. Bush's then solicitor
general and longtime GOP dirty-tricks operative, was godfather to Spaeth's
daughter. But that wasn't all. Spaeth had participated in a similar independent campaign attacking John McCain during the 2000 Republican primaries, and her late husband, Tex Lezar, had shared the Republican ballot
in 1994 with George W. Bush as the unsuccessful candidate for lieutenant
governor of Texas. Moreover, the main protagonist of SBVT, John O'Neill,
had been recruited in 1971 by the Nixon aide Charles Colson to act as a
public relations counterweight to Kerry, who had become an influential
leader in Vietnam Veterans Against the War. O'Neill was also a partner at
the same law firm as Lezar and Margaret Wilson, who succeeded future
U.S. Attorney General Alberto Gonzales as Bush's general counsel when
he was governor of Texas.

In other words, this was a reputedly disinterested veterans group being
steered by some of President Bush's closest friends and advisors.

The Kerry campaign knew of these complex and long-standing ties
from the start. The same day that SBVT announced its formation, the
Kerry campaign held its own press conference featuring some of the veterans who had served on the same swift boat with Kerry. The campaign

showed photos of O'Neill with Colson and Nixon and spoke about the ties between Spaeth and the Bush campaign. "The Nixon White House attempted to do this to Kerry, and the Bush folks are following the same plan," said Kerry senior advisor Michael Meehan. "We're not going to let them make false claims about Kerry and go unanswered."

While the initial SBVT press conference attracted little attention, the intent was clear: to torpedo Kerry's campaign by discrediting his combat leadership, thus portraying him as unfit to be commander in chief. Little happened over the summer, although an IRS report filed July 15 indicated that the Houston, Texas, developer Bob Perry had given $100,000 of the initial $158,750 raised by SBVT.

Three months later, at the Democratic convention in Boston July 26–29, Kerry's campaign made his Vietnam service a central theme. As he strode onstage to deliver his nomination speech, he embraced several of his swift boat mates, dubbed the Band of Brothers, and stepping up to the podium, he saluted and said, to wild applause, "I'm John Kerry, and I'm reporting for duty." In an election dominated by terrorism and war concerns, Kerry advisors expected this narrative to inoculate Kerry against the typical "Democrats are weak on defense" attacks Republicans would hurl against the candidate.

But as the Democrats set out to build and reinforce that narrative, SBVT struck back with an air attack. Their first TV commercial, titled "Any questions?" began running August 5, less than a week after Kerry's nominating speech. It began with a clip from Kerry's running mate, John Edwards:

JOHN EDWARDS: If you have any questions about what John Kerry is made of, just spend three minutes with the men who served with him.

TEXT ON-SCREEN: *Here's what those men think of John Kerry*

AL FRENCH: I served with John Kerry.

BOB ELDER: I served with John Kerry.

GEORGE ELLIOTT: John Kerry has not been honest about what happened in Vietnam.

AL FRENCH: He is lying about his record.

LOUIS LETSON: I know John Kerry is lying about his first Purple Heart because I treated him for that injury.

VAN O'DELL: John Kerry lied to get his bronze star . . . I know, I was there, I saw what happened.

JACK CHENOWETH: His account of what happened and what actually happened are the difference between night and day.

ADMIRAL HOFFMAN: John Kerry has not been honest.

ADRIAN LONSDALE: And he lacks the capacity to lead.

LARRY THURLOW: When the chips were down, you could not count on John Kerry.

BOB ELDER: John Kerry is no war hero.

GRANT HIBBARD: He betrayed all his shipmates . . . he lied before the Senate.

SHELTON WHITE: John Kerry betrayed the men and women he served with in Vietnam.

JOE PONDER: He dishonored his country . . . he most certainly did.

BOB HILDRETH: I served with John Kerry . . .

BOB HILDRETH (OFF CAMERA): John Kerry cannot be trusted.

The buy for the ad was modest, only about $500,000, and it ran in only three states. Yet the impact of the ad extended far beyond those paid media buys. Cable news made it a major story, playing the ad for free time and time again. It was distributed virally online. Newspapers wrote about it.

The Kerry campaign reacted instantly. On the same day the ad aired, the campaign's chief counsel tried to get stations to take down the ad, while the research and press arms of the campaign issued a thirty-six-page rebuttal of the SBVT ad. First, they pointed out that none of the men in the ad ever served with Kerry on the same swift boat. Several of the veterans who claimed to have served with Kerry in fact did not know him, and many weren't even in Vietnam at the same time as Kerry. Finally, many of the SBVT members were shown to have contradicted previous statements and actions, including official reports they signed while in the navy.

For two weeks the controversy raged, fueled by the release of a book by John O'Neill and Jerome Corsi titled *Unfit for Command: Swift Boat Veterans Speak Out Against John Kerry*. But while the campaign and its surrogates fought back against the bogus charges, Kerry himself did not address the accusations. Campaign manager Mary Beth Cahill didn't want to respond, according to Joe Klein in his book *Politics Lost* (2006), believing that "an aggressive response would only balloon the story." And Kerry's advertising consultant Bob Shrum not only thought that "the Republicans were trying to get them to chase another rabbit," but he also argued against spending money on television in August when viewership was low.

Eventually other voices prevailed over Shrum and Cahill. On August 17, the campaign held a press conference led by General Wesley Clark (ret.) and Admiral Stansfield Turner (ret.) to rebut the charges. On August 19, the campaign unveiled an ad in response to the SBVT charges. And on the same day, Kerry responded in a speech to the International Association of Fire Fighters in Boston, "More than thirty years ago, I learned an important lesson—when you're under attack, the best thing to do is turn your boat into the attacker. That's what I intend to do today."

Only, Kerry was turning his boat two weeks after the initial volley. During that time, the Swifties had successfully raised bogus doubts in the minds of voters about whether Kerry was honest, forthright, and even worthy of the high honors he had received for his valor in combat in Vietnam. In fact, in Election Night polling in six swing states, the Republican polling firm Public Opinion Strategies found that the SBVT's "Any Questions?" ad was the second most memorable ad of the cycle, recalled by an astonishing 23 percent of voters, even though only $500,000 was spent airing the ad in an election that saw $620 million in political advertising.

The Kerry campaign wanted to make his wartime record his greatest asset in the campaign. SBVT turned Kerry's heroism into a weakness, a reason why Americans could not trust him to keep America safe.

The Kerry campaign clearly thought having Kerry directly respond would give the SBVT charges credence and "feed" the story, and ignoring the ad, officially at least, might cause the story to melt away, with little publicity after its initial run. Yet the story had already crossed over from its small ad buy into the public consciousness, backed by some of the Texas Republican establishment's most seasoned, proven, and well-financed political operatives. Hindsight is always 20/20, but in the heat of the moment, you must differentiate between credible and effective threats and those that won't make a ripple in the media landscape.

DON'T BRING A SPORK TO A GUNFIGHT

On January 10, 2008, I did something seemingly crazy: I urged every Democrat in Michigan to vote for a Republican. Just for the hell of it.

In January 2006, Michigan scheduled its primaries for the 2008 presidential election before February 5, against the rules of both political parties. In response, Republicans stripped the state of half its delegates to the Republican convention. The Democratic National Committee meted out a harsher sentence—it removed *all* of its delegates. Furthermore, in a weak effort to curry favor with Iowa and New Hampshire, all top-tier Democratic candidates, except for Hillary Clinton, removed their names from the Michigan ballot. So the Democratic primary, when it rolled around in January 2008, was for all practical purposes irrelevant.

Not so for the Republican primary. A recent victory for Sen. John Mc-

Cain in New Hampshire had given him a big boost heading into the Michigan contest. A victory in Michigan would essentially seal the deal for McCain, giving Republicans an early nominee—and the one who, as luck and polls would have it, would be the strongest candidate against Democrats in the general election.

Fighting to take the lead in Michigan against McCain was former Massachusetts governor Mitt Romney. The free-spending millionaire had spent tens of millions of dollars running attack ads against his fellow Republican candidates. Meanwhile, early polls indicated the Mormon candidate would prove the weakest general election opponent for Democrats. A Romney victory in Michigan would blunt McCain's momentum and keep Romney engaged, spending cash freely to buy hundreds of ads criticizing his primary foes.

Given the lay of the political land, on January 10, the week before the election, I launched the "Mitt for Michigan" campaign, posting this on *Daily Kos*:

> "[W]ithout a real Democratic contest on the ballot, and a lack of party registration in Michigan, this is an open primary. Anyone can pick up a Republican ballot. So Michigan Democrats and independents who want to see the Republican battle royale continue should just take a few minutes on Tuesday, January 15th to cast a ballot for Mitt Romney in the Republican primary.
>
> "If you know someone in Michigan, send them the email I've included below the fold. If you don't know someone in Michigan, send the email to your liberal friends and see if THEY have friends in Michigan. Get the word out, whether by blog, mailing list, MySpace or Facebook page, or whatever.
>
> "If we can help push Mitt over the line, not only do we help keep their field fragmented, but we also pollute Romney's victory. How 'legitimate' will the Mittster's victory look if liberals provide the margin of victory? Think of the hilarity that will ensue. We'll simply be adding fuel to their civil war, never a bad thing from our vantage point."

There was no point in pretending our effort was high-minded or noble. It really wasn't a "dirty trick" since urging people to vote really doesn't qualify as a dirty trick, no matter how Machiavellian the decision-making process might be leading up to casting a legal vote. But it definitely violated the spirit of fair play. While many *Daily Kos* readers embraced the idea immediately, others were outraged. "I place a high value on democracy, and I don't think that interfering with the other party's primary shows democracy respect," one commenter wrote. "Sure the rules allow for this to happen, but that certainly does not make it right. Others might argue that the other side has done it in the past and actively works for voter-suppression even in general elections. But I tend to be from the an-eye-for-an-eye-leads-to-more-blindness camp." Another wrote, "A terrible idea. We are better than this." Those sentiments were repeated by hundreds of others, leading to this response from me:

> "There are some concerned that this is 'dirty tricks' and that we shouldn't 'stoop to their level.' This is perhaps the key difference between traditional liberals and movement progressives. The former believe that politics is a high-minded debate about ideas, the latter have seen movement conservatives use every tool at their disposal to steal power and cling to it. The problem is, politics matter, and so does the winner of elections. You can't bring a spork to a gunfight, because like Florida 2000, we lose every time. And while some may feel proud their personal ethics weren't compromised and that we 'took the high road' through the recount battle, how many thousands of soldiers and Iraqis wish that Democrats had fought a little harder for Gore's victory? . . . [A]s long as we operate within legal boundaries, all's fair in politics. The stakes matter too much to unilaterally disarm."

The campaign was a big PR success for *Daily Kos*, covered heavily in print and broadcast media. And while Romney would eventually win Michigan by a larger margin than that provided by self-proclaimed "liberals" in the exit polls (about 3 percent), our campaign tainted Romney as "the candidate Democrats would most like to face." Additionally, had

Romney won by less than three points—the percentage of self-identified liberals—we would've hit the mother lode by casting doubt on the legitimacy of his win, but *only* because we were willing to play rough and work within the rules to gain every possible advantage.

If the cause is just, then the goal should be victory. All reasonable options should be on the table. Anything less is simply unilateral disarmament, and unless you care little about the eventual outcome of your efforts, such disarmament is the height of irresponsibility. It's vital to focus on what tactics will best help accomplish the results you seek, and proceed accordingly. Similarly, when evaluating the work of your allies, don't criticize *effective* tactics merely because you find them distasteful or feel they have crossed your own self-defined ethical lines.

Effecting change is not for the meek. Any effort to challenge the entrenched status quo will be met with resistance. The democratization and global reach of new media cuts both ways—while it gives regular people a chance to directly participate in their world, it also allows enemies the ability to smear and attack before huge global audiences. No matter the stakes, those whose interests are being challenged will hold on to their privileges and power with all the strength they can muster. Notions of chivalry, gentlemanly combat, and fair turnabout cannot and should not come into play—unless you want to lose. The victors don't just get the spoils, they get to write the histories.

Ask yourself this: How many people remember that in the 2000 Florida presidential election recount battle, Republicans solicited military ballots *after* the voting deadline had passed? Yet Democrats, in a bid to "take the high road," allowed such ballots to be counted rather than challenging their validity. For an election decided by a scant 150 votes, this was just one of dozens of actions that Democrats refused to fight, lest they be seen as playing rough. Yet Republicans "won" an election they had actually lost, and Democrats got nothing for their efforts at chivalry.

Of course, for the citizen activist, the law serves as an effective boundary in how we can act. Unlike the rich and powerful, laws apply to us, and we don't have the ability to shrug off such formalities without potentially destroying our own lives. So we cross that line carefully and only after much deliberation. But anything within the boundaries of the law is fair game. There are ethical constructs we all operate under to govern our actions, and some forms of activism may be legal yet violate a personal sense of decency and decorum. But the only issue when considering a legally permissible tactic is whether the action will help further your cause. Efficacy, and not morality, is the governing principle. The opposition will stop at nothing to make you fail. You need to use everything in your bag of tricks to ensure they don't get that satisfaction.

Michael Moore is internationally famous for his documentaries, like *Roger & Me* (1989), *Bowling for Columbine* (2002), *Fahrenheit 9/11* (2004), and *Sicko* (2007). Yet few know that Moore was the editor of the liberal *Mother Jones* magazine in 1986—for four short months. He was fired from the publication for refusing to print an article criticizing the human rights record of the Sandinista government in Nicaragua. Moore didn't balk because of any solidarity with the communist regime, but because he had a keen tactical sense. He'd reasoned that if his magazine ran that story, his ideological nemesis, Ronald Reagan, "could easily hold it up, saying, 'See, even *Mother Jones* agrees with me.'" The writer of the piece that Moore withheld, Paul Berman, told the *Newark Star Ledger* on March 30, 2003, that Moore was a "very ideological guy and not a very well-educated guy." He also complained about being "censored."

No one was censoring Berman, of course; he could have had the article published anywhere else. Moore was simply conscious of the ramifications of publishing a story in a liberal magazine that would have brought aid and comfort to the Reaganites. Berman, with his master's degree from Columbia University, turned his nose up at the "not very well-educated" Moore, but Moore was the savvier one by far. Specifically, whether Moore agreed with Berman's article or not was irrelevant. Moore simply didn't want to hand Reagan a cheap propaganda victory, and if that required taking a step (rejecting an article) that offended Berman's ethical sensibilities, so be it. There was a real-world difference between that article running in *Mother Jones*, the *Weekly Standard*, or that repository of hawkish liberals, *the New Republic* (where, fittingly, Berman eventually became a contributing editor).

This incident cost Moore his job, but he finagled a $58,000 wrongful termination settlement out of it, which helped fund the $250,000 cost of making *Roger & Me* (he also sold his house for $27,000, held garage sales, and hosted bingo nights to fill out the rest of the movie's cost). The movie was a smashing success and was parlayed into a franchise of mega-successful documentaries that explored serious issues from a progressive-populist viewpoint, including the war in Iraq, the economic and personal devastation of plant layoffs in the heartland, the nation's gun culture, or the poor quality of health care in the United States. *Bowling for Columbine* earned him an Oscar for best documentary feature. *Fahrenheit 9/11* became the highest-grossing documentary film ever, taking in more than $200 million in international box office receipts.

But more important than his movies, it is Moore himself who has morphed into a powerhouse brand—a crusading, blue-collar, in-your-face (and fat, as conservatives seem to delight in stressing) filmmaker who fearlessly challenges entrenched powers in occasionally cringe-inducing, hysterically funny ways, as Yahoo Movies' review of Moore's *The Big One* shows:

> "The rabble-rousing Moore had great on-camera fun writing checks for 80 cents ('The first hour's wage for a Mexican worker') that he tried—along with a Downsizer of the Year Award—to present to Johnson Products of Milwaukee. He also sent a $100 check for Pat Buchanan's presidential campaign from Abortionists for Buchanan and checks from Satan Worshippers for Dole, Pedophiles for Free Trade (Perot), and Hemp Growers for Clinton—all of which were hilariously cashed. But the big coup of 'The Big One' was his on-camera corralling of Nike CEO Phil Knight. Unlike Roger Smith, who had consistently dodged Moore, Knight welcomed the pesky miscreant with open arms, then amazingly spoke with more candor than business savvy about his company's use of cheap Indonesian labor—some as young as 14 years of age—to manufacture its trendy sneakers. Nike's attempted damage control afterwards did not persuade Moore to remove the CEO's imprudent comments, though a deal could have been

struck if Knight had acceded to the filmmaker's request that he build a factory in Flint. Knight, however, remained true to his original statement that 'Flint's not on our radar screen.'"

Yet much like Berman's sanctimonious whining at *Mother Jones*, progressives have complained that the filmmaker is too brash, too unkempt, too aggressive, or doesn't focus on their pet issues. Jesse Larner, the author of *Forgive Us Our Spins: Michael Moore and the Future of the Left* (2006), wrote on August 7, 2007, in the *Huffington Post* that Moore has a "habit of loading up his films with deceptions delivered through half-truths, misleading edits, and broad conspiracy theories." An example of one of those "half-truths"? Well, in *Sicko*, the climactic scene includes Moore taking to Cuba several 9/11 rescue workers with lingering effects from working around the contaminated Ground Zero. He explains that the excellent care the workers receive is similar to that enjoyed by all Cubans. This is horrible to Larner because, "Any discussion of Cuban medicine that completely omits the totalitarian system in which it is offered would be disgustingly false. Moore isn't concerned with human rights, though." I'm not sure why the type of government in Cuba should be discussed in an examination of its health care system, any more than it would make sense to demand an analysis of Cuba's health care system when talking about its government's human rights record.

Elitist liberals such as the *Washington Post* columnist Richard Cohen loathe Moore as well. "[T]he stunning box-office success of 'Fahrenheit 9/11' is not, as proclaimed, a sure sign that Bush is on his way out but is instead a warning to the Democrats to keep the loony left at a safe distance," he wrote on July 1, 2004. "[*Fahrenheit 9/11*] is so juvenile in its approach, so awful in its journalism, such an inside joke for people who already hate Bush, that I found myself feeling a bit sorry for a president who is depicted mostly as a befuddled dope." Moore's biggest sin? "The case against Bush is too hard and too serious to turn into some sort of joke, as Moore has done," he wrote.

Having fun in politics? Simplifying the material to make it accessible to the masses? Why, that's "prosaic and boring" and "utterly predictable"! He might as well have added "plebeian." Yet others get it. "The genius of this most American of films is that it has turned politics into a blockbuster subject," wrote the reviewer Alex James on the *Guardian Unlimited* (UK) website. "It's the first punk rock movie: it must have cost less to make than *The Blair Witch Project,* and yet he's managed to distil reality and come up with something more powerful."

For people who don't generally follow politics the way political or news junkies do, simplicity isn't just a virtue, it's an absolute necessity. That means stripping out all extraneous information and focusing one's message like a laser. Sometimes it can mean abandoning the notion of "fairness to the other side." Your opponents have their own ways to get out their propaganda, and they won't be too concerned about giving your views "equal time." Your job is to make your own case as strongly, as clearly, and as unambiguously as possible.

Noting that the Declaration of Independence was a document notorious for its omissions—listing all of the grievances the colonists had with England but acknowledging none of the benefits they had received (such as food and medicine during times of famine and disease)—Saul Alinsky stressed in *Rules for Radicals* (1971) that all's fair in pursuit of one's noble goals:

> "To expect a man to leave his wife, his children, and his home, to leave his crops standing in the field and pick up a gun and join the Revolutionary Army for a 20 per cent difference in the balance of human justice was to defy common sense. The Declaration of Independence, as a declaration of war, had to be what it was, a 100 per cent statement of the justice of the cause of the colonists and a 100 per cent denunciation of the role of the British government as evil and unjust."

CHAPTER 6

DON'T BELIEVE THE HYPE

Your own ego can be your own worst enemy. Guard against the danger of buying into hype about your personal success or brilliance. Instead, understand your place as merely one element in a broad and ever-changing movement, with your effectiveness forever linked to your individual credibility, good reputation, and the respect you show your fellow activists.

I t began as a stark, dramatic symbol of national grief: a mother standing in a shallow ditch at the gate of the most powerful man in the world, dusty and worn down by the heat of a long Texas summer, wanting to ask him: *For what "noble cause" did my son die?*

But by the end of that August in 2005, the vigil of Cindy Sheehan outside the Crawford ranch of President George W. Bush had devolved into a mishmash of every lefty group organized during the Summer of Love and since, a compost of myriad causes, as they all jiggered and shoved to get their fifteen seconds of fame, spotlighted against the backdrop of Sheehan's once-dignified and solemn personal protest.

As Cindy Sheehan caravanned down to Crawford, Texas, to establish on August 6 what would become Camp Casey, her friends and early advisors already were worried sick about her state of mind. She'd been wrecked emotionally by the death of her son, Casey Sheehan, twenty-four, in Iraq, and as her fame grew, so did the pressures on her. Still, those early days had gone well. The national media was present in droves, starved for news to fill the content of the twenty-four-hour news cycle during a boring summer. The grieving mother filled news slots nicely.

Then came the celebrities. Viggo Mortensen, Joan Baez, Al Sharpton, and Martin Sheen undertook pilgrimages to dusty Crawford to meet with the woman who had finally succeeded in changing the national dialogue about the war in Iraq. Among the first to arrive was Mortensen. Unannounced and with little fanfare he met with Sheehan and left just as quietly. In an interview with Nina Siegal of the *Progressive* that October, he explained why he went down there. "I also had a sense of just how threatening someone like this would be to people who are used to running the show, in terms of perception and media information—or disinformation. It's like she pulled an end around just by being herself, a relatively ordinary woman displaying extraordinary courage and being quite eloquent and brave, knowing she's being savaged and hearing it and standing up to it and having her say as an individual and as a woman."

As the vigil continued and more and more people descended upon Crawford, things began to fray. The steady stream of celebrities, of groups touting causes other than the Iraq war, began overshadowing the message—began *replacing* the message. Even well-meaning allies began muddying the message and couldn't help but contribute to the growing carnival atmosphere.

Among those concerned about Sheehan herself and the message she was bearing was Dante Zappala, who had a firsthand look at how conditions in Crawford became more surreal and confusing by the day. Zappala, whose brother Sherwood Baker had been killed in Iraq, was sent to Crawford by Military Families Speak Out to help coordinate media access for service members' relatives who'd felt drawn to the protest, looking for answers for their own grief.

Yet almost immediately he found himself fighting a battle to protect the protest's message from other organizations jostling to get in the limelight. First up was the women's antiwar group Code Pink, which had taken over the entrance to the camp with its neon pink banners, tables, and paraphernalia, in the manner of a corporate sponsor at a sports facility. They eventually agreed to recede to the background with other organizations at the camp after tough negotiations, but the episode was disheartening.

"This wasn't about Code Pink," Zappala told me. "It was about the movement."

Before long, Zappala found himself contending with an activist from the People for the Ethical Treatment of Animals (PETA), parading around in her lettuce bikini, handing out veggie burgers—right next to the cross memorial bearing the names of the U.S. soldiers killed in Iraq. "Have some respect, get some clothes on," Zappala pleaded. "That's my brother's cross right there."

Next up for attention was the Revolutionary Communist Party. "At one point I organized a crew of old vets from Veterans for Peace," Zappala explained. "We picked up the RCP literature and dumped it in the outhouses." And how far can the socialists be if the communists are already there? The International Socialist Organization felt entitled to pitch its fringe ideology at the camp because it had already put Sheehan on the cover of its newsrag. Unable to get the socialists to depart, Zappala approached a group of nearby sheriffs for help.

"You've got some Bush supporters giving you trouble?" they asked.

"It's a little more complicated than that," sighed Zappala.

Meanwhile, the Code Pink cofounder Jodie Evans made few friends, as other groups accused her of fostering divisions in the camp. "For some reason we became the scapegoat," Evans told me in February 2008, noting that her organization "was battered after Camp Casey from all the hatred coming our way from different groups." A large share of the animosity stemmed from Code Pink's success in plastering its trademark garishly pink banners in high-profile spots, like behind the main stage. The organization was also responsible for bringing many of the celebrities into the camp, giving Camp Casey the feel of the second coming of Woodstock with performances by Joan Baez. This reenactment of the culture of the 1960s began to undermine the efforts of more media-savvy groups that aimed to keep the focus on Sheehan's core message. Yet Sheehan resented Zappala's efforts to kick out disruptive or unhelpful groups, and she gave her take on it in her book, *Peace Mom*.

"[M]y heart was broken by my dear friends coming and trying to fix a situation that wasn't broken, and taking what was working so well and trying to mold it into their idea of what a peace camp should look like," wrote Sheehan, who instead became smitten by Evans's efforts. "She literally gave me the sandals off her feet, and she did it all for peace. She did it because she believed in what we were doing at Camp Casey, and we are and always will be friends for life."

Zappala, on the other hand, dreaded news coverage and late-night monologues turning the camp into . . . well, a parody of itself. "Cindy was angry that we tried to kick them out," Zappala told me. "She thought it would be peace and love, and we could all share the experience at Camp Casey." It wasn't that Sheehan was embracing the views of those fringe groups, he made clear, but she thought anyone who was against the war should be welcomed, regardless of what effect the groups or their special-issues agenda might have on the broader narrative.

Even media voices friendly to the antiwar cause, like *The Daily Show*'s Jon Stewart, ended up mocking the protest ("If they work hard, they can end Vietnam!"). The most media-savvy organizations, like MoveOn and True Majority, knew that they had lost the battle to control the message and preserve the very elements of the protests that had made it so successful in its earliest days. "This is everything we were working against," laments Zappala. "We were smart enough to know that this is where things were headed. It was becoming Woodstock all over again. It was great meeting Joan Baez, but I was thinking, 'You aren't helping here.' "

MoveOn, which had rallied its 4 million members on behalf of Sheehan, organizing 1,625 supportive candlelight vigils around the country, was drawing Sheehan's ire over tactics. True Majority, a progressive advocacy group founded by Ben Cohen of Ben & Jerry's ice cream fame, funded two public relations specialists from the high-powered Fenton Communications firm to help Sheehan manage her media appearances, but she bristled at their efforts to keep her on message. "She worked well with them, but they did try to craft her responses and the messages of each day," Evans, of Code Pink, told me. "Sometimes it caused a struggle because they wanted her to back down on her voice. Or to put up American flags."

Sheehan admitted as much to me in an email: "Fenton did try to shape my message and tried to put words in my mouth."

People had been riveted by the Crawford protests early on because of the narrative of the regular mom who had lost her child in Iraq—it brought the war home in all its humanity and sadness. But Sheehan's tolerance of the likes of the communists, socialists, PETA, and others watered down the narrative with subplots, as it were, and tarnished her credibility in the long run. Her lack of message and outright hostility toward efforts to help her focus effectively created the type of circuslike protests that Americans had already seen a million times before.

Toward the end of the month, professional activists like Al Sharpton began arriving at the camp, getting in the way of the message, no matter

how well-intentioned they may have been. "I feel that it is our moral ob-
ligation to stand and to be courageous with these families, and particularly
Cindy, that have become the conscience of this nation," Sharpton, a former Democratic presidential candidate, told reporters on August 28.

That same day, Martin Sheen stopped by as well. "It is an Irish tradition," Sheen told the Camp Casey gathering. "When a person had a dis-
agreement with a landlord, for example, that person would stand vigil
outside that landlord's home until he came out to talk with them. You all
know what I do for a living, but this is what I do to stay alive."

By the end of the month, the message had become diffused, the camp
had turned into a hodgepodge of voices all protesting for their own cause,
and everyone was vying for the attention of the media. The stresses of instant fame and the pressures created by her genuine desire to change the
world took their toll on Sheehan. "Health-wise, she couldn't deal with this
sort of thing," said Glenn Smith, a longtime Texas organizer who worked
with the faith community setting up the Camp Casey Peace Chapel.
"It was too much pressure. Seasoned politicians have a hard time dealing
with it. She was undone by her son's death and she should've been given
space to grieve."

In a way, Hurricane Katrina making its destructive landfall on August
29 did Sheehan a favor by ending the protests in Crawford just as they
were crossing into utter absurdity. On September 1, Sheehan packed it in
as the country turned its attention in horror to the natural disaster unfold-
ing along the Gulf Coast.

After Crawford, Sheehan drove up to Washington, D.C., to take part
in a mass protest scheduled for September 24 against the Iraq war. Again,
a second natural disaster intervened. As Sheehan and fellow protesters
were marching ineffectively in the capital, Hurricane Rita, the third Category 5 hurricane to hit that year, was ripping through the Gulf Coast—
killing seven people, causing mass evacuations, forcing repeats of levee
breaches, and causing $11.3 billion in damage in five states. Sheehan
fumed that the antiwar march wasn't receiving the media attention she felt
it deserved.

In a September 24 diary on *Daily Kos*, she wrote: "i am watching cnn
and it is 100 percent rita . . . even though it is a little wind and a little

rain . . . it is bad, but there are other things going on in this country today . . . and in the world!!!!"

It's highly unlikely the Washington protest would have garnered attention even without the hurricane news. The march was exactly the kind of obsolete protest that gets little attention today. It wasn't part of a broader narrative, nor did it provide a novel or interesting news hook for the media to latch on to. It was simply a gathering of people opposed to the war who were marching and shouting slogans. For someone who'd just had huge success with an innovative protest action and been rewarded for it with scads of media attention, Sheehan had regressed to an old, outmoded, and irrelevant approach to activism.

Even Sheehan's insistence that her issue should suddenly take precedence over all else—which had not been a hallmark of her early Crawford action—uncannily echoed the divisiveness that haunted the squabbling lefties of the Vietnam era.

As her understanding of media priorities appeared to slip—and apparently her ability to empathize with Americans in danger and distress—it became easier and easier to dismiss her and marginalize her once-powerful voice. She fed the growing mistrust of her judgment by beginning to branch out and speak about areas far outside her original, piercing question about why her son had died.

Her devolution, alas, was still not over. By January 2006, she was flying to Venezuela as a guest of its foreign ministry to join more than ten thousand antiglobalization protesters.

Hoping to meet President Hugo Chavéz later that week, she told the Agence France-Press (AFP) news service, "I admire him for his resolve against my government and its meddling." Now one can debate Chavéz and his ideology, his policies, and his heated rhetoric against U.S. foreign policy, but the fact is that he is a hugely controversial and polarizing figure in the United States. A master of propaganda, Chavéz used Sheehan's visit to garner international press for yet another anti-American broadside, as reported on January 29 by the Associated Press: "Hugo Chavéz, an arm around Sheehan's shoulders, told a group of activists that she had told him 'she is going to put up her tent again in front of Mr. Danger's ranch' in April."

In some of his strongest recent comments aimed at Washington, Chavéz condemned the Bush administration and said his audience should work toward ending U.S. dominance.

"Enough already with the imperialist aggression!" Chavéz said, listing countries from Panama to Iraq where the U.S. military has intervened. "Down with the U.S. empire! It must be said, in the entire world: Down with the empire!"

In just a few short months, Sheehan had morphed from a grieving mother seeking closure about her son's death to a globe-trotting, peace-sign-flashing, anti-imperialist activist. As time passed, the distance between her original clear-eyed purpose and her later embrace of the entire spectrum of liberal orthodoxy became harder and harder to overlook.

On January 30, Sheehan showed up on a panel in Washington, D.C., at a forum calling for the impeachment of Bush and Dick Cheney. Sheehan, accepting for the sake of argument that only thirty thousand people had died in the Iraq war, told the audience: "On September 11, one of the most tragic days in American history that we will all never forget, three thousand Americans were killed, so does that make George Bush ten times a bigger terrorist than Osama bin Laden?" It was a controversial sentiment she later echoed on MSNBC that distracted from her core message.

Meanwhile, an email was circulating around the internet supposedly written to ABC's *Nightline* program, in which she mentioned the neocon group Project for the New American Century, saying her son "was killed for lies and for a PNAC Neo-Con agenda to benefit Israel. My son joined the army to protect America, not Israel." While she admitted sending the email, she vigorously denied writing the anti-Israel portion. Her denials were met with skepticism—a skepticism that might not have arisen if not for her association with fringe causes and groups. Rather than mainstreaming her views in the way her original Crawford protest helped bring anti-war sentiment to the surface, she appeared to be headed in the opposite direction.

Still, not all her efforts were counterproductive.

The day after the impeachment forum, on January 31, she earned headlines when she was kicked out of Bush's 2006 State of the Union address for wearing a T-shirt that read, "2,245 Dead. How many more?"—

helping inject that tragic statistic into coverage of the president's biggest annual speech. It was a simple and direct action that spoke directly to her core issue—young men and women dying for an unclear cause—and it was precisely the kind of action that reinforced her original narrative. But it seemed as time went on that much of the goodwill and respect she had earned had slowly ebbed away through a mixture of unrelated messages and embarrassing actions. By the time she returned to Camp Casey in August 2006, one year after her original game-changing protest, the reception she received was decidedly cooler—the media and the crowds stayed away. She was playing herself out.

"When she did start to speak out beyond just that she was a mother in pain, [it became] difficult for a lot of people to swallow, even people in the antiwar movement," Dana Balicki, a Code Pink spokeswoman, told the *Politico* on May 29, 2007. "It gets a little murkier than just going after George Bush, Dick Cheney and Donald Rumsfeld."

After nearly a year on the speaking circuit, Sheehan had burned herself out and was clearly smarting over the increasing chorus of critics from her left. While pragmatic netroots progressives were struggling with the frustrations of dealing with a slim Democratic congressional majority that seemed fearful of the president, prodding and suggesting maneuvers that could work within the legislative setting and the ever-present threat of presidential vetoes, Sheehan seemed to be getting more and more absolutist and purist, venturing further into making naïve pronouncements about what was achievable given the political balance.

On May 26, 2007, she posted a diary on *Daily Kos* titled "Dear Democratic Congress," an announcement that she was leaving the Democratic Party because pro-war legislators and President Bush scuttled a Democratic attempt to attach a withdrawal timetable to a war-funding bill with a veto. She wrote:

> "Congratulations Congress, you have bought yourself a few more months of an illegal and immoral bloodbath. And you know you mean to continue it indefinitely so 'other presidents' can solve the horrid problem BushCo forced our world into. It used to be George Bush's war. You could have ended it honorably. Now it is

yours and you all will descend into calumnious history with BushCo . . . We gave you a chance, you betrayed us."

Sheehan's announcement that she was leaving the party was mostly politely received, though some expressed regret about her exit. "Your leaving the Democratic Party will only make it easier for those Democrats who actually do want to continue the Iraq occupation—due to 'vital U.S. national security interests' . . . to succeed," read one typical comment. Others were fully supportive: "So many good people got her back she's gonna have to expand the space behind her!!!!" Others were more cutting: "I've said to her directly before, but it is clear that she is no longer helping the cause that she ostensibly supports. In fact she's more of a hindrance than a help." On other forums outside of *Daily Kos*, the responses were even harsher.

Two days later, on Memorial Day, she wrote her "Goodbye America" letter on *Daily Kos*, saying that she was tired of being attacked by the left and called an "attention whore":

> "The first conclusion is that I was the darling of the so-called left as long as I limited my protests to George Bush and the Republican Party. Of course, I was slandered and libeled by the right as a 'tool' of the Democratic Party. This label was to marginalize me and my message. How could a woman have an original thought, or be working outside of our 'two-party' system?
>
> "However, when I started to hold the Democratic Party to the same standards that I held the Republican Party, support for my cause started to erode and the 'left' started labeling me with the same slurs that the right used. I guess no one paid attention to me when I said that the issue of peace and people dying for no reason is not a matter of 'right or left,' but 'right and wrong.' [. . .]
>
> "People of the world look on us Americans as jokes because we allow our political leaders so much murderous latitude and if we don't find alternatives to this corrupt 'two' party system our Representative Republic will die and be replaced with what we are rapidly descending into with nary a check or balance: a fascist corporate

wasteland. I am demonized because I don't see party affiliation or nationality when I look at a person, I see that person's heart. [. . .]

"This is my resignation letter as the 'face' of the American anti-war movement. This is not my 'Checkers' moment, because I will never give up trying to help people in the world who are harmed by the empire of the good old US of A, but I am finished working in, or outside of this system. This system forcefully resists being helped and eats up the people who try to help it. I am getting out before it totally consumes me or any more people that I love and the rest of my resources.

"Goodbye America . . . you are not the country that I love and I finally realized no matter how much I sacrifice, I can't make you be that country unless you want it."

Her "retirement" didn't last long. She continued posting diaries on *Daily Kos*, including poems and 1960s antiwar songs. Then in July, she announced that she would run as an independent against House Speaker Nancy Pelosi unless Pelosi introduced articles of impeachment against Bush. By this point, people were wishing she had truly called it quits, but alas, her fall from grace was complete.

Sheehan utterly misunderstood the reason people turned against her. It wasn't because she attacked pro-war Democrats. Some of her biggest fans had been people who had worked to defeat Sen. Joe Lieberman in the Connecticut Democratic primary in 2006—mainly because of his support of Bush's military adventures—and the war would continue to be one of the biggest points of contention between the Democratic Party and its base for some time to come.

People originally saw her as a symbol of the war's ravages, a very human and sympathetic representation of the cold statistics of war. That is why she was successful early on—both with the media and the broader public. But by the end of Camp Casey in August 2005, Sheehan had received so much media attention, so much adoration, as well as the pressures that come with it, that she began to believe the hype. In the heady air of celebrity, she lost her perspective. To make matters worse, she was influenced too much by the extreme left, the fringe elements that are so ideologically pure as to be rendered inconsequential.

Sheehan's belief that she was the "face of the antiwar movement" was an indication of how she had lost touch with reality. The antiwar movement began long before her son died and would continue as long as the war did. She had become a crucial part of the movement, but she was not its "face," nor did she have the burden of fronting or representing it. Even before she commanded national attention, support for the war had been plummeting. Blogs were abuzz with antiwar information, and in communities across the country, regional media was covering the deaths of local heroes coming home in body bags. This wasn't the world of the '60s where we needed Walter Cronkite and visible national antiwar leaders to captivate media coverage. In today's fragmented world thousands of people were doing their part, aided by the tragic reality in Iraq, toward changing public opinion.

Sheehan personified the tragedy of the war, pushing into the traditional media a gripping, authentic story that could be woven into the broader antiwar narrative. She played her role brilliantly, and could have kept playing it for good effect for years to come. But unrelated protests for various causes, trips to Venezuela, heartless responses to a region devastated by hurricanes, and becoming a self-styled expert on the intricacies of congressional bills and presidential vetoes all ended up distracting her. Her story, so beautiful and poignant in its simplicity, became muddled and sullied. As her biggest fans began to distance themselves from her, her public bitterness grew. No longer a sympathetic figure, her effectiveness was blunted; no longer effective, she became a lonely, irrelevant voice relegated to the margins of the political debate.

WORK YOUR NICHE

It's tough to suggest that once you have a role, you should stick to it to the exclusion of other interests. But when you live in a media-saturated world, it takes clarity of message and specialization to cut through the clutter. If you find a niche that resonates with a wider audience, a niche where you find yourself being *effective*, exploit that niche. Extend from that niche carefully, mindful that such expansion may cost you the audience that initially empowered you.

I made my name writing about electoral politics on behalf of the Democratic Party and anti–Iraq war advocacy. If I suddenly began to write about the Israeli-Palestinian conflict or the World Bank and its treatment of developing countries or my vegetarian lifestyle, readers would walk away scratching their heads. The vast majority couldn't care less about my views on those matters. It's also the reason I am careful about how much radio or television I do and what I talk about when I am on the air. Rush Limbaugh has focused his energies on his radio program, despite early forays into book writing and television. His brief stint as an analyst for *Monday Night Football* ended in disaster—a reminder that he's at his best when he focuses on what has made him successful.

Yet it can be tempting, when some measure of success is achieved, to branch out, particularly if the direction or field seems related to areas you've already conquered. In 2007, the John Edwards for President campaign set out to find a campaign blogger and settled on two: Amanda Marcotte of the blog Pandagon, and Melissa McEwan of the blog Shakesville. Both were outspoken feminists and accomplished and popular bloggers. Based on their mastery of the blogging medium, they seemed to be great fits for the job.

But political campaigns are worlds apart from the Wild West frontier mentality of the blogosphere. While bloggers are famously and proudly independent, campaign bloggers serve their candidate and his or her campaign. While bloggers write about whatever it is that strikes their fancy, campaign bloggers have to remain "on message." While bloggers can be controversial and push the envelope, campaign bloggers must operate cautiously and avoid any controversy that might distract or derail a campaign. And these two bloggers, Marcotte and McEwan, in particular, reveled in creating a stir.

As soon as they were hired, the right-wing media began culling their sites for controversial statements, and they hit gold mines with statements

from Marcotte, such as, "The Catholic church is not about to let something like compassion for girls get in the way of using the state as an instru-
ment to force women to bear more tithing Catholics," and "The Christian
version of the virgin birth is generally interpreted as super-patriarchal
where god is viewed as so powerful he can impregnate without befouling
himself by touching a woman, and women are nothing but vessels."
McEwan's supposed "anti-Catholic" statements were less so, although she
had a tendency to use a lot of foul language on her blog.

Conservatives demanded John Edwards fire the two women. "Over the
next week, we will contact hundreds of organizations throughout the nation informing them of the kind of people that John Edwards is proud to
have on his payroll," threatened blowhard Bill Donohue of the conservative Catholic League (which has no connection to the Vatican) on February 9, 2007. "We will give them the exact comments made by Amanda
Marcotte and Melissa McEwan—nothing will be censored. They will read
for themselves the most hate-filled, blasphemous and obscene remarks—
all of which were brought to the attention of Edwards—that have ever
been written by any employee of a presidential candidate. The purpose of
this communication is to ignite a national discussion on the incredible
double standard that exists regarding bigotry in American life."

The Edwards campaign resisted efforts to fire the bloggers, but less
than a week after their hiring, both women resigned their positions to
spare the campaign the continued hassle. It was for the best. Their talents
would be wasted on a campaign that would muzzle their creative streaks.
Of course, there may have been legitimate reasons they wanted the gig—
steady paychecks are a rarity for bloggers, and working for a presidential
campaign is hard to resist—but in regards to movement building, their
talents were best used on their blogs. More importantly, they had branded
themselves and behaved in a way that made it impossible for them to
switch gears and work for a risk-averse operation like a presidential campaign. Their role was set. Oftentimes, the role we choose for ourselves
early on will set limits on what we can do in the future.

Sometimes, specializing more deeply into a niche can bring more satisfaction and be more effective. A general-assignment reporter might blos-

som on the environmental news beat, a campaign volunteer might turn out to be a terrific phone banker, or a former senator and vice president may turn out to be the premier international ambassador for the environment.

Al Gore was always on the cutting edge of the global warming debate. While serving in the U.S. House in the late '70s, he held the first hearings on reducing carbon dioxide and other greenhouse gases, pushing for new technologies to combat ecological degradation. His environmental record was second to none during his years in the House and Senate. In 1992, he authored *Earth in the Balance: Ecology and the Human Spirit*, which was a *New York Times* bestseller.

After his defeat in the 2000 presidential election, Gore joined the private sector, where many of his business dealings focused on environmental issues. In 2004, he cofounded Generation Investment Management to assist in investing in environmentally responsible companies. He also chaired the board of the Alliance for Climate Protection in 2006, and became a partner in 2007 in the famed Silicon Valley venture capital firm Kleiner Perkins Caufield & Byers, in charge of the company's rapidly growing environmental solutions group.

In 2006, Gore's environmental advocacy was taken to the next level when he starred in the documentary *An Inconvenient Truth*. It was a marvelous example of the meshing of modern activist mediums—taking a simple PowerPoint presentation he had delivered to hundreds of audiences and creating a mass-market vehicle to better disseminate the information. The film was a rousing success, earning more than $24 million in limited theater release and winning an Academy Award for Best Documentary Feature. A companion book was an instant bestseller. In October 2007, Gore shared the Nobel Peace Prize for his work on the global warming issue.

Clearly, Gore has been a catalyst in thrusting the issue of global warming onto the national—and international—public agenda. Demand for Gore as a speaker shot through the roof as people clamored to see his live version of *An Inconvenient Truth*. In Idaho, a Gore event in January 2007 sold out twelve hundred tickets in minutes. The event was moved to a basketball arena, where the ten thousand tickets were sold out in ninety minutes. The next month, when tickets for a Gore lecture at the University of Toronto were made available online, twenty-three thousand people tried to buy them in the first three minutes The website collapsed under the demand for the nine hundred available tickets.

Gore's star couldn't possibly have burned any brighter in 2007. So naturally, with a presidential campaign looming, a lot of Americans wanted him, the rightful winner of the 2000 contest, in the White House. The logic made sense—Gore was a unifying force in his party and would run strong not just in the primary but also in the general election. Indeed, he had won before in an environment far less hostile to Republicans before the partisans on the U.S. Supreme Court stripped his victory away. And what better place for Gore to push for meaningful global warming change than from the most powerful office in the world?

But Gore begged off, and despite ongoing pressure for him to join, including a spirited Draft Gore campaign, he remained firm in his decision. "Please trust me to make good decisions about where I can do the most good," he pleaded to his supporters, as reported in *Newsweek* on December 13, 2007. "And don't automatically assume that running for president again is the right thing for me to do."

Gore believed he could do more good for global warming from outside the White House, as he told *Time* magazine on May 16, 2007:

> "If I do my job right, all the candidates will be talking about the climate crisis. And I'm not convinced the presidency is the highest and best role I could play. The path I see is a path that builds a consensus—to the point where it doesn't matter as much who's running. It would take a lot to disabuse me of the notion that my highest and best use is to keep building that consensus."

Gore had become the preeminent voice on global warming on the entire planet. He could devote 100 percent of his energy to the issue, and he had the access and respect that got him into pretty much any door he wanted outside of ExxonMobil. By running for president, Gore would have to run a national campaign and he would have to focus on Social Security, and Iraq, and the economy, and health care, and a million other issues. Yet with his "outsider" status, he has been able to ignore all the rest of the stuff and focus on his true passion. "There's no question I'm freed up," he told *Time*. "I don't want to suggest that it's impossible to be free and authentic within the political process, but it's obviously harder. Another person might be better at it than I was."

Gore realized that reentering politics would complicate things and distract attention from his core issue, the environment. Many of his current fans would probably have drifted away as he squared off against their favorite Democratic candidate. Others, especially those who are not Democrats, might have dismissed his environmental message because of a reentry into partisan politics.

It may seem callous to suggest that Cindy Sheehan should have stuck to her niche and not tried to branch out to wider activism, but as Gore noted, retaining focus can actually be liberating. He understood that in the current world, we need to devote our time and energy to where we are the most effective. That means sometimes resisting the pressures to broaden out. You quickly find as you rise in prominence that everyone wants you to speak about their cause. Just like the hangers-on who flocked to Camp Casey to steal a bit of Sheehan's spotlight, people will demand that prominent movement personalities address or focus on *their* issue. They may even accuse those personalities of "not caring" about their issue if it remains unaddressed. But we remain at the top of our form when we focus on what we know best and what we most enjoy doing, rather than trying to make other people happy by expanding beyond our natural boundaries.

Sheehan struck out by trying to become "the face of the antiwar movement." Al Gore, on the other hand, saw his stock rise by refusing all distractions so he could remain clear and focused on his mission to reverse global warming.

GUARD YOUR CREDIBILITY

Stephen Glass joined the *New Republic* as an editorial assistant in 1995. At the time it was still a respected and influential magazine, and Glass wrote a string of well-received stories with colorful characters and compelling story lines. He became a star writer for the publication, with his pieces sometimes seeming too perfect to be true. They were. In fact, Glass was fabricating much of what he wrote.

"I remember thinking, 'If I just had the exact quote that I wanted to make it work, it would be perfect,' " Glass told *60 Minutes* on August 17, 2003. "And I wrote something on my computer, and then I looked at it, and I let it stand. And then it ran in the magazine and I saw it. And I said to myself what I said every time these stories ran, 'You must stop. You must stop.' But I didn't."

Glass went to great lengths to get around fact checkers at the *New Republic,* creating fake notes, voice mails, websites, and business cards, and over the next few years wrote numerous high-profile articles for other magazines as well, including *Rolling Stone, Harper's Magazine,* and *George,* with first-person accounts—young conservatives ("pissed off and pissed: dejected, depressed, drunk and dumb"), homeless people smoking crack and talking about murders they committed, an evangelical church that worshipped George H. W. Bush, and so on. At the *New Republic,* he had moved up to the position of associate editor. In 1998, a *Forbes* reporter was doing a follow-up article on a Glass story about a convention of computer hackers, particularly a teenage hacker who was blackmailing software companies, and discovered that Glass's story ("Hacker Heaven") was fabricated. After an internal review, the *New Republic* later determined that at least twenty-seven of forty-one of Glass's articles were also fabricated. Glass was fired.

Glass's career was destroyed (he now works as a paralegal and performs with a comedy troupe), but the *New Republic*—which had essentially enabled his deceptions—was able to carry on, given its long-standing credibility.

At the *New York Times,* the reporter Judith Miller was caught being a stenographer for Bush administration higher-ups who claimed that Iraq had weapons of mass destruction. Officials would leak bogus information to her, she would write the stories, which then allowed the administration to point to her stories (in the "liberal" *New York Times* no less!) as evidence that war was necessary against Iraq. Another *New York Times* reporter, Jayson Blair, was fired in 2003 for both plagiarism and fabricating news stories. The *Times* formed a committee of staffers and outside journalists to look into Blair's work and discovered that thirty-six of seventy-three national news stories written over a period of seven months were either fake or copied from other sources.

Janet Cooke, a reporter for the *Washington Post*, wrote a shocking story ("Jimmy's World") in 1980 about an eight-year-old heroin addict. Bob Woodward, an assistant managing editor at the time, nominated the story for the Pulitzer Prize, which Cooke won. Two days later the newspaper admitted the story was fake and publicly apologized. Cooke resigned and returned the prize, saying the environment at the *Post* "corrupted her judgment."

Yet in all these cases, no matter how egregious the violation (Miller's "reporting" helped drag the nation into a war that has cost thousands of lives and hundreds of billions of dollars), the institution in question always emerged unscathed. Chastened a bit, a little red in the face perhaps, but ultimately, those organizations survived because of their institutional credibility. This principle applies not only to media outlets, but to social justice organizations, think tanks, corporate America, and the government as well: Where there is a gatekeeper, there is an institution that confers its credibility and reputation upon anyone associated with it. The first day Janet Cooke and Jayson Blair and Stephen Glass showed up for work at their publications, they were deemed legitimate members of the media by virtue of their association with their respective publications.

Citizen activists and citizen journalists don't have that first-day legitimacy, nor do they have long-standing institutions behind them that carry on if they're discredited. If they bring disgrace to their fledgling organization or publication, they may well drag down the institution with them. Everything they build hangs by a very narrow thread—reputation—and their work is threatened if they fail to uphold the highest standards for truth and behavior. As such, activists have to build reputation the hard way, day by day, with little room for error.

More than anything else, those without credible institutional backing need to hold fast to a basic commitment to truth in their dealings. In today's information-rich environment, most people are only one or two

Google searches away from having lies exposed or problematic special interests revealed. Young organizations may not be able to survive a bout of scandal the way a more established institution could. Honesty and transparency are not only the best policy for personal ethical reasons, but for practical ones as well.

James Rucker and the Color of Change reaped the benefits of carefully guarding their reputation in 2007.

The balding yet dreadlocked Rucker graduated from Stanford University in 1993 hoping to spend the next ten years making lots of money so he could retire at the age of thirty and do good. After ten years of working in the technology sector, his plan to make lots of money had failed, yet he thought it was time for him to start doing good anyway. He joined the team at MoveOn as its director of grassroots mobilization and faced a vexing problem. As an African-American, he desperately wanted to bring more of his community into the realm of digital mobilization, yet the challenges were tough.

"The set of issues and the tone/voice of MoveOn wasn't likely to reach a lot of communities, especially communities of color or black folks in particular," Rucker told me in a February 18, 2008, conversation. "It was also clear that trying to be all things to all people—or specifically, trying to appeal to different groups who are in reality segregated—wasn't going to work." At the urging of MoveOn's founders, Wes Boyd and Joan Blades, Rucker began searching for someone who could use MoveOn's tools but tailor them for specific communities. They hadn't found that person yet, and Rucker was on a sabbatical from MoveOn, when Hurricane Katrina hit on August 29, 2005.

As a horrified world watched the Bush administration bungle its response to the Hurricane Katrina disaster in the Gulf Coast, and especially in heavily African-American New Orleans, Rucker founded a new organization in response—Color of Change—with the help of the community activist Van Jones of the Ella Baker Center for Human Rights in Oakland, California. The group was envisioned as a MoveOn-style email list for the black community, and although Katrina was the catalyst for its founding, it was the "Jena 6" campaign to provide help to six black teenagers in Jena, Louisiana (see chapter 4), that brought Color of Change to national prominence. By the time the Jena 6 campaign was over, Color of Change had grown from 100,000 members to nearly 400,000, giving it serious credibility as a power base in the African-American community. Yet compared with such venerable and long-serving institutions like the National Association for the Advancement of Colored People (NAACP) and the Congressional Black Caucus (CBC), and leaders like Jesse Jackson and Al Sharpton, Color of Change was the new kid on the block, completely unknown. So was James Rucker.

As Color of Change jumped into organizing on behalf of the Jena 6, the group began raising money for the defendants' legal fund, garnering $212,000 from its members. Prominent establishment African-Americans were suspicious of these new interlopers, and leading the charge was the well-known, nationally syndicated radio personality Michael Baisden. On a Friday in late September 2007, Baisden told listeners that there was an organization raising money for the Jena 6 families, but that the funds weren't getting to them. He promised listeners that he would name names the following Monday. Having caught wind of the broadcast, Rucker called Baisden to explain how the fund worked, and how the lawyers would get the money. Problem solved, or so Rucker thought. But a few weeks later, he got a call from a Baisden staffer trying to get information about the money. Rucker put that staffer in contact with the attorneys and the families so they could confirm that everything was aboveboard. Yet on November 5, 2007, Baisden featured Marcus Jones, the father of the Jena 6 defendant Mychal Bell, claiming that he hadn't seen any of the money raised by Color of Change.

"The money has not been going to where it needs to go, according to the families," Baisden can be heard saying on a recording of the program posted on the Color of Change website. "I told you guys, don't be sending your money to people who you don't know who these people are." The next day, he continued his attack, claiming he had a letter from the Jena 6 families demanding that Color of Change stop fund-raising, and he took the opportunity to discredit Rucker himself: "I had a chance to talk to James Rucker and I have a right to my opinion, and he sound shady to me. You sound like a shady brother."

Faced with such repeated assaults from a prominent personality, many fledgling groups would have withered and collapsed. But Color of Change from its inception had been well aware that it didn't have the built-in institutional credibility of a well-known radio host or the NAACP. Knowing its handicap as a newcomer, the group had carefully logged every check that had been sent to each of the lawyers representing the Jena 6, and when cashed, the organization had posted scans of the canceled checks on its website for verification purposes.

The group moved quickly to rebut Baisden's allegations. In response to his claim that he had a letter signed by the Jena 6 families demanding that Color of Change stop its fund-raising efforts, the group posted an email from one of the mothers who said she'd never seen nor signed such a letter. As for Marcus Jones, who had claimed on Baisden's show that he'd never seen a dime of the money, Color of Change posted a signed fax authorization from Jones asking Color of Change to release the funds directly to the lawyers representing his son. Jones had never seen a dime — because the money was sent directly to his son's legal team.

The *Chicago Tribune*'s Howard Witt, one of the national journalists closely following the case, was quick to offer independent support. "Only one national civil rights group, Color of Change, has fully disclosed how the $212,000 it collected for the Jena 6 via a massive Internet campaign has been distributed," he wrote on November 11. "The grassroots group, which has nearly 400,000 members, has posted images of cancelled checks and other signed documents on its website showing that all but $1,230 was paid out in October in roughly equal amounts to attorneys for the Jena youths." Witt noted that despite this "transparency," Baisden's show offered "no evidence" for its claims of malfeasance. Additionally, the $1,230 balance referenced by Witt was paid out after the article ran, and the organization ultimately raised another $38,000 by the end of the campaign.

Times have clearly changed from the days when media gatekeepers could hurl charges with impunity, leaving the target with little (nonlegal) recourse. Color of Change rallied its members, the online Afrosphere, and the broader blogosphere to its defense, and its case was obviously strong.

The evidence—canceled checks, emails, authorization from families—
was posted online for all to see, and it was easy for reporters like Howard
Witt who were covering the story to see how Color of Change had handled
the donations. Baisden was forced to issue a reluctant apology on November 9, 2007.

What was amazing is that at the end of the day, Color of Change stood
head and shoulders above its more "established" and "respected" peers.
The group raised almost $250,000 for the Jena 6, while Baisden and the
NAACP each raised a mere $40,000 (despite Baisden's on-air boast that
he would raise $1 million in one day). And while the NAACP claimed it
would send the money to the Jena 6 families *after* deducting unspecified
administrative expenses, Color of Change gave every dime it raised to
those families and documented it all on its website.

Something as simple as sloppy—but honest—record keeping could
have doomed Color of Change when charges began to fly from established personalities. New organizations are often considered upstarts by
more established groups that claim certain issues or areas as their turf.
Given the resistance the newcomers will encounter, they need to be especially sensitive in guarding their credibility. Because they have no long-
standing history or recognized figures associated with them, one bad apple
can sink a new organization. Care must be taken every step of the way.

While it can seem unfair when applied to us, higher standards are
necessary to protect the public from unscrupulous characters who would
be happy to part fools from their money. There is no logical reason for
people to trust us with no documentation. So we build that trust over the
long haul, and we reinforce that trust by being transparent and open in our
actions and behavior.

After all, we *want* a society in which everyone is accountable to the
citizens. If we become corrupt, lazy, and ineffective like the existing power
structure, we'll be targeted, bypassed, and rendered irrelevant. It bears
noting that there's nothing that we're doing today that can't be done *to* us
at a later date.

If that doesn't keep us honest, then we deserve a taste of our own
medicine.

FACTOR REALITY INTO YOUR PLANS

As Americans tried to cope with the terrorist attacks on 9/11, the president was MIA, hiding in Nebraska aboard *Air Force One*. Into the leadership void stepped New York mayor Rudy Giuliani, who took to the microphones to calm a nervous city and nation.

"We will strive now to save as many people as possible and to send a message that the city of New York—and the United States of America—is much stronger than any group of barbaric terrorists," he said in a press conference just hours after the attack. "I want the people of New York to be an example to the rest of the country, and the rest of the world, that terrorism can't stop us." On *Larry King Live* that same night, he confidently declared, "Tomorrow New York is going to be here, and we're going to rebuild, and we're going to be stronger than we were before." In the absence of a president that day, Giuliani emerged as a symbol of strength and resolve in the face of a heinous attack.

The New York mayor's reputation was never higher than in those dark days after the attacks. Two weeks later, at a memorial for the 9/11 victims at Yankee Stadium, Oprah Winfrey famously dubbed Giuliani "America's Mayor." That December, *Time* named Giuliani its "Person of the Year," and speculation about a presidential run began as soon as he entered private life after being term-limited out of the mayor's office on December 31, 2001. A November 2004 Gallup poll pitting Giuliani against McCain gave the New Yorker a 47 percent to 26 percent advantage. On February 14, 2007, when Giuliani announced he would enter the presidential race, a Gallup poll gave him 40 percent of the vote, compared to 24 percent for McCain. None of the other Republicans in the race got more than 5 percent.

With the propagandists at Fox News trumpeting "America's Mayor" every step of the way, and with the national media enamored with the "moderate" Republican, Giuliani believed that he actually had a near-lock on his party's nomination. His campaign focused almost solely on his

big historical moment, with the terrorist attacks being referred to constantly and ads of the burning towers being run. Mentioning 9/11 became
a near-obsession with Giuliani—in person, in ads, and in media interviews. When he rudely interrupted a meeting with NRA members to take
a cell phone call from his wife, he justified the action by claiming that
"since September 11 . . . we talk to each other and just reaffirm the fact
that we love each other." He explained his "conversion" on gun control
from staunch supporter to sudden ardent foe by referring to 9/11. He even
claimed he had spent as much time at Ground Zero as recovery workers.
The incessant "9/11" references, which *The Daily Show*'s Jon Stewart
called "9/11 Tourettes," led Sen. Joe Biden to quip that "there's only three
things he mentions in a sentence—a noun, a verb, and 9/11."

But why wouldn't Giuliani take a national tragedy to such absurd ends?
He was constantly told he was the hero of 9/11, that he was "America's
Mayor," that his leadership had helped the nation cope with the traumatic
attacks, and that people believed he was a true leader.

Floating on all that hot air, Giuliani apparently forgot to give himself
a reality check. For starters, Giuliani had serious problems in appealing to
the base of the Republican Party—he supported abortion rights, he didn't
hate gay people, he was tolerant toward immigrants, and he had supported
gun control. In other words, there was no way in hell he could ever win a
nomination contest for a party that considered every one of those positions
anathema to its core ideology.

Another reality check for Giuliani should have been his own check-
ered record as mayor of New York. On the eve of 9/11, his approval rating
in his own city, according to a Quinnipiac University poll, was an anemic
39 percent. He had been married three times, including a second mar-
riage that ended in a very public, very messy divorce during his term as
mayor. He had a documented history of using city resources to help out
his extramarital relationship, with city police chauffeuring his mistress and
her family around town, and putting in time walking her dog. Some of his
closest associates were corrupt, several facing federal indictments, like Bernard Kerik, Giuliani's former police commissioner, who faced sixteen
counts of fraud and corruption in the fall of 2007.

Even his successes, when examined closely, seemed to be built upon shaky ground. His trumpeted victories in the battle against crime were marred by controversies over civil rights abuses and police misconduct. Reports were issued that revealed that police and fire teams had been unable to communicate on 9/11 effectively because of faulty radios, a possible factor in the deaths of hundreds of firefighters. He'd also stubbornly ignored advice to locate the city's emergency command center in Brooklyn, opting instead for an office in the World Trade Center—a high-probability target given the fact that it had been attacked in 1993—a decision that further complicated the emergency response.

These negatives, as they emerged, would eventually crater his support, and in the end he was unable to manage anything better than a distant third-place finish in any of the presidential primaries in which he competed. As *Harper's Magazine* reported on January 31, 2008, Giuliani had spent a total of $48.9 million as of December 31, 2007. And in the first seven states in which he competed, he averaged 5.14 percent of the vote, receiving a total of 342,357 votes (exclude Florida and he only got 60,602 votes). In other words, Giuliani spent a total of $142.83 per vote he received. *Harper's* referred to the collapse of Giuliani's campaign as "one of the most spectacular political humiliations in recent American history."

Giuliani's electoral fate provides a handy object lesson about keeping things real in your own mind. No matter how nice people are to you, no matter how much the media builds you up, it is highly unlikely that you are as great as they say. In fact, there's often reason to be suspicious of such hype, given the old adage about the media building you up so they can tear you down. The more you buy into your own hype, the juicier a target you become and the more people will revel in your downfall. By remaining realistic, humble, and grounded—and by factoring reality into your plans—you deny your enemies the satisfaction of piercing your egotistical armor.

In Giuliani's case, he was so seduced by all the talk about "America's Mayor" and his heroic status that he was unwilling to assess the fundamental weaknesses of his candidacy. Similarly, Cindy Sheehan was seduced by the fame her Crawford protest generated and began thinking that she as an individual was more important than the movement she was part of. Even Michael Baisden, the radio host who was so quick to attack and dismiss Color of Change for their fund-raising efforts, overreached and set a goal publicly to deliver far more money than he was able to provide to the Jena 6. Big promises from big egos often can backfire in spectacular and public ways.

One of the things I've always loved about blogging and the netroots culture is that there's virtually no danger of living in a bubble surrounded by sycophants. Every time I write anything on my own site, I have dozens of people telling me what an idiot I am. And that's a wonderful thing. Even if I disagree with them, I'm forced to face the fact on an hourly basis that there are people who vigorously disagree with me and don't think I'm beyond reproach. Everyone who signs up to post at *Daily Kos* has the opportunity to challenge opinions, find new facts, provide new evidence, and analyze the "conventional wisdom" of every other poster, including mine. This robust demand for interaction and accountability is probably one of the greatest strengths of the rising movement, and it helps to keep its leaders grounded.

★ CHAPTER 7 ★

FIGHT SMALL, WIN BIG

Permanent change is created only through long-term effort, with small gains leading to larger achievements. Resist the lure of notching up quick and easy conquests that may harm long-term goals. On the other hand, small, well-planned skirmishes leading to incremental advances can hone strategies and skills while rewarding activists with occasional, welcome victories.

If the 1964 presidential campaign had been a title bout between two rivals—New Deal liberalism in one corner, hard-right conservatism in the other—the electoral repudiation of Barry Goldwater and his radical right ideology would have been the knockout punch that should have ended that movement forever.

Goldwater, after a hard-fought primary victory over Republican Party establishment favorite Governor Nelson Rockefeller of New York, took his brand of conservatism on the road to the American people in his campaign against President Lyndon B. Johnson. His laundry list of policy prescriptions was clear-cut and stark: he was virulently antiunion, proposed using nuclear weapons to defoliate Vietnam, suggested that battlefield commanders be given the right to use nuclear weapons without presidential authority, and opposed the Civil Rights Act of 1964, which enabled desegregation of schools and public accommodations and prohibited workplace and voter discrimination.

The historian Rick Perlstein in his 2001 book, *Before the Storm: Barry Goldwater and the Unmaking of the American Consensus*, best captured Goldwater's extremism:

> "Think of a senator winning the Democratic nomination in the year 2000 whose positions included halving the military budget, socializing the medical system, reregulating the communications and electrical industries, establishing a guaranteed minimum

income for all Americans, and equalizing funding for all schools regardless of property valuations—and who promised to fire Alan Greenspan, counseled withdrawal from the World Trade Organization, and, for good measure, spoke warmly of adolescent sexual experimentation. He would lose in a landslide. He would be relegated to the ash heap of history."

Goldwater, of course, was a true believer. At his nominating speech, he famously remarked, "Extremism in the defense of liberty is no vice," and received forty-one seconds of thunderous applause, before finishing off with "And let me remind you also that moderation in the pursuit of justice is no virtue." The problem was, to the American people, Goldwater's extremism seemed, if not a vice, certainly not a trait they wanted to see in a president. His brand of rabid anticommunist militarism and radically antigovernment views made him a champion of the nascent conservative movement, but proved to be grossly out of step not only with the broader American electorate but within his own party as well.

But the Goldwaterites were an inspired flock, as described by *Time* magazine in its July 24, 1964, issue:

"They wear tennis shoes only on tennis courts. They don't read [John Birch Society founder] Robert Welch or hate Negroes. They aren't nuclear-bomb throwers, and they don't write obscene letters to editors who disagree with them. They are reasonably well-educated and informed. They are, in fact, nuts about Barry Goldwater without being nutty in the process. These are the citizens who make up the great majority of Goldwater's following. As such, they are the troops in a middle-class revolution that borrows from Populism, has a strong desire to maintain the economic and social advances it has achieved, looks with deep concern at the moral decline of the country, has geographical definitions and strong religious and patriotic overtones. The movement injects a new thrust into U.S. politics; and win, lose or draw in November, that thrust will be felt for a long while."

That enthusiasm was no match for an electorate repelled by Goldwater's radicalism. On Election Day, Johnson royally thumped Goldwater, getting 61.1 percent of the popular vote to Goldwater's 38.5 percent. Goldwater carried just six states—his native Arizona, plus Alabama, Georgia, Louisiana, Mississippi, and South Carolina.

With Goldwater utterly rejected, the Republican establishment breathed a sigh of relief: crisis averted, insurgency crushed. Except, of course, that the insurgents hadn't been crushed, as *Time* had correctly predicted in its article. The Goldwaterites realized that the country wasn't yet ready for their ideology, and they blamed the "liberal media," academia, and eastern Republican elites for creating an atmosphere and a society predisposed against their "truth."

Taking a long, hard look at the political landscape, disappointed conservative activists took a deep breath and set into motion a far-reaching plan—a plan to build their "vast right-wing conspiracy," with think tanks and idea machines, alternate media institutions, pressure groups, and a new class of pundits, academics, staffers, and politicians to promote their ideology nationwide. From the start, they knew their plan was a long-term one. It would require investment, patience, and a sustained below-the-radar effort to win the country, one small chunk at a time. The 1960s was not yet a people-powered era with the technological tools we now have available, so the right had to build its infrastructure the old-fashioned way, by dumping hundreds of millions of dollars and building brick-and-mortar institutions. It took time. *Lots* of time. And all along, these activists kept their motivation and clung to the long view. They ran for local and regional office, took over school boards and city councils, and infiltrated the judiciary and academia. Gradually, they worked their way up the ladder, replacing their party's old-school moderates.

In 1980, all that hard and inglorious work, all that patience and dedication, paid off spectacularly when a speaker who had been spotlighted by Goldwater at the 1964 convention—Ronald Reagan—won the White House. And their "revolution" still wasn't complete until fourteen years later, when Newt Gingrich led the Republican takeover of the U.S. House in 1994, a full thirty years after Goldwater's crushing defeat. By the time conservative Republicans swept to power, Goldwater's "extreme" agenda was no longer extreme—the views had slipped into the mainstream, so much so that even Democrats were desperate to show how they too were militaristic, antitax, and pro-business.

This was never a short-term battle. The conservative movement's ideology lingered in the shadows of the nation's political spectrum. It was a slow and monumental process that eventually brought it out into the light of acceptability.

Radical ideas cannot be forced down the throat of the nation; that's where Goldwater had tried and failed. People yearn for stability and resist sweeping change. Goldwater's failure in 1964 was mostly due to expecting too much too fast. His devotees who built modern conservatism in the wake of his presidential run tried a different tack and ultimately succeeded. Conservatives learned to slowly steer public opinion around to the point that voters would be *asking* for the product only the Right could deliver.

Effecting lasting change in society is a daunting undertaking, with frustrations and hurdles every step of the way. It's not a task for those with short attention spans, or those without the fortitude for the long haul.

We live in a society in which people prefer the familiar and fear rapid change. Forced change, while often necessary, can create a backlash and present continued challenges for decades, as we see with the ongoing battles over abortion and civil rights, which were "solved" by the courts, yet lingered on as the culture failed to keep pace.

Some battles are worth fighting to force rapid change, and choice and civil rights certainly qualify, but the fact remains that the most desirable pathway to change is slow, steady, and incremental, a process that can bring whole societies along. It's the difference between having courts force something on the people, and having the people—through their elected representatives in a legislature—make that decision themselves. Only in extreme cases do we want to make that decision for people, because the most effective change occurs when people lead the way with ideas they've already bought into—and that takes a long-term commitment to engaging in political persuasion. It is evolution, rather than revolution.

ADVANCE AND HOLD ENEMY GROUND

In 1974, the first "gay rights bill" was introduced in Congress, proposing to add "sexual orientation" to the Civil Rights Act of 1964, prohibiting such discrimination. It was too broad a demand for rights too early, perhaps, and didn't get very far. Twenty years later, in 1994, supporters narrowed the scope of the legislation by focusing only on employment discrimination, and the Employment Non-Discrimination Act (ENDA) was introduced, prohibiting "employment discrimination on the basis of sexual orientation." The legislation didn't get a floor vote until 1996, when the Senate rejected it, 50–49.

ENDA bills were subsequently introduced and failed in 1999, 2001, and 2003 (never in an election year, conveniently). Then, with the Democratic takeover of both chambers of Congress in 2006, prospects for passage brightened considerably. The House introduced the latest version of ENDA in April 2007, which included workplace protections for gays, lesbians, bisexuals, and transgendered people.

However, it became quickly apparent that the inclusion of the transgender category would doom the measure. When that language was stripped, all hell broke loose in the LGBT community. The largest of the gay rights groups, the Human Rights Campaign (HRC), which had pushed for a bill that included the transgendered community, seemed to reluctantly support a noninclusive ENDA after seeing the writing on the wall in Congress. HRC president Joe Salmonese issued a statement on September 27, 2007, saying, "This is not what any of us wanted, and certainly not what we've been fighting for. But, it has been made clear that the House leadership and bill sponsors are moving forward with a noninclusive ENDA even without the full support of our community. They view this as the best opportunity they will have this year to help the largest number of people—and have stated that they do not intend to miss this opportunity." The organization's stand resulted in the resignation of the board's only transgender member.

But the Lambda Legal Defense Fund and most of its sister groups opposed the exclusion of transgender people from the legislation, summing up their position succinctly in an October 4 statement:

> "Our common goal is passage of a fair and inclusive employ-
> ment nondiscrimination statute and we pledge to work with mem-
> bers of Congress to ensure that the new law serves its important
> purpose—securely to protect our community against workplace
> discrimination. A law that does not actually do that is a law not
> worth having."

As the last sentence made clear, the groups wanted all or nothing. Ultimately, 350 organizations came together to form United ENDA to lobby for the original, all-inclusive version of the legislation. Despite its name, the community was not united. Publicly, gay rights groups insisted on the inclusion of the transgender community, with the glaring exception of the Human Rights Campaign. But in private, many activists seethed. They had fought for more than thirty years to get a nondiscrimination employment bill passed, and now, right on the cusp of a historic victory, all their efforts were threatened by a transgender community that had come to the battle late. Many gay rights activists didn't just want the victory; they desperately *needed* it after many years of setbacks and scapegoating—even if it wasn't perfect or ideal.

Perhaps no one captured the heart of the controversy and articulated that position better than the blogger John Aravosis, who wrote about it on October 2, 2007, on his site *AmericaBlog*. Admitting that he was "afraid" to even write about the issue, Aravosis first clarified why the provision got dropped, saying it "wasn't because Dem leaders didn't want trans in there. It's because we don't have the votes to get ENDA passed if it includes job protections for transsexuals." Then he explained the political realities— and the choices facing the proponents—as he saw them:

> "No amount of 'insistence' is going to change that fact; all the
> pressure in the world on Democratic leaders isn't going to con-
> vince Republicans and conservative Dems to support transsexual
> rights. Pressuring Dem leaders to add the T back into ENDA is

addressing the symptom but not the cause. The Dems dropped the T because we don't have the votes when we include the T. Forcing them to put the T back in does nothing to change the vote count. So insist away that the Dem leadership put the T back in to ENDA, but please don't call it a victory when ENDA goes down in flames as a result of your actions, and 25 million gays and lesbians are told to wait a few more decades for their civil rights (assuming they live that long, don't lose their jobs in the meantime, etc.). If losing is your definition of victory, then we can all pack our bags and go home, because we can achieve that victory—have been achieving that victory for decades—without lifting a finger or donating a dime to a knowier-than-thou gay group."

Soon enough, some other voices joined Aravosis in favor of the "incremental step" strategy. Susan Ryan-Vollmar, the editor in chief of the Boston weekly *Bay Windows*, the largest gay newspaper in New England, wrote an impassioned editorial on October 4, calling the all-or-nothing approach "madness":

"The House is on the verge of passing groundbreaking workplace protections for millions of Americans. It's the first piece of legislation Congress has seriously considered since the Family Medical Leave Act (FMLA) was passed in 1993 that offers American workers protection from arbitrary firings. It's not perfect. Few pieces of civil rights legislation are. But it would provide a concrete base upon which to expand ENDA protections not just to transmen and women but to also add provisions to the bill that would require employers to offer domestic partnership benefits to the partners of their LGBT employees if they offer such benefits to their heterosexual employees—a provision that is not in the current bill. [. . .]"

The petulant insistence on purity, principle, and perfection had limited appeal.

A poll commissioned in late October by the Human Rights Campaign of five hundred national members of the LGBT community found that 70 percent of them preferred the imperfect bill—without the transgender protections—rather than no bill at all. It was as if the community's rank and file understood the notion of incremental change better than the leadership of the 350 groups that were demanding all or nothing. The poll respondents' logic made sense: It would be imperfect, yes, but it would pass. And once it was law, it would be far easier to add transgender protections than it would be to pass a fresh bill with all such protections already included.

In other words, partial ENDA legislation would be a foothold into the law, making it easier to expand not just employment nondiscrimination protections to other classes of people, but also expand the rights themselves, such as health benefits for domestic partners.

What's more, and perhaps ironically, just getting the bill passed in the House was part of an incrementalist strategy. The legislation had little chance of passing the Senate, and even if it did, it faced a promised veto by President Bush. However, that wasn't the point. The point was to pass the legislation in order to build momentum toward future efforts. It was a time to identify friends, lobby the fence-sitters for the next round, and target foes for defeat. Perhaps even more important, it would be a tangible victory for a community that had historically enjoyed precious few of them.

The legislation eventually passed the House 235–184 on November 7, with 200 Democrats and 35 Republicans voting for it, and 25 Democrats and 159 Republicans opposed. Predictably, the legislation died in the Senate, where the bill was never taken up and never made it to a floor vote.

"History teaches that progress on civil rights is never easy. It is often marked by small and difficult steps," said House Speaker Nancy Pelosi after the House victory, and she was right. In an ideal world, there would be no discrimination against the LGBT community, or any other, for that matter. Any effort to bring forth such sweeping change will entail taking baby steps like ENDA, or like efforts to include sexual orientation in hate crimes law. Each baby step has even smaller steps—getting approval from one legislative body, then the other, then a signature from the president, or the governor, or the mayor. The gay rights fight is a long-running battle. Nearly forty years have passed since the groundbreaking 1969 Stonewall rebellion in New York City that kick-started the modern gay rights movement. It wasn't until 2007 that the movement notched its first legislative victories, passage in the House of both ENDA and Hate Crimes legislation.

That the ENDA legislation died does not negate the historic value of the victory. The battle wasn't over, and would be reengaged in subsequent congressional sessions, baby stepping ever closer to eventual victory. This repetitive tactic has proven to be particularly effective for conservatives, who remain politically committed and willing to try and try again to dismantle the legacy of the New Deal and to accomplish other pet ideological goals, such as rolling back the hard-fought gains of American workers.

In fact, the methodical dismemberment of the labor union movement is perhaps the best illustration of conservative incremental success. In some ways, it has been a classic example of the "death by a thousand cuts" metaphor. While in the mid-1950s 35 percent of the American wage-and-salary workers were members of organized labor, by 1974 that number had declined to 25 percent, and stands today at 12.1 percent, with only 8.5 percent of private-sector employees in unions. And the decline continues.

This is a result of a long and sustained war that the right wing has waged against labor for decades, exerting pressure on all three branches of government. It began in the 1930s, when the landmark National Labor Relations Act of 1935 was passed, which provided broad protections for workers and established the National Labor Relations Board (NLRB). Twelve years later, a Republican Congress began chipping away at the rights of workers, enacting the Taft-Hartley Act over President Harry Truman's veto. According to the historian Dan Clawson in *The Next Upsurge: Labor and the New Social Movements*:

> "The general principle, for the Taft-Hartley Act in particular and for labor law in general, is that any tactic that gives workers power is illegal. To that end, supervisors are forbidden to form or

join unions. . . . Radicals and Communists were ordered expelled from unions. . . . Secondary boycotts were outlawed: cannery workers may picket the cannery (which does not sell to individual consumers) but not the grocery store that carries the canned goods. This limit applies only to unions; any other American, or group of Americans, has a free speech right to picket the grocer."

The establishment of "right to work" states created antiunion, pro-business sanctuaries, and after the passage of Taft-Hartley, conservatives turned to the courts and executive agencies to continue chipping away at labor power. Additionally, efforts were made by Big Business, according to Clawson, to infiltrate the culture itself by hiring public relations firms that focused on influencing journalists and placing antiunion messages on television, in textbooks, and even comic strips.

In 1980, movement conservatives elected their first president, Ronald Reagan, and he immediately moved against the unions by firing striking air traffic controllers. An emboldened business world took its cues and began serious attempts to break unions, confident that Reagan's NLRB would back them.

Conservative foes of organized labor have always known that a head-on assault on unions would prove difficult if not impossible. Labor still has too many allies and the public, while not exactly pro-union (a lack of visibility has made organized labor largely irrelevant in broader society), would likely bristle at an overt effort to target workers. Hence, the antilabor movement takes baby steps toward its ultimate goal, staying mostly in the shadows, quietly chipping away at labor's legal foundation while working to erode its popular support.

Long-term goals are most often reached through a series of small, short-term advancements, each one building ever closer to that finale. You advance and hold your ground, and then you advance again. Each step forward not only helps shift public opinion, but it also gives activists and their allies a series of victories with which to recharge their batteries. Even the longest-term plan requires a series of intermediate battles to advance the agenda and keep commitments focused.

PICK YOUR BATTLES

In one of the more bizarre political proposals since the Democratic strate-gist James Carville popped the question to the Republican strategist Mary Matalin, right-wing Fox News Channel courted the 2008 Democratic presidential candidates for a debate to be held in Nevada in early 2007. Like giddy fools, the party initially accepted the poisonous overture.

Both the Nevada Democratic Party and the Congressional Black Cau-cus (CBC) jumped in bed with Fox as cosponsors of the debates. Ronald Brownstein of the *Los Angeles Times* accurately summarized the choice facing Democrats, writing on March 16, "The question the party faced was whether access to Fox's viewers was worth the validation the network would receive from hosting a Democratic debate." The party answered yes.

But a rapidly growing coalition of grassroots progressive groups, spear-headed by the bloggers, found the concept scandalous and fought back.

Since its inception in 1996, progressives have been frustrated with the Fox News Channel. As a clearly partisan propaganda machine for the Republican Party, the network mocked its critics with its "Fair and Bal-anced" tagline, a branding that seemed to fool the broader media and even some Democrats. As Brownstein wrote in his March 16 article:

> "Fox cloaks itself in the mantle of objectivity with the nudge-nudge insistence that it—and it alone—provides 'fair and bal-anced' coverage of the news. Then it advances its financial and ideological interests by promoting lurid accusations from conser-vatives against Democrats, accusations that are routinely debunked later by the mainstream media. Many Fox reporters are fair. But overall the network—through its language, its news decisions and its hosts—generally functions more like a cog in the Republican message machine than as a conventional news organization that attempts to abide, however imperfectly, by the traditional stan-dards of (yes) fairness and balance."

A poll by John Kerry's pollster found Fox's audience dramatically skewed to the right. "An audience that decides for itself, based on 'fair and balanced' coverage, ought not to reach monolithic conclusions," wrote Mark Mellman on March 20 in the Washington, D.C., newspaper the *Hill*. "Yet, in our 2004 polling with Media Vote, using Nielsen diaries, we found that Fox News viewers supported George Bush over John Kerry by 88 percent to 7 percent. No demographic segment, other than Republicans, was as united in supporting Bush. Conservatives, white evangelical Christians, gun owners, and supporters of the Iraq war all gave Bush fewer votes than did regular Fox News viewers."

Besides the blatantly partisan nature of Fox and its relentless demonizing of Democrats, there were two additional factors at play regarding the presidential debate issue. First, even in late February 2007, less than a year from the Iowa caucuses, this was already a heated Democratic primary. Candidates were looking for any advantage to stand out from the rest of the crowd, which meant they might consider refusing to participate in the debate as a means of doing that. Secondly, I knew from ultimately successful efforts to get the candidates to attend a presidential forum debate at the annual YearlyKos gathering later that summer that the campaigns were inundated with requests for debates, and they were keen to lessen that load. So while the Nevada Democratic Party and the CBC might want those debates, the top-tier candidates almost assuredly did not. True, the second- and third-tier candidates craved any free media attention they could get, and the debates provided that, but the top candidates at the time—Hillary Clinton, Barack Obama, John Edwards, and Bill Richardson—might be persuaded to quit one of those debates, I reasoned, to earn brownie points with progressive activists.

So I launched the first volley on *Daily Kos* on February 20:

> "Fox News is unabashedly movement oriented . . . But they cannot exert serious pressure on media narratives unless it creates some semblance of respectability. Its so-called 'fair and balanced' nonsense. It's much easier to ignore Newsmax as partisan dribble. But when reporting news, any 'serious' news operation gets deference by its peers. And Fox News has taken advantage of that defer-

ence to promote some of the worst smears against Democrats. Yet for years, Democrats have helped fuel this right-wing propaganda arm by appearing on their various programs, lending it an air of legitimacy. But I suppose politics is about measuring baby steps. And the Nevada Democratic Party's decision to give Fox News rights to one of *our* field's debates sets back much of our hard work. Would Republicans hold a debate on Air America? Would they live blog on *Daily Kos*? Only if they were idiots. But apparently, that very simple notion eludes our top Democrats."

For years bloggers had watched Fox News with a mixture of admiration and contempt. We admired the network's ability to promote its conservative message, but we had contempt because instead of being honest about what it was—a conservative news network—it kept up a ridiculous charade of being an objective news source. The goal of progressive bloggers had never been to destroy Fox News, but simply to brand it—honestly—as an outlet with a heavily partisan and conservative bias.

Let's be clear: There was nothing wrong with being a conservative propaganda outlet, but there was everything wrong with Democrats helping validate the organization as a legitimate news outlet. If we could get Democrats to drop out of the debate, we would score two points—we'd deprive Fox of the validation that a Democratic debate would offer, and we'd reinforce the "Fox is a conservative mouthpiece" narrative in the broader media. But could we pull it off?

The broader netroots engaged immediately after my initial post. Bloggers piled on. MoveOn lent its weight to the effort. Brave New Films released video clips on YouTube of Fox News mocking and disparaging Democrats, such as labeling Mark Foley, the Republican congressman from Florida caught preying on young male pages, as a Democrat. It wasn't a rare "mistake," but a pattern—enough instances to compile a rich video record that proved invaluable in offering a quick and powerful way to make our point about Fox News that words never could. Progressive bloggers gleefully slapped those videos on their sites, where hundreds of thousands of visitors viewed them. Many responded by contacting the campaigns, asking them to bow out.

I let the pressure build for one week, then sent a quick-and-dirty email to the four campaigns asking their intentions on the debate, which I then blogged on March 6:

> "I've asked several campaigns whether they plan on attending the Fox News debate in Nevada. I've started collecting responses, and expect to post them tomorrow. I can say off the bat that the question clearly has campaigns conflicted. It's not a position they want to be in, and I'm sure they're cursing whoever it was that negotiated the deal with Fox News."

The Edwards campaign responded the very next day:

> "We will not be participating in the Fox debate. We're going to make lots of appearances in Nevada, including debates. By the end of March, we will have attended three presidential forums in Nevada—and there are already at least three proposed Nevada debates. We're definitely going to debate in Nevada, but we don't see why this needs to be one of them."

The Obama and Clinton campaigns begged off on an immediate decision, saying they were still mulling their calendars, but the Edwards pullout had already doomed the debate. Now there needed to be a face-saving way for the Nevada Democrats to back out of the event.

That was provided the very next day by none other than Fox News Chairman Roger Ailes, during a speech he gave in accepting the Radio and Television News Directors Foundation's 2007 First Amendment Leadership Award in which he taunted the Democrats:

> "It is true that just in the last two weeks Hillary Clinton has had over two hundred phone calls telling her in order to win the presidency she must stay on the road for the next two years. It is not true they were all from Bill. [Laughter]
>
> "And it is true that Barack Obama is on the move. I don't know

if it's true that President Bush called Musharraf and said, 'Why can't we catch this guy?' [Laughter]"

Here was the head of Fox News mocking the very Democrats he was trying to lure to his network's soundstage with the typical right-wing slurs — Hillary's husband cheats on her, and Obama is a Muslim terrorist. In any case, those remarks finally cleared the way for Democrats to bail out of the debate. The next day, New Mexico governor and presidential candidate Bill Richardson dropped out after having previously agreed to participate, and hours later, Democratic Senate Majority Leader Harry Reid of Nevada and his state party chair Tom Collins pulled the plug, sending a letter to Fox saying:

"[C]omments made last night by FOX News President Roger Ailes in reference to one of our presidential candidates went too far. We cannot, as good Democrats, put our party in a position to defend such comments. In light of his comments, we have concluded that it is not possible to hold a Presidential debate that will focus on our candidates and are therefore canceling our August debate. We take no pleasure in this, but it is the only course of action."

Fox News' response was predictable. Vice President David Rhodes released a statement on the *Drudge Report* that read in part, "the Nevada Democratic Caucus [appears] to be controlled by radical fringe out-of-state interest groups, not the Nevada Democratic Party." Exactly the way a serious news operation would react, of course. Meanwhile, Ailes was beside himself in rage, threatening that any candidate "who believes he can blacklist any news organization is making a terrible mistake" and "impeding freedom of speech and free press."

It was a laughable charge to make, of course, since no one was seeking to pull Fox off the air or in any way muzzle its voice. But Fox was smarting. The pullout, as we'd hoped, made big news, and hundreds of stories — including wire stories printed in thousands of outlets — now talked about

Democrats backing out of the debate because Fox News was a right-wing media outlet.

The network's attempt to use the Democratic debates to legitimize its propaganda efforts had blown up in its face.

Some establishment Democrats, conditioned for years to submit to Fox's will in a bizarre "battered wife syndrome" sort of way, picked up the torch for the right-wing network, arguing that Democrats had to be able to speak to all Americans—including those watching Fox News—in order to look for votes in unexpected places. But those arguments betrayed a fundamental misunderstanding of what Fox News was about, and I responded:

> "[W]hy do you think conservatives watch Fox News? Because they worship at the altar of their pundit heroes—Sean Hannity, Bill O'Reilly, Brit Hume, John Gibson, and their special little friends like Bill Bennett, Ann Coulter and the like.
>
> "That's who the viewers tune in to hear. That's who they trust.
>
> "So logic would dictate an easy answer to this question—Who will those conservative Fox News viewers trust—the Democrats at the debate, or their hero pundits who will spend the next hour (and days) afterward trashing those Democrats?
>
> "It's not a trick question."

This wasn't a matter of controlling the message at an unfriendly media outlet, but of letting them frame questions in the light most unfavorable to the Democrats on the stage—then cutting away to conservative celebrity pundits who would proceed to eviscerate those Democrats before a hungry partisan audience. But the Democrats who urged capitulation and attendance at the debate became the target—of other establishment Democrats who fought back.

The aforementioned Mark Mellman released the results of his poll and spoke forcefully on behalf of the pullout: "If Fox wants the legitimacy afforded by official sponsorship of Democratic debates, it needs to become a relatively objective news organization, not a dispenser of partisan cant."

The longtime liberal commentator Paul Begala echoed the sentiment: "Thank God Democrats are finally growing a spine and fighting back. No longer can Fox function as a Republican mouthpiece and expect us to put it on stage as a neutral news source."

Incredibly, Fox refused to give up and made yet another effort to host a debate—this one in Detroit with the Congressional Black Caucus (CBC)—which was similarly defeated. This time it was the black blogosphere, spearheaded by Color of Change, that helped kill the debate. Their efforts received another great assist from Brave New Films, which distributed a video on YouTube of Fox News clips with African-Americans and their issues being disparaged by its conservative hosts and commentators.

But faced with an obstinate and tone-deaf leadership at the CBC refusing to even acknowledge the bloggers' existence and addressing their concerns, the bloggers shifted tactics. They were too small as a percentage of the black community to directly threaten the CBC's entrenched leadership. So instead of a frontal attack, they went to the black newspapers that reached a larger percentage of their black community and lobbied them to editorialize against the debate. The results of that campaign were packaged together and sent to the offices of every CBC member—editorials against the Fox News debate from major black newspapers: the *Dallas Weekly*, *Philadelphia Tribune*, *Los Angeles Sentinel*, *Louisiana Weekly*, and the *Chicago Defender*. While the CBC stuck resolutely to the debate, the effort was doomed when all the major candidates eventually dropped out of this debate as well.

Now, in the greater scheme of things, this was actually a modest victory. Fox News is still attacking and smearing Democrats, and likely will continue to do so for the foreseeable future. If we set out to destroy the network, we'd be doomed to failure and mocked for our naïveté and powerlessness. Instead, we set a much more modest goal—to damage the network's brand as "fair and balanced"—and we did that with yet another modest goal—to get Democratic candidates to drop out of their debate on Fox. By tying it to the long-running and passion-arousing anti–Fox News narrative, we had a compelling story to tell.

In the end, it didn't matter how modest the victory was. It was a victory, and it energized me and my progressive allies for future battles. No one ever wins every battle he or she fights. But even the small ones matter, and are necessary when moving toward a larger goal.

Part of taking those small steps toward a final goal is picking battles you can win. Shoot too high and your ambitious plans could expose you as a paper tiger and demoralize you and your allies. There are times when failure can build momentum toward future success. Years of ENDA failures have led us to passage in the House — then more failure as the Senate drops the ball and the president promises a veto. But each failure builds momentum for the next push, and thus still works toward the eventual goal. However, nonstrategic failures do none of that. Add too many failures together, and your opponents and allies no longer will take you seriously. No one wants to be associated with impotent losers. So pick your battles carefully.

DON'T CROSS ENEMY LINES

Pro-choice, pro–gay rights, anti–death penalty . . . by all rights, Lincoln Chafee, the junior U.S. senator from Rhode Island, should have been trailing a D after his name. During his six-year tenure in the Senate, he supported increases in the minimum wage, more federal funding for health care, and measures for affirmative action. Most notably, he was the only Republican to vote against giving President Bush the authority to invade Iraq — which put him not just to the left of his party, but well to the left of twenty-nine Democratic senators on this issue as well. Given the dogmatic conservatism of the current Republican Party, he was an anachronism, a Rockefeller Republican stranded in the most Democratic state in the union.

His father, John Chafee, had a long history of public service in the state, serving as governor from 1963 to 1969, then as U.S. senator from 1976 until his death in 1999. The Republican governor of Rhode Island at the time nominated Chafee's son, Lincoln, to carry on the mantle. With the exception of one four-year break from 1972 to 1976, Rhode Island had gone a span of forty-three years with a Chafee in public office.

Lincoln Chafee also had an impeccable record as an environmental-ist, making his mark as a member of the Senate Committee on Environ-ment and Public Works. On that committee, his was the decisive majority vote that prevented President Bush's Clear Skies initiative, a polluter-friendly measure, from getting to the Senate floor. He fought drilling in the Arctic National Wildlife Refuge in Alaska and he resisted attempts to undermine the Endangered Species Act. He was a throwback to the earlier Republican period of commitment to conservation, ushered in by Theo-dore Roosevelt, outdoorsman extraordinaire and founder of America's na-tional park system.

His environmentalist profile—and his record—got Chafee a ringing endorsement from the Sierra Club in 2006. "We pledge to do all we can to help ensure Senator Chafee is reelected," announced Alison Buckser, chair of the Sierra Club's Rhode Island chapter, on April 19, 2006. "Sierra Club volunteers will work with the campaign to contact voters about his exemplary environmental record. We look forward to a victory party for the environment on election night and to many more years of Lincoln Chafee fighting for the environment as a U.S. Senator."

Chafee was also quite popular with women's groups, receiving a 100 percent rating from Planned Parenthood in 2006 and a 100 percent and 65 percent rating from NARAL in 2004 and 2005 respectively, and, con-versely, a 9 percent rating from the National Right to Life Committee, according to Project Vote Smart. So NARAL joined the Sierra Club and the League of Conservation Voters (LCV) in endorsing Chafee. "We are proud to add even more names to the list of candidates who are cultivating a winning pro-choice message that reinforces their support for the values of freedom, privacy, and personal responsibility," announced NARAL president Nancy Keenan.

But there was a big problem. These pillars of the old progressive coalition—the Sierra Club, NARAL, and LCV—were working against their own interests.

In any other era, progressive groups would likely have been satisfied with having a moderate Republican voting with them on key issues, giving them some bipartisan cover when needed. But in 2006, a fierce battle for control of the U.S. Senate had been engaged. Although Republicans enjoyed a ten-seat majority in the upper body of Congress, Democrats found themselves within reach of a majority.

One seat—just one Senate seat—would mean the difference between a Democratic and Republican majority. And Chafee, no matter how liberal a Republican he might be, would vote for a Republican majority leader if elected, and Republicans would control key committees and thus have real-world repercussions. The importance of controlling the Senate was paramount for movement progressives, and should've easily overridden any loyalties or attachments to Chafee.

The voters of Rhode Island had a decision to make—stick with a name that was a cultural treasure in the state, or be true to its ideological beliefs and elect a senator who shared them. Predictably, the Democratic Senatorial Campaign Committee targeted Chafee's seat and pumped resources into the state to back the Democratic challenger, Sheldon Whitehouse.

Whitehouse was a formidable challenger to Chafee, with a strong record of advancing progressive causes as attorney general. He'd pursued lead paint manufacturer Sherwin Williams, and he'd helped found the Rhode Island Quality Institute, a nonpartisan organization dedicated to "helping reinvent health care" for the state. He also had a reputation as a dogged initiator of public corruption cases, most likely a holdover from his days serving as U.S. attorney. Like Chafee, he could boast a family public service pedigree: both his father and grandfather had been career diplomats. He won his primary handily and was ready to face off against Chafee, with the wholehearted blessing and help of the DSCC.

The netroots became heavily invested in the race for the same reasons as the DSCC—the crucial gaining of the majority. This meant that the Democratic Party and the netroots understood the importance of getting rid of Chafee and his enabling of an odious Republican government.

Yet the traditional liberal groups like the Sierra Club and NARAL had crossed enemy lines—just because they had a positive relationship with one nice soldier on the other side.

Every single Senate seat in the 2006 election mattered. If the Republicans kept control of the Senate—with help from the Sierra Club's support of Chafee—the chair of the Senate Committee on the Environment and Public Works would've been Oklahoma Senator James Inhofe.

When the histories of the battle over global warming are written, no villain will feature more prominently than Inhofe. In July 2003, he claimed on the Senate floor that he had "compelling evidence that catastrophic global warming is a hoax. That conclusion is supported by the painstaking work of the nation's top climate scientists." And it wasn't just *any* hoax. "With all of the hysteria, all of the fear, all of the phony science, could it be that man-made global warming is the greatest hoax ever perpetrated on the American people? It sure sounds like it."

In an interview with the *Tulsa World* in 2006, he compared environmentalists to Nazis. "It kind of reminds . . . I could use the Third Reich, the big lie," Inhofe said. "You say something over and over and over and over again, and people will believe it, and that's their strategy. A hot summer has nothing to do with global warming. Let's keep in mind it was just three weeks ago that people were saying, 'Wait a minute; it is unusually cool.' " He has compared the Environmental Protection Agency to the Gestapo, and blames the Weather Channel for promoting global warming to improve its ratings.

The Sierra Club's endorsement of Chafee implied the organization was willing to keep Inhofe, with these views, in control of all environmental legislation moving through the Senate. The League of Conservation Voters also shortsightedly backed Chafee—even though the group itself had awarded Inhofe the worst scorecard in the Senate. By supporting Chafee, they were, in effect, working to keep the gavel of the environmental committee out of the hands of Democratic senator Barbara Boxer, who'd voted the LCV position 93 percent of the time over the past ten years.

The environmental groups in particular worked to justify their endorsement in the face of fierce criticism from its usual allies.

"Environmentalism is not yet a party-transcending issue, not totally, but it could become one. The Sierra Club is trying to help that process along," wrote Dave Roberts of *Grist* magazine on its blog. "Time will tell if they succeed, but I don't begrudge them the attempt." Sierra Club Executive Director Carl Pope shot back at his critics, "Linc Chafee has proven himself an environmental hero, and we are not going to dump our heroes overboard."

Similarly, had the women's groups had their way, the U.S. Senate Committee on Health, Education, Labor & Pensions, which handles some abortion legislation, would've been chaired by Wyoming senator Mike Enzi, who was named in 2007 by the *National Journal* as the Senate's sixth most conservative member. He'd garnered a 0 percent rating by NARAL, 100 percent by the vehemently anti-abortion National Right to Life Committee, and 100 percent by the Christian Coalition. He's been one of the fiercest critics of federal funding of stem-cell research and Planned Parenthood clinics.

In fact, Enzi was on the wrong side of every issue of major importance to women's groups. Yet he wasn't just an antichoice and antiwoman vote in the Senate: He was in charge of the committee that handled many of those matters. If Democrats took over the Senate, the gavel would be passed to the liberal legend Sen. Ted Kennedy of Massachusetts, who wasn't only a perfect vote on choice, but also a stalwart supporter of Planned Parenthood. Yet guess who also endorsed Chafee? Planned Parenthood.

The other committee handling abortion-related legislation is the Senate Judiciary, and the somewhat pro-choice Republican Arlen Specter would theoretically chair that one, since the anti-abortion crusader Orin Hatch was term-limited out of the chairmanship by his party's rules. However, a brooding rebellion in conservative circles would've challenged Specter's ascendancy. There was a push to waive Hatch's term limits or hand the gavel to Iowa senator Chuck Grassley (next in line, but already chairing a different committee) or fourth-in-line Arizona senator Jon Kyl, all of them vehement abortion foes.

Thankfully, the voters of Rhode Island rescued the women's groups and environmental organizations from themselves — as well as a couple of other traditional progressive organizations, like the Human Rights Campaign, which also endorsed Chafee, and the Rhode Island laborers union, which contributed money to his campaign.

Chafee was handed a 53 percent to 47 percent defeat. Had he won, Republicans would have kept their Senate majority and controlled the agenda. Chafee's loss sent him into forced retirement, a decision he *praised* in his book, *Against the Tide*. "The system works best when power remains in the hands of the voters," wrote Chafee. "I was a casualty of the system working in 2006, and while defeat is never easy, I give the voters credit: They made the connection between electing even popular Republicans at the cost of leaving the Senate in the hands of a leadership they had learned to mistrust."

Ironically, Whitehouse, as should have been expected from such a solid liberal Democratic candidate, has since proven to be perfect on environmental issues—but only after winning against the candidate endorsed in his election by the very groups most concerned with the issues.

It is important to always keep the big picture in mind, and to remain ruthlessly on target. By all accounts, Lincoln Chafee was an exceedingly nice and kind person. No one who dealt with him hated him. But the reality was that his presence in the Senate, especially given his refusal to abandon the Republican Party, enabled a truly reactionary set of people to run this country, and ultimately, that's what counted. It mattered little that he voted against abortion restrictions or against efforts to destroy the environment if the Republican majority was constantly sponsoring and passing such legislation despite him. A Democratically controlled Senate, with its grip on the committees, was far more valuable in protecting choice and the environment than Chafee's lonely and futile votes.

If anything, the Chafee-Whitehouse race is a textbook example of why crossing enemy lines is not to be taken lightly.

DO WHAT YOU CAN

There are few things more frustrating than when someone walks up to me and says, "I have a blog, but it's not like *Daily Kos*—it only gets two hundred visits a day." It drives me up the wall, and I consider it one of the negative side effects of my site's popularity—that it has redefined the definition of "success" when it comes to blogging. I remember when *Daily Kos* first hit one hundred readers. I thought, "I couldn't *fit* one hundred people in my house!" And if I do a public event that draws one hundred to two hundred people, it's clear that this is not an insignificant number.

The reason that networking technologies like the internet have become so dominant is that they mimic how we behave as a species. Our offline world has always been about networks—families, friends, affinity groups organized around shared interests (knitting, sports, political groups, book clubs, schools, and so on). It's inside those networks that we have the greatest influence. I am more able to make a persuasive political argument to one of my close friends than I would be to a casual visitor on *Daily Kos* who doesn't know or care who I am. It's why movie studios aim to build word-of-mouth buzz about their movies. All the best reviews and outsized marketing budgets in the world ultimately mean little more than a big opening weekend if the public reaction is negative and early moviegoers trash the product to their friends.

Activists need to understand that they can wield enormous influence in their social networks. That might be defined as the two hundred visitors to your modest blog. That could be the eight people in your book club. It could be your family around the Thanksgiving dinner table. It could be your church, your PTA, your corner bar, your bowling league, your kid's soccer league, or your coworkers. That blogger with her two-hundred-reader blog will have a far more intimate relationship with her readers than I can with the hundreds of thousands of people who visit *Daily Kos*.

These relationships matter and can be powerful conduits for change. Seek to bring five new people over to your point of view every year. Some of those people will then become advocates as well, expanding your circle of influence beyond you. That's how movements are built, by projecting and moving outward through connections. The immigration marches may have been publicized by Spanish radio, but they were ultimately driven by individuals who sent text messages to their friends via cell phone and instant messenger to spread the word about individual actions. *Daily Kos* has grown via word-of-mouth (and word-of-link) referrals since I've never had a marketing budget. Color of Change grew from 100,000 to 400,000 members during the Jena 6 campaign because their subscribers forwarded the emails to their social circles. This is networked activism.

It's also the *Daily Kos* diaries I've seen photocopied and left on subway benches, expecting bored commuters to pick them up to read. It's engaging your taxi driver or grocery store checkout clerk about some topical issue. It's making stickers and slapping them on street posts, toll booths, and other public places. (I've always liked the "driving" stickers people slap under the "Stop" on stop signs.) It's giving $20 to your favorite cause. It's doing all the little things that when combined with the power of other citizens can create a critical mass for change.

I was twenty-one when I became a vegetarian, and immediately became an avid evangelist for meat-free living. Over the next several years I must've bought two dozen copies of John Robbins's *Diet for a New America* for my friends and some family members. One of my converts herself started handing out copies of the book and got some of her friends to convert. At one point, we figured out that thanks to my efforts, about fifteen people had become vegetarian. In a world of billions, that was a minuscule number. But all change has to begin somewhere, and I hope that some of those people are still out there evangelizing the benefits of a meat-free diet. And there was success—while finding things like veggie burgers, soy milk, and other vegetarian and vegan fare once required shopping in small, dingy co-ops, now such things are easily available in the largest chain supermarkets.

Don't worry that your actions may seem lacking or that your audience might be too small. The first person to illegally download a file from Napster wasn't going to bring the music labels to their knees. That first fan to write a letter to Sony records wasn't going to get Fiona Apple's record released. Lasting change in the world is built on one-to-one relationships and small actions. Be proud of what you can do for your cause, even if you can't move a mountain alone. With a friend, and the friends of your friend, and the friends of the friends of your friends though . . . you may be able to shift a hill or two. And you might just find yourself actually enjoying the effort along the way.

RALLY THE TROOPS

Given the myriad entertainment options available to people today, the ability to build a movement is directly proportionate to the ability to make activist efforts entertaining. If people aren't having fun, they'll quickly move on to other pursuits.

In 2004, I was asked to speak at a city chapter of the Democratic Party. The event, located in a dimly lit church basement, drew about fourteen people with an apparent average age of eighty. One young enthusiastic couple in their mid-twenties also showed up, looking a bit out of place but eager to work for a cause.

The first thirty minutes of the meeting were worse than a root canal. Operating under the dreadful and archaic (for nongovernmental functions) *Robert's Rules of Order*, the officers of the club went through voting on motion after motion, from approving the minutes of the previous meeting to literally arguing over commas in their latest resolution condemning the war in Iraq and debating whether to "strenuously object" or "vigorously object." Throughout this already painful and unnecessary process, one surly elderly man kept raising "points of order" to question and challenge each procedural step taken by the officers, filibustering the approval of the club's agenda.

I sat in back, aghast, with the young couple. They were clearly uncomfortable and ready to run, but thought it would be rude. It didn't take long for the three of us to hightail it out of there after my brief remarks were concluded. I asked the couple, trying to look sincere, if they'd be back for another meeting, but I couldn't keep a straight face. We burst out laughing at the absurdity of the question. The meeting reeked of irrelevance—the silly adherence to parliamentary procedure, the stuffiness, the clock watching—all of which made the experience excruciating.

That's the old model.

In 2003, Justin Krebs and the Emmy-winning documentary filmmaker Matthew O'Neill started a get-together for their liberal friends at Rudy's Bar and Grill in New York's Hell's Kitchen. Krebs already had a history of bringing people together by running an NYC political calendar as well as the Tank—a space for artists and activists to ply their trades. The monthly get-togethers were branded "Drinking Liberally," and while they described themselves as "one part support group, and one part strategy session," there was much more going on. It was a true social gathering. The alcohol flowed, people joked and flirted, had fun, and—oh yeah—they got involved politically.

It may sound distasteful to progressive ears, but what Krebs and O'Neill hit upon with Drinking Liberally was little different from the way conservatives had worked in many churches, particularly in the new breed of megachurches that have spread throughout the country. Most of these houses of worship are nondenominational or unaffiliated (though they usually are of Protestant or evangelical origin), and many can boast of congregations in the thousands, with people flocking to them as much for their community-center aspect as their spiritual offerings. Their services are modern, using pop or rock bands instead of archaic organs. They utilize stage lighting, video, and projections to entertain the audience, rather than featuring someone merely preaching from a pulpit. Worshippers are encouraged to dress casually and comfortably, rather than worry about their "Sunday best."

While most churches struggle with congregations in the low hundreds, the most successful megachurches are drawing stadium-sized crowds. The largest in the nation—Lakewood Church in Houston, Texas—has even moved its congregation to the former home of the NBA's Houston Rockets, the 17,500-seat Houston Summit.

Drinking Liberally experienced exponential growth as well, spreading to other cities, fueled by the netroots. Chapters can now be found in 236 cities in forty-six states, Washington, D.C., and even in Canada and Australia. And aside from the socializing, these events now are a source of organizing and political networking, as well as a whistle-stop for politicians looking to staff up and find volunteers.

No matter how important your cause or how earnest your efforts, you have to realize that building the crowds necessary to effect mass change requires entertaining your troops and allies. Few might share your passion, but more will come along for the ride if organizing incorporates a social aspect. I predict attendance at progressive and Democratic Party events would skyrocket if club events became a social gathering and concentrated on creating an environment in which everyone is allowed to contribute ideas without being shut down by parliamentary maneuvers.

Ditch the dingy and dank church or labor hall basement and find social places to congregate—popular restaurants, or the barbecue pits at a local park on weekends so people with families can bring their kids along.

Encourage real-life gatherings during political events like election nights, debates, or the State of the Union address. Hanging out at the Tank in New York during the Republican National Convention in 2004, a crowd of over one hundred inebriated liberals had a blast throwing popcorn at the projector TV playing speeches of Republican after Republican. Silly as it might've been, it was also a reaffirmation of our shared commitment to fight those characters speaking just a few short blocks away at Madison Square Garden. These social experiences, whether in a bar or at a barbecue or at a restaurant or in someone's home, have a way of bonding us. And the more bonded the troops are, the more purposefully they will pursue their mission.

CHAPTER 8

THE UNLIKELY WARRIORS

The mantle of leadership can arrive unsought. Learning to embrace it by stepping outside of your comfort zone, standing tall for your beliefs, and taking a prominent role in public affairs—especially when it's sure to draw fire—can be the most effective form of action, and the most rewarding experience.

arol Shea-Porter never sought to be a leader and never intended to be a change agent of any sort. In fact, she was advised to aim low. At age sixteen, her high school guidance counselor told her to "forget about college and try secretarial school," as she recalled to the Associated Press on November 8, 2006. "They didn't think as big for our futures as they did for some of the guys." Little did "they" know where she was headed.

Thirty-six years later, with no political background on her résumé, she was elected to the U.S. House of Representatives after unseating an incumbent in the most stunning upset race in recent years.

A native of coastal New Hampshire, Shea-Porter grew up in a household that had more in common with a previous era than the twentieth century in which she was raised, with extended family stretching her home to include, according to her campaign website, "parents, a great-uncle, a grandmother, and a constantly changing roster of children and teens who needed a place to live during difficult times in their lives." It would stand to reason that such a tradition of caring for others helped shape her ideas about the role of ordinary citizens in the world.

Ignoring her high school counselor's advice about secretarial school, Shea-Porter enrolled at the University of New Hampshire, graduating with a master's degree in public administration and going on to a career as a social worker. After serving as director of senior centers in Maryland and New Orleans, she returned to New Hampshire. She vaguely began considering a run in the state's First Congressional District (NH-01), dissatisfied with the incumbent, Republican Jeb Bradley, whom she'd follow to events and then pepper with questions. This was a bold step for a woman whose largest political action to date had been wearing a "Turn Your Back on Bush" T-shirt that earned her a personal escort out of a campaign event.

Her resolve to run for office, however, didn't harden until she returned to New Orleans in the aftermath of Hurricane Katrina to volunteer her efforts. For Shea-Porter, as for many Americans, seeing the government's incompetent and heartbreaking response to the emergency galvanized a commitment to pursue a course of true change in this country. If she needed any more motivation to act, all she had to do was look at the disastrous and immoral acts of the Bush administration in Iraq. Upon her return to New Hampshire, she decided to seek Bradley's congressional seat.

From the start, her campaign appeared quixotic and doomed to failure. Led by the Democratic Congressional Campaign Committee (DCCC) and its aggressive chairman, U.S. Rep. Rahm Emanuel of Illinois, the party was convinced Bradley's seat was winnable—but only with the "right" kind of Democrat. They set their eyes on the New Hampshire House Minority Leader Jim Craig, one of the state's top Democrats. Shea-Porter wasn't even on the DCCC's radar.

The primary wasn't supposed to be much of a contest. The DCCC gave $5,000 to Craig, an accomplished and well-known politician in the state, and Emanuel worried little about angering grassroots activists who were beginning to rally around Shea-Porter. He was convinced that Democratic chances in the district depended on a Craig primary victory, and was so confident of it that he earmarked $7,000 for Craig's general-election campaign and leaned on the party's fund-raising apparatus to raise much more.

None of that made Shea-Porter back off. She knew she faced formidable odds, with little institutional support and virtually no chance of victory. Yet her unwavering belief in her issues—commitment to end the war in Iraq, the value of public service in a nation sorely lacking in it— made her willing to take on an enormous uphill battle. There was little glory promised her in the long run, and a lot of hard work for this most unlikely of electoral warriors.

In terms of money for her campaign, she knew she was outgunned and that Craig would have a huge advantage, plus the backing of the DCCC. However, Shea-Porter had something that money couldn't buy—a dedicated cadre of supporters, not to mention the fact that she was more in tune with her district's prevailing sentiment on the election's burning issue—Iraq.

"I was against going there and I'm against being there," said Shea-Porter at a May 7 candidates' forum. "The only thing I'm for is getting out." Craig more closely parroted the prevailing "safe" answer to the question by "serious" Democrats, agreeing that a withdrawal timetable from Iraq was important because "there's nothing like pressure to get the job done," but then arguing that American troops needed to remain in Iraq "indefinitely" to protect U.S. interests.

On July 23, quarterly fund-raising numbers suggested that the DCCC had made the right bet—Craig had raised nearly $261,000 and had over $194,000 in the bank. Shea-Porter limped behind with a pitiable $27,700 total raised and just over $19,000 in the bank. But she used that money gap to make a point. "I have to tell you we're actually thrilled," she told the *Portsmouth Herald*. "It helps deliver the message. Our campaign is not about the money. We've said that from the beginning. We know how to run this campaign without blowing people's money and we can do this in Washington." Her campaign could not possibly be about the money, all things considered. No one even knew who she was. In a University of New Hampshire Granite State Poll taken July 21–31—less than two months before the primary—86 percent of respondents said they'd never heard of Carol Shea-Porter. She also trailed Bradley, the incumbent Republican, 58 percent to 24 percent. Craig, however, fared little better against Bradley, polling at 55 percent to 27 percent, dealing a blow to the argument that he was inherently more electable than Shea-Porter.

Soon, there were signs that Shea-Porter and her shoestring campaign were making headway. In the first few days of September, the two largest newspapers in the district announced their support. The *Portsmouth Herald* editorialized:

"A political campaign, particularly one for New Hampshire's two seats in the U.S. House of Representatives, is supposed to involve a true exchange of ideas. Candidates should each represent specific points of view on how best to resolve the issues facing their home district and the nation in general. That is why we are endorsing Rochester Democrat Carol Shea-Porter in the Sept. 12 primary. We are looking forward to the kind of heat she will bring to a general election campaign against incumbent Republican Jeb Bradley."

The *Concord Monitor* called Shea-Porter "smart, well-spoken, resourceful and passionate—just the kind of person the Democratic Party ought to welcome and nurture as a candidate." Lamenting the obsession with "money, money, money," the *Monitor* then delivered a blistering rebuke to the DCCC interference in the primary contest:

> "[I]t is reprehensible that the Democratic Congressional Campaign Committee and its train of interest groups and big-name pols have given thousands of dollars to Jim Craig. . . . This money discrepancy, brought to us by outsiders trying to influence a New Hampshire election, creates a special burden for 1st Congressional District voters next Tuesday. They need to look beyond what money can buy and make a reasoned assessment of which candidate deserves their vote. . . . [They] should do their homework and not be swayed by the national Democratic party's effort to put a giant thumb on the scale."

Shea-Porter played up that thumb on the scale and embraced the role of aggrieved grassroots activist perfectly, using the establishment support for Craig and the DCCC's endorsement as a rallying point. It played well in a state with its independent spirit reflected in the state motto: "Live free or die." As the former pollster Rich Killion told *Congressional Quarterly* on September 11, the DCCC interference "had a negative impact on Craig's campaign and energized Shea-Porter's." Pointing out that New Hampshire "is very much a grassroots political state," he said, people didn't like state candidates being "ordained" by outsiders. For her part, Shea-

Porter told *CQ*, "I wish they had stayed out," before admitting that the endorsement had given her campaign an inadvertent boost.

Meanwhile, Shea-Porter was building a grassroots army of activists and students who were spreading the word about her campaign face-to-face with potential voters across the district with a single-minded message about Iraq—we need to get out. Disgust with the Iraq war was strong enough in her district that it helped carry her to victory on September 13, rocking the political world with a strong 54 percent to 35 percent margin despite the fiercest efforts of her own party's establishment against her.

But, of course, the victory over Craig was a mere preliminary round in a much larger and much more difficult fight. To say that her prospects didn't look good in the general election against Jeb Bradley is a wild understatement.

Shea-Porter had essentially two months to turn around a gaping deficit in the polls without any money to do it. By the middle of October, she had $49,000 cash in hand, compared to $538,000 for Bradley. Despite the DCCC's willingness to earmark funds for Craig should he have won, Emanuel left Shea-Porter high and dry without a dime of help. As a columnist at the University of New Hampshire student newspaper wrote, "Her victory in the primary made National Democrats look foolish, and they are repaying the favor by not putting any money into her race." And it wasn't just the DCCC's money at stake. Had the committee backed Shea-Porter, it would have signaled to other party donors, political action committees, and interest groups that the race was worth investing time and money in, further boosting her electoral chances. By ignoring the race, Emanuel and the DCCC were telegraphing the exact opposite— "Don't waste your time on this one. It's hopeless."

Given the district's demographics and Bradley's electoral troubles, such a decision wasn't being made on the merits. It was Emanuel's way of sending a message—"You buck the party, the party will screw you." It was gatekeeping of the most disrespectful sort, with an insufferably arrogant elite utterly disregarding the will of the people most concerned with the race—the Democratic voters of the district. Adding insult to injury, the DCCC poured $1.1 million in advertising into the neighboring contest in

New Hampshire's Second Congressional District, while Shea-Porter scraped for pennies and hustled for votes. The DCCC's dismissal was particularly galling when contrasted with the gracious help offered to Shea-Porter by the primary candidate she'd bested: Jim Craig joined Shea-Porter's general election campaign as its campaign cochair.

On October 2, a second University of New Hampshire poll showed Shea-Porter gaining ground on the incumbent Bradley, but it was all relative—the 52 percent to 33 percent deficit was better than being down 58–24 as she was in July, but only marginally so. With just a month left in the election, she still trailed by a daunting 19 points, and incumbents are only considered seriously vulnerable when their numbers drop below 50 percent. So although the trend line was definitely running against Bradley, the challenge for Shea-Porter still looked impossible to overcome with the election just a few weeks away. Such a drastic deficit called for uncommon tactics.

Instead of spending eight hours a day dialing potential donors for money, Shea-Porter spent time on the streets talking to people. Instead of relying only on student volunteers, she had experienced middle-aged community organizers, who enlisted influential members of their community on behalf of their efforts. "It's about finding the people in your community who are trendsetters and opinion leaders, and getting them to talk to other people for you," Harry Gural, the campaign's communications director, told the *Concord Monitor* in a postmortem piece on November 9. "We were always looking for those people. If you found them, then you unlocked the community." Since they had no money for a real field operation to get out their vote, they deputized their supporters and trusted them to do the job. The campaign's two commercials were low-budget productions, one with Shea-Porter speaking directly to the camera with no music or effects, the other with her sitting at a table with her mother.

Bradley struggled with whether to give Shea-Porter any attention. After her primary victory, he had unloaded a volley of ads, essentially accusing her of being a Far Left loon. Then, he lost interest beyond a series of perfunctory debates. All his subsequent ads were "Thanks Jeb!" biographical pieces touting his work saving a local shipyard and providing strong constituent services. He delivered no direct mail to voter mailboxes. There was little need, it seemed, for Bradley to further target Shea-Porter. His big leads in the polls suggested that he'd be "punching down" if he targeted his opponent too aggressively.

Even days before the election, things didn't look good for Shea-Porter. A University of New Hampshire/WMUR tracking poll taken November 2–5 showed the race at 51 percent to 37 percent, seemingly confirming Bradley's decision to ignore Shea-Porter. But then there was an upturn. The next day's results, based on phone interviews taken November 3–6, pegged the race 49–40 in Bradley's favor, but there was a twist—among those listed as "extremely interested" in the election, Shea-Porter was ahead an astonishing 62 percent to 38 percent. The *New York Observer*, in a roundup of New England elections, wrote on November 6:

> "Jeb Bradley (NH-1): The second-term incumbent from the Lake Winnipesaukee area may well be the last New England House Republican left standing after tomorrow—and he'll a stroke [*sic*] of luck to thank for it. In September, 1st District Democrats defiantly thumbed their noses at Washington, handing their nomination to a former social worker named Carol Shea-Porter and snubbing Jim Craig, the state House minority leader who had been championed by the DCCC. On the stump, Shea-Porter is inarguably a better candidate than Craig, explaining her chocking [*sic*] win in what was a historically low-turnout primary. But her rancorous relationship with the DCCC has kept them from flooding the 1st District the way they have the 2nd District. On top of that, Bradley is fortified by a slight GOP advantage in the district, which favored Bush by three points over Kerry (thus making New Hampshire's 1st District the most Republican district in New England). For all that, though, Shea-Porter is not far off Bradley's pace. If independent voters are even angrier with the GOP than conventional wisdom tells us—and if the GOP base is as torpid as many claim it is—a win by Shea-Porter, who does not even crack national observers' lists of the top 60 House challengers in the country, is not impossible. And if she does win, it will be mean [*sic*] nothing short of a national catastrophe for Republicans."

Overall, Shea-Porter spent about $292,000 in her primary and general election combined, a pittance compared to her two opponents. Bradley spent nearly $1 million. Yet when the smoke cleared on election night, none of Rahm Emanuel's treachery mattered.

Carol Shea-Porter was now a member of the U.S. House of Representatives, having upset a sitting incumbent 51 percent to 49 percent in perhaps the evening's biggest and most improbable victory.

We live in a world where there's no reason anyone should whine or complain that they are being shut out of the system. The tools are available to mount credible challenges to even the most entrenched of powers. Such efforts will always lack resources, and will mostly face well-funded, deeply entrenched foes, but innovative tactics and smart use of money can carry the day. Shea-Porter's wildly surprising victory—over two outsized opponents—should serve as both an inspiration and a valuable primer about overcoming obstacles put in the way of activists who buck the system.

Perhaps most important, effective activism requires that those who have the heart and passion for it step out of their comfort zone and into the fire.

★   ★   ★

Everyone knew Michael J. Fox as Alex Keaton on TV's *Family Ties* or as Marty McFly in the *Back to the Future* movie trilogy, or as Mike Flaherty on *Spin City*. But in real life, he'd long been starring in a tragedy of his own and keeping his personal struggles out of the limelight.

In 1991, Fox was diagnosed with Parkinson's disease, a degenerative disorder that attacks the nervous system and impairs motor skills and speech. Muhammad Ali is one of the 1.5 million Americans with the diagnosis, and fifty thousand new cases are reported each year. For seven years, Fox had kept his illness under wraps until, in 1998, the disease had progressed to the point where he could no longer continue a full-time acting career. When he went public with the news, he also announced that he'd undergone brain surgery to lessen the tremors caused by the illness.

The actor's public admission of his illness launched a new role for him, that of an advocate for more research into his affliction. He testified before Congress in September 1999 and a year later established the Michael J. Fox Foundation, an organization committed to cutting the red tape so common in the research grant-funding process. For his work, Fox was awarded an Impact Award in 2006 by the American Association of Retired Persons, which notes on its website:

> "This is no celebrity sideline: it's the largest private institution in the PD research hunt today, and it has galvanized scientific work in the field by cutting the typical yearlong grant-review process and investing strategically in the most promising research avenues. 'The key to the Fox Foundation is that they give out real money, at least $100,000 per project,' says Jeffrey Kordower, M.D., a pioneer in the study of gene therapy for Parkinson's and a member of the foundation's scientific advisory board. 'They've established a new business model for science.'"

While Fox went public with his illness and began serving as a role model by "soldiering on," it was still fairly safe work. After all, there's no risk in advocating for greater research for any disease, much less the one that afflicted Fox. Yet even this noncontroversial step was meaningful. As he testified before Congress:

> "While the changes in my life were profound and progressive, I kept them to myself for a number of reasons: fear, denial for sure, but I also felt that it was important for me to just quietly 'soldier on.' When I did share my story the response was overwhelming, humbling and deeply inspiring. I heard from thousands of Americans affected by Parkinson's, writing and calling to offer encouragement and to tell me of their experience. They spoke of pain, frustration, fear and hope. Always hope. What I understood very clearly is that the time for 'quietly soldiering on' is through. The war against Parkinson's is a winnable war and I have resolved to play a role in that victory. What celebrity has given me is the

opportunity to raise the visibility of Parkinson's disease and focus attention on the desperate need for more research dollars."

Time magazine named him one of its 2007 "Heroes and Pioneers": "He could have been forgiven for never disclosing it or for hiding once the symptoms became obvious. Instead, in 1998 he told the world. Then he stepped onto the front lines of the effort to find a cure." Fox even inspired Muhammad Ali—no wilting flower—to become more outspoken with his advocacy for Parkinson's funding. "It was interesting because when he met Michael, Michael sort of became the voice," said Ali's wife, Lonnie Ali. "And he saw Michael go out in front of a whole lot of people and start talking about Parkinson's disease. Michael was just being very courageous about it, and not hiding it. After that, Muhammad started doing the same thing."

Yet it has been the misfortune of Fox and Ali—and millions of others who suffer from afflictions like Parkinson's—to be ill in an age when modern science holds promise for cures that the fundamentalist wing of the Republican Party fights as if it's fighting the very demons of hell. All of it stemmed from their obsession with abortion—and electing antichoice Republicans.

In 2002, researchers were successful in using embryonic stem-cell research to reverse symptoms of Parkinson's in rats. While the research was early, it showed great promise as a future treatment or cure for the debilitating disease. It also inserted Fox into the poisonous abortion debate. Embryonic stem-cell research requires the destruction of leftover embryos taken from fertility clinics, where families undergoing fertility treatment may leave unused, fertilized three-day-old embryos behind for disposal. Because abortion opponents consider life to begin at conception and vehemently oppose the use of embryos for such research, federal funding for advancing stem-cell research had been brought to a halt by the stranglehold the Christian right has on the Republican Party.

Nevertheless, in the summer of 2006, both chambers of Congress passed a bill allowing for federal funding of lifesaving stem-cell research. While the victories were large—63–34 in the Senate and 247–176 in the House—they were not large enough to overcome a veto from President

Bush, the first veto of his first six years in office. While a great deal of money is spent on Parkinson's research in the private sector—Fox's foundation had funneled more than $95 million on its own—private efforts are dwarfed by the scale of money the federal government can bring to disease research.

Reacting to this veto, Fox realized he had to step into the political realm. "I remember in 2000, I wrote a letter to then Governor Bush asking him to come through on his promise of compassion when he got to the office," he told Katie Couric in a *CBS News* interview. "And then he did limited stem cell in 2001. . . . This summer when the president vetoed the HRA10, which is the legislation [for] stem cell research . . . it really stung the hearts of a lot of people counting on this. I knew I'd be involved in 2006."

But if Fox thought advocating for federal funding for stem-cell research was difficult, his entry into electoral politics would subject him to far worse treatment. From talk radio blowhards to blogs to pulpits, the Right assaulted his integrity, belittled his dedication, mocked his symptoms, and insisted that he was a publicity-seeking faker. In their eyes, Fox had dared a dastardly deed: He endorsed senatorial candidates such as Claire Mc-Caskill of Missouri, Ben Cardin of Maryland, and Arlen Specter of Pennsylvania, as well as Gov. Jim Doyle of Wisconsin, all of whom supported stem-cell research.

His first salvo was a political ad for McCaskill, who had made stem-cell research a key component of her campaign against the incumbent, Republican Jim Talent, a darling of the Far Right. Without a doubt, it was the most powerful ad of the election cycle, with the impact of a blow to the gut, as Americans got a firsthand glimpse of the effect of Parkinson's on the actor. Fox sat in a living room, discussing the disease, as his body rocked heavily from side to side, symptoms out in the open as he made a solemn and wrenching pitch to the voters of Missouri:

> "As you might know, I care deeply about stem-cell research. In Missouri, you can elect Claire McCaskill, who shares my hope for cures. Unfortunately, Senator Jim Talent opposes expanding stem-cell research. Senator Talent even wants to criminalize the sci-

ence that gives us a chance for hope. They say all politics is local, but it's not always the case. What you do in Missouri matters to millions of Americans. Americans like me."

Those words were actually quite tame, particularly for a political ad. But the emotional impact was overwhelming.

The first to fire back was the "bad cop" of the conservative media machine, Rush Limbaugh. "In this commercial he is exaggerating the effects of the disease, he's moving all around and shaking and it's purely an act," he said on his show, mocking Fox by swaying side to side and flailing his arms around. "This is the only time I've ever seen Michael J. Fox portray any of the symptoms of the disease he has . . . he can control himself enough to stay in the frame of the picture, and he can control himself enough to keep his eyes right on the lens of the teleprompter . . . This is really shameless of Michael J. Fox. Either he didn't take his medication or he's acting." Video of that radio segment was immediately beamed around the country not just on the internet, but also on the evening newscasts.

Accusations aside, Limbaugh was simply wrong about Fox's shaking side-to-side motion—it wasn't a symptom of a lack of medication, it was a symptom *of* the medication. As Fox explained to Couric, as he sat shaking in front of her: "I just take [the medication] and it kicks in when it kicks in. Sometimes it kicks in too hard and then you get what you call dyskinesia, which is that rocking motion. That's caused by the medication. One of the reasons they are looking for cures particularly for Parkinson's is that the medication only has an efficacy that lasts so long and then at a certain point it ceases to, or it works with horrible side effects, which is the dyskinesia that you see."

If anything, the problem for Fox during the commercial was that he was *overmedicated*, hence the harsh symptoms. Yet without it, advanced Parkinson's sufferers lock up, unable to move their faces or speak. Regrettably, Parkinson's sufferers can't fine-tune their dosages to the point that no symptoms appear. It's a tough balancing act, and not always successful. Too many factors, from the humidity in the air to how much protein was in their diet that day, can have an impact on the severity of their symptoms.

None of that mattered to Limbaugh, of course. He shot first and didn't bother to ask questions later. Fox noted that his mother had been particularly incensed at Limbaugh's salvo. "My mother was visiting that day, was in the back room and she was saying throughout the filming of it . . . 'he's trying so hard to be still,' and so [when Limbaugh's comments] were made, she was the only one who was really angry and she said 'I can't even see straight.'"

When criticized for his mockery, Limbaugh took aim at a new target, making Fox a victim of the Democratic Party, claiming it had "exploited" the actor. But by then, the damage was done. In a race where the incumbent senator Jim Talent in a conservative-leaning state was expected to survive, Claire McCaskill defeated him by a surprising 50 percent to 47 percent margin; Wisconsin's Doyle, Maryland's Cardin, and most candidates Fox endorsed also won their races.

Yet Fox's endorsements ultimately came at quite a high price. He'd been dragged through the mud, ridiculed, and accused of being a charlatan by hateful political opponents. The more effective his efforts became, the crueler was the backlash. But as we've seen, a backlash isn't necessarily a bad thing, and in this case it was particularly advantageous—it helped spread Fox's message about lifesaving stem-cell research far beyond the borders of Missouri. It's probably not entirely unrelated to Fox's efforts that federal spending on Parkinson's research has increased from $65.5 million in 1998 to $205 million in 2007, at a time when the National Institute of Health's budget has been flat.

The most effective activists are those who understand that to operate successfully in a given landscape, you have to stand out from that landscape. The actor could've suffered his disease in silence, stayed out of politics, and played the far more comfortable role of celebrity pitchman and fund-raiser for his cause. But with each small step he took further into the advocacy arena, the more he stood out. The more he stood out, the further he inched away from his comfort zone, provoking attacks and ridicule. Yet that backlash made him that much more effective, ensuring that his message reached an ever-growing number of people. He paid a personal price for it, as did his closest friends and family, but the world doesn't change for those who aren't willing to sacrifice and take risks.

★   ★   ★

The comic and actor Stephen Colbert made his name as a "correspondent" on Comedy Central's fake news program, *The Daily Show*, winning
three Emmys for his writing, in 2004, 2005, and 2006, and becoming a
favorite of the show's fans. He parlayed his success into the spin-off *The
Colbert Report*, where he's found his niche parodying Bill O'Reilly—and
by out-O'Reillying the master, whom he calls "Papa Bear." The show was
an instant hit and consistently spawns pop culture references. The word
"truthiness," for example, was featured on the first episode, and he explained its resonance in an interview with the *Onion*:

> "It used to be, everyone was entitled to their own opinion, but
> not their own facts. But that's not the case anymore. Facts matter
> not at all. Perception is everything. It's certainty. People love the
> president because he's certain of his choices as a leader, even if
> the facts that back him up don't seem to exist. It's the fact that he's
> certain that is very appealing to a certain section of the country. I
> really feel a dichotomy in the American populace. What is impor-
> tant? What you want to be true, or what *is* true?"

The word was named "Word of the Year" by both the American Dia-
lect Society and the *Merriam-Webster* dictionary.

In January 2008, despite a strike by its writers, *The Colbert Report* was
averaging 507,000 viewers (with a 21 percent increase from the previous
year in the coveted eighteen–forty-nine bracket), just slightly less than its
more established and better-known *Daily Show* lead-in, which had
535,000 viewers. That was more than the 494,000 that Bill O'Reilly's top-
ranked cable news show averaged that month in the similar twenty-five–
fifty-four age demographic.

Part of the appeal of Colbert and his show is the nebulous nature of the
shtick. The parody, nearly always directed at political and media figures,
is so spot-on that those not "in" on the joke can end up taking his pose
seriously. When the comedian mockingly grilled the film producer Robert
Greenwald in May 2006 about *The Big Buy: Tom DeLay's Stolen Con-*

gress, even the indicted former House majority leader himself was taken in. Completely missing the satirical and over-the-top defense Colbert had provided him, DeLay promoted the episode through an email put out by his legal defense fund, claiming that Greenwald had "crashed and burned" under pressure. Even with Colbert throwing such questions at the producer as "Who hates America more, you or Michael Moore?" DeLay didn't tumble to the obvious and realize he was the butt of the joke, not the beneficiary.

But it was a real-life performance, not one on his show, that catapulted Stephen Colbert into the national spotlight. It was in April 2006 at the White House Correspondents' Association dinner and Colbert was the scheduled entertainment. The dinner is usually a genial affair, with entertainers allowed to gently rib the powers that be—in both media and government—with the understanding that everyone in the room is really, at heart, good company, a great American, and a civilized member of the elite. In 2005, Cedric the Entertainer performed. In 2004, it was Jay Leno. The dinner traditionally includes a skit by the sitting president to entertain the press corps in the audience. In 2004, in the wake of failures to find the weapons of mass destruction used to justify the invasion of Iraq, Bush played a slide presentation of him doing "funny" mini-acts, like looking for WMDs around him in the Oval Office, including under his desk: "Nope, no weapons over here!" The assembled journalists roared in laughter, because it was apparently hilarious to mock the rationale that Bush had used to send thousands of American kids to their deaths in Iraq. The whole event crystallized everything that was wrong about American journalism—the all-too-chummy relationship between an American administration and the press that was supposed to help keep it in check.

Into that clubby atmosphere walked Colbert with nothing but a persona and a bullshit detector, with no ally at his side, and armed only with his trademark satirical shtick. It was an amazing performance, opening up with a full-bore roast of the president himself:

> "Now, I know there are some polls out there saying this man has a thiry-two percent approval rating. But guys like us, we don't pay attention to the polls. We know that polls are just a collection

of statistics that reflect what people are thinking in 'reality.' And reality has a well-known liberal bias [. . .]

"Okay, look, folks, my point is that I don't believe this is a low point in this presidency. I believe it is just a lull before a comeback. I mean, it's like the movie 'Rocky.' All right. The president in this case is Rocky Balboa and Apollo Creed is—everything else in the world. It's the tenth round. He's bloodied. His corner man, Mick, who in this case I guess would be the vice president, he's yelling, 'Cut me, Dick, cut me!' and every time he falls everyone says, 'Stay down! Stay down!' Does he stay down? No. Like Rocky, he gets back up, and in the end he—actually, he loses in the first movie.

"Okay. Doesn't matter. The point is it is the heartwarming story of a man who was repeatedly punched in the face. So don't pay attention to the approval ratings that say sixty-eight percent of Americans disapprove of the job this man is doing. I ask you this, does that not also logically mean that sixty-eight percent approve of the job he's not doing? Think about it. I haven't."

It was gutsy to stand right next to the president of the United States and mock him mercilessly. But Colbert was not done yet. Next, he turned his guns on the media:

"As excited as I am to be here with the president, I am *appalled* to be surrounded by the liberal media that is destroying America, with the exception of Fox News. Fox News gives you both sides of every story: the president's side, and the vice president's side.

"But the rest of you, what are you thinking, reporting on NSA wiretapping or secret prisons in Eastern Europe? Those things are secret for a very important reason: they're super-depressing. And if that's your goal, well, misery accomplished. Over the last five years you people were so good—over tax cuts, WMD intelligence, the effect of global warming. We Americans didn't want to know, and you had the courtesy not to try to find out. Those were good times, as far as we knew.

"But, listen, let's review the rules. Here's how it works: the president makes decisions. He's the Decider. The press secretary announces those decisions, and you people of the press type those decisions down. Make, announce, type. Just put 'em through a spell check and go home. Get to know your family again. Make love to your wife. Write that novel you got kicking around in your head. You know, the one about the intrepid Washington reporter with the courage to stand up to the administration. You know— fiction!"

The reaction in the room was, well, awkward. To the assembled press corps, the performance was a painful flop. Here and there were a few nervous laughs, but Colbert's calling-out was mostly greeted with silence. Yet he soldiered on, never breaking character. If he was aware of the reaction he was getting, he didn't let on. Or perhaps he expected it.

But outside of that room, Colbert was a spectacular hit. There was an immediate near-blackout of the speech by the media, but it had been captured by C-SPAN and word spread quickly. The Saturday event was posted all over the web right away. On the following Sunday and Monday, there were 3 million downloads from YouTube, and 300,000 downloads from the video-heavy Crooks and Liars blog alone. The C-SPAN site was down Sunday morning as I tried to access the video. And when it was posted on iTunes as a $1.95 download it quickly became the #1 download on the entire music site, despite new albums by Pearl Jam and the Red Hot Chili Peppers.

Unable to continue to ignore it in a YouTubed, iTuned, people-powered world, the media narrative became "Colbert wasn't funny." The *Washington Post* columnist Richard Cohen launched his May 4 column on the matter by pointing out just how funny people think he, Cohen, is, then proceeded to lay down the establishment line:

"Colbert was not just a failure as a comedian but rude. Rude is not the same as brash. It is not the same as brassy. It is not the same as gutsy or thinking outside the box. Rudeness means taking advantage of the other person's sense of decorum or tradition or civility that keeps that other person from striking back or, worse, rising in a huff and leaving. The other night, that person was George W. Bush."

Interestingly, five days later Cohen was back whining in a column titled "Digital Lynch Mob" that people online had the nerve to disagree with his definition of what is funny and what is not: "Kapow! Within a day, I got more than 2,000 emails. A day later, I got 1,000 more. By the fourth day, the number had reached 3,499." Surely if it's 3,499 opinions versus Richard Cohen, the beltway knows who to believe.

Another *Washington Post* columnist, Dan Froomkin, noted on May 4 the press reaction to the event as well:

> "The traditional media's first reaction to satirist Stephen Colbert's uncomfortably harsh mockery of President Bush and the press corps at Saturday night's White House Correspondents Association dinner was largely to ignore it. The result, however, was a wave of indignation from the liberal side of the blogosphere over what some considered a willful disregard of the bigger story: That a captive, peevish president (and his media lapdogs) actually had to sit and listen as someone explained to them what they had done wrong; that the Bush Bubble was forcibly violated, right there on national television."

The reason traditional media journalists didn't find Colbert's routine funny was precisely because they were the butt of the joke, and they were forced to have it rubbed in their face. Their lack of humor about the event just enhanced the joke. Colbert had managed to use them as the foil to best illustrate his jokes.

"To the audience that would watch Colbert on Comedy Central, the pained, uncomfortable, perhaps-a-little-scared-to-laugh reaction shots were not signs of failure. They were the money shots," wrote *Time*'s pop culture columnist James Poniewozik. "They were the whole point." And the more of a backlash he generated, the more popular the clip became, and the more gleefully his fans celebrated.

"I somehow doubt that Bush has never heard these criticisms before," said *Time*'s Ana Marie Cox, a former foulmouthed blogger who used to be quite funny herself. "Comedy can have a political point but it is not political action." It's not? This was the epitome of modern-day political action—a masterful use of media to capture and distribute a ballsy message straight in the belly of the beast—targeting both the president and his loyal press corps (it was, as the blogger Peter Daou put it, "a work of staggering genius that could only be pulled off by a man with testicles the size of Alpha Centauri").

Colbert had indeed taken an enormous risk. It was different. It was fun and entertaining. And most important, the message was clear and *substantive.*

"His performance was judged a bomb by the Washington press corps, which yukked it up instead for a Bush impersonator who joined the president in a benign sketch commissioned by the White House. But millions of Americans watching C-Span and the Web did get Mr. Colbert's routine," explained the *New York Times* columnist Frank Rich. "They recognized that the Beltway establishment sitting stone-faced in his audience was the butt of his jokes, especially the very news media that had parroted Bush administration fictions leading America into the quagmire of Iraq." It was a sentiment expressed a million times a day in America's streets but that rarely seeped into the hallowed halls of traditional journalism. The assembled cast of characters in that room was forced to listen to the message, unable to hang up the phone, delete that email, change the channel, surf to a different website, or otherwise shut their ears, eyes, and minds to the criticism.

Viewership to Colbert's show increased 37 percent that week, but more significantly, it spurred an honest discussion about the role of the traditional media in uncritically enabling the war in Iraq as well as much of Bush's destructive agenda. It pushed on to the larger public agenda the issue of whether journalists were living up to their role of questioning authority, of examining—not just parroting—official pronouncements, of being watchdogs, not lapdogs.

The fact remains that Colbert didn't have to do it. That comedic confrontation was not necessary for his career. The easier way—the safer way—would have dictated prudence: he could have remained masked in his conservative persona, comfortably taking potshots at hippies or peace-niks or terrorists—or bloggers—in such establishment company. He could have, had he so chosen, *become* one of them, one of the comfortable, the "in," the elite, at least for a night. But he didn't. He made a conscious and extremely risky choice—he challenged and mocked those whom many, many others would have been glad to accept and embrace.

He later admitted that he refused to read any reaction to the speech, good or bad.

But then, he didn't need to. He was fully, wholly *there*.

★   ★   ★

When nine-year-old Graeme Frost of Baltimore learned how to talk again after a 2004 car accident, he had no idea that three years later the most hardened haters of the Right would swoop down on his family like they were roadkill.

Graeme, his sister Gemma, and his parents hit a patch of black ice, slammed into a tree, and quickly discovered the limits of America's health insurance system. Graeme himself suffered from a brain stem injury, a paralyzed vocal cord, and was in a coma. His sister had a cranial fracture, and both children were hospitalized for more than five months. The family, unlucky in the accident, was fortunate enough to fall under the guideline qualifications for a government program called SCHIP—State Children's Health Insurance Program—which helped pay the horrific medical bills. The program not only covered the immediate recovery pe-riod, but helped the children enter rehabilitation as well. Without the SCHIP coverage, Graeme could have died. Almost certainly, he would have been wheelchair-bound.

When the Democrats retook Congress in 2006, one of their priorities was to expand SCHIP to cover more families, setting off a high-stakes battle with Republicans. The notion of health care for the children of low- and middle-income American families is a political winner. Indeed, ac-cording to a September 2007 *ABC News/Washington Post* poll, 72 percent of respondents approved of the Democratic SCHIP plan, compared to 25 percent who opposed it. Yet Republicans had no choice but to resist the program's expansion, deadly as it is to their cause. Christopher Hayes, writing in October 2007 in the *Guardian*, explained:

> "It was back in 1993, as the Clintons prepared to roll out their new universal healthcare plan, that Bill Kristol wrote a memo to fellow conservatives and Republican lawmakers on Capitol Hill warning them that their goal must be to 'kill,' not amend, the Clinton plan. 'Healthcare,' Kristol wrote, 'is not, in fact, just another Democratic initiative . . . It will revive the reputation of the . . . Democrats, as the generous protector of middle-class interests.' "

This is really the issue: from the New Deal through the Great Society, the Democrats dominated American politics by being first and foremost the stewards of social-democratic middle-class entitlements. In the wake of the Civil Rights Act, white southerners in particular and white middle-class voters in general began to associate the Democrats with pursuing the interests of Others—minorities, homosexuals, welfare queens. Conservative political dominance in the post-Reagan era has rested on two pillars: preserving, at a rhetorical level, the conception of the Democrats as being beholden to "special interests" (who don't look like you), and, at the policy level, making sure Democrats never have an opportunity to pass legislation that would belie that claim.

That's the real reason this episode unleashed such a fit of viciousness from the Right: conservatives recognized just how politically dangerous the SCHIP is for their cause.

Families USA, an advocacy group that promotes the expansion of the SCHIP program, passed on the names of the Frosts to House Speaker Nancy Pelosi as a family that benefited from the program and that would be willing to speak up for it. Pelosi passed on Graeme's name to Senate Majority Leader Harry Reid, and two staffers from Reid's office contacted the youngster and his family to see if the twelve-year-old would be willing to give the Democratic weekly radio address on September 28 to ask President Bush to sign the recently passed SCHIP expansion measure. The family agreed and Graeme told a national audience why SCHIP was important:

> "My parents work really hard and always make sure my sister and I have everything we need, but the hospital bills were huge. We got the help we needed because we had health insurance for us through the CHIP program. But there are millions of kids out there who don't have CHIP, and they wouldn't get the care that my sister and I did if they got hurt. Their parents might have to sell their cars or their houses, or they might not be able to pay for hospital bills at all.
>
> "Now I'm back to school. One of my vocal cords is paralyzed so I don't talk the same way I used to. And I can't walk or run as fast as I did. The doctors say I can't play football anymore, but I might still be able to be a coach. I'm just happy to be back with my friends.
>
> "I don't know why President Bush wants to stop kids who really need help from getting CHIP. All I know is I have some really good doctors. They took great care of me when I was sick, and I'm glad I could see them because of the Children's Health Program. I just hope the President will listen to my story and help other kids to be as lucky as me."

It's a pretty safe bet Graeme and his family didn't feel quite as lucky once they discovered what it's like to fall into the hands of an angry right-wing mob calling for the blood of those who praise government services and urge their expansion.

Bush would end up vetoing the bill not just once but twice. But that presidential firewall wasn't enough for conservatives livid that Graeme would have the temerity to tell his story on the radio. "If federal funds were required [they] could die for all I care," said a typical commenter on the conservative site Red State. "Let the parents get second jobs, let their state foot the bill or let them seek help from private charities . . . I would hire a team of PIs and find out exactly how much their parents made and where they spent every nickel. Then I'd do everything possible to destroy their lives with that info."

The problem wasn't that conservatives were blowing off steam on these websites. The problem was that they began acting on such threats. The conservative blogosphere led the charge, with bloggers harassing the Frosts at work, creepily staking out their house, and digging up their private financial information. Soon thereafter Rush Limbaugh was reciting all of it on the air—from the fact that their Baltimore town house was valued at $485,000 (they bought it in 1990 for $55,000 when the neighborhood was a dump, according to an October 10, 2007, *Baltimore Sun* article by Matthew Hay Brown) to the fact that both children attended expensive private schools (they are special-needs students going to schools that catered to such children, and are on scholarship). Even the Frosts' 1992 wedding announcement in the *New York Times* was fodder for criticism. The blogger John Cole posted the following observations on his Balloon Juice blog on October 9:

> "If you look through this family's dossier, it appears they are doing everything Republicans say they should be doing—hell, their story is almost what you would consider a checklist for good, red-blooded American Republican voters: they own their own business, they pay their taxes, they are still in a committed relationship and are raising their kids, they eschewed public education and are doing what they have to do to get them into Private schools, they are part of the American dream of home ownership that Republicans have been pointing to in the past two administrations as proof of the health of the economy, and so on.
>
> "In short, they are a white, lower-middle-class, committed family, who is doing EVERYTHING the GOP Kultur Kops would have you believe people should be doing. They aren't gay. They aren't divorced. They didn't abort their children. They aren't drug addicts or welfare queens. They are property owners, entrepreneurs, taxpayers, and hard-working Americans. I bet nine times

out of ten in past elections, if you handed this resume to a pollster,
they would think you were discussing the prototypical Republican
voter."

Of course, the problem wasn't that the Frosts were not doing everything right, following GOP dogma on how to live—it was that they had
the temerity to lend their voice in favor of a government program that
could prove so popular it would help the Democratic Party's brand with
the voters. If they let Democrats deliver on their agenda, people might end
up *liking it* too much. As such, the Frosts had to be destroyed.

"It's really frustrating," Bonnie Frost told the *Baltimore Sun* on October
10, explaining that she was getting angry internet posts, emails, and telephone calls targeting the family. "The whole point of it for me was that
this program helped my family, and I wanted it to help others. That's the
message, and I can't believe the way the spotlight has been taken off of
that." But in today's world, even the mildest public statement in support
of a contentious issue invites such attacks. "Hang 'em. Publically [*sic*],"
wrote that Red State contributor. "Let 'em twist in the wind and be eaten
by ravens. Then maybe the bunch of socialist patsies will think twice."

But the Frosts hung tough, refusing to be intimidated, and while Bush
ended up vetoing the expansion, Democrats were more than ready to keep
the fight going into the future, while the conservative backlash helped not
only build sympathy for the Frosts but created a news hook for the media
to continue talking about how SCHIP saved the lives of Graeme and his
sister.

The irony is that the specific SCHIP bill vetoed twice by Bush was a
"compromise" bill between Democrats and some Republicans in Congress. This defeat gave Democrats a new issue with which to beat Republicans over the head during the following election cycle. So Bush improved
the chances of Democrats winning the White House and more congressional seats in 2008—and that in turn increased the chances that Democrats will no longer need to "compromise" on SCHIP. This issue may well
prove to be the perfect example of taking baby steps . . . with a healthy
assist from Bush and the conservative smear machine.

Change is never brought about by those who play it safe. The Frosts would've been far better off staying anonymous in the comfort of their home, far away from the public spotlight. Their decision to lend their voice to the debate exposed them to harassment, stalking, invasions of privacy, and emotionally taxing attacks. They paid a price, but their voices helped advance the cause of a noble government program that has the potential to help millions more children when it eventually passes.

The Frosts displayed the kind of civic courage that is in regrettably short supply these days, willing to stand up for a program they believed in—and from which they'd already reaped the benefits—so that their fellow citizens would have the same kind of care in their own emergencies.

Sometimes, we have to adjust and adapt to circumstances that put us well outside our comfort zones, whether we like it or not. Sometimes we become leaders not because we seek it, but because the role in the end seeks us out.

★ EPILOGUE ★

Those first ten words I ever wrote on *Daily Kos*—"I am progressive. I am liberal. I make no apologies."—changed more than my job, my financial situation, and my personal place in politics. Because of where they led—to the unimaginable success of the online political community I founded—those words in the end also changed my view of myself. They eventually thrust me into the role of "leader" that I reluctantly accepted, after fighting it every inch of the way.

What I'd begun in the spring of 2002 as a haven for progressive complaints and observations about the state of the nation was at the time a small part of a rapidly growing but self-contained world online—the political blogosphere. The popular blogs at the time measured their readership in the hundreds and the outside world was blissfully unaware of this community of political junkies arguing with each other in their insignificantly tiny corner of the internet. When I jumped into this world, there was literally zero expectation that I would ever have any readers beyond a couple of my more politically minded friends. I was doing it for myself, not for anyone else.

Of course, things turned out quite differently than I'd planned. *Daily Kos* struck a chord with readers. And while I'm most certainly not the best writer in a medium replete with incredibly talented voices, I *did* have a talent for the technology and rules that would best foster a vibrant and active community. So *Daily Kos* grew as people adopted tools that allowed them to have, as I desperately wanted in May 2002, a voice in their politics.

However, I soon began hearing the dreaded "L" word—"leadership."

People were complaining about the quality of my leadership, demanding my leadership, or praising my leadership. Every time I heard the word applied to me, I'd cringe. It was a word that had nothing to do, I thought, with who I was or what I was doing at *Daily Kos*. I liked to write; I liked to fiddle with internet technologies. That was it. And I had come a long way based on those two interests of mine. I didn't see a need to do more, to be this "leader" that so many wished I would be. Couldn't I just keep doing my thing, and let it be?

My usual line of defense was simple: "I'm just a guy with a blog." I increasingly wielded it as a shield after the 2004 elections, as *Daily Kos*'s readership and influence continued to explode. In August 2005, *Daily Kos* was part of a broad netroots coalition that almost propelled Democrats to victory in a special election in a solidly conservative Ohio congressional district. The near-victory by the Iraq war vet Paul Hackett shook both parties to the core—the Republicans because they never expected to contend in a district so safely Republican, and Democrats because Hackett had been fueled almost exclusively by netroots allies without the party establishment's help. Hackett lost, but it was a huge victory for movement progressives seeking to create a Democratic Party that could compete in all fifty states and in every congressional district.

Three days later, Eleanor Clift of *Newsweek* wrote a very gracious column touching on our work:

> "Two days earlier, an antiwar Democrat had come close to winning a special election in Ohio for a congressional seat assumed to be safe for Republicans. Former Marine reservist Paul Hackett, who returned from Iraq to run for Congress, had gotten a huge boost from bloggers around the country. Leading the charge was Markos Moulitsas, founder of the progressive *Daily Kos*, which attracts hundreds of thousands of daily visits and is considered one of the most popular political blogs on the Internet. For Democrats desperate to find their way back to a winning coalition, Moulitsas, 33, has emerged as one of the most creative thinkers and activists in the progressive ranks."

There was that "L" word again! And I responded on *Daily Kos*:

> "I'm not leading anything. I didn't lead the charge on Hackett, and I don't think I lead the charge on anything. What I have helped do is create a platform that allows situational leaders to emerge outside the establishment class (be it media, political, or activist establishments) [. . .]"
>
> "Did I play a role? Sure, a supporting role. A small role. But the beauty of this medium is that a lot of 'small roles' add up to something incredible. It's a collaborative medium, one in which no one person can make the definitive difference, but together we can shake things up."

But then again, my defense *was* getting stale, and people were tiring of it because it was ringing increasingly hollow. No matter how hard I tried to at least convince myself that I was not a leader, that conviction was getting harder and harder to shore up. In the summer of 2005, I *had* taken a lead fighting back against efforts by reformer groups and the Federal Election Commission to impose government regulations on political blogging. As I prepared for my June 28 testimony before the FEC, it was clear that I was already seeing a shift in my role. "I like to think of myself as just a guy with a blog, but it's clear that 'just a guy with a blog' is different today than it was when I started three years ago," I told the Associated Press the day before my FEC appearance. "One sign of having arrived is when government regulators start wanting to poke their fingers into what you do."

But there were other signs that I had graduated past the "just a guy with a blog" stage. My allies and my critics parsed and amplified everything I wrote as though my words were the edicts of a deity. Media bookers and reporters looked to me for quotes about blogging issues. Perhaps the biggest sign: the blog had become my day job. Advertising revenues had reached the point in late 2004 that I could abandon a brief and unsuccessful flirtation with political consulting to focus on *Daily Kos* full-time. Unlike the vast majority of bloggers, I had money to pay myself and a full-time

programmer, with enough left over to fund development of the site's hard-
ware and software infrastructures.

So, all right, I wasn't "just a guy with a blog." I was, I could admit at
last, something else. But a leader? Ugh. While some people thought it was
false modesty on my part, it was actually a desire to avoid that label — and
for good reason. My temperament was ill-suited for the job, given that I
lacked the diplomatic skills necessary to lead anyone anywhere they didn't
already want to go. Inevitably, every so often I'd write something that would
anger this group or that, and readers would loudly proclaim that they were
leaving the site. And every single time I'd say, "Glad to see it. My job isn't
to cater to your pet whims. It's a big internet. And if *Daily Kos* doesn't do
it for you, there are plenty of sites that would be more than happy to host
your presence." That's the sort of thing a guy with a blog would say, I
thought. But a leader? No way.

I also didn't want to deal with the hassles of being a high-profile leader
of anything. I'd seen some people become mildly corrupted by such
things, and others become raging megalomaniacs. And to be honest, I'm
a little lazy. Being a real leader is hard work. But ultimately, the biggest
problem I had with it was that I didn't like people telling me what to do.
Why then would I suddenly decide to take on the role of telling other
people what *they* should do?

And then it hit me. My kind of leadership wasn't about telling people
"Get behind me as I set your agenda!" My leadership was more like that
of a mayor of a big city, in the sense that a mayor creates a favorable living
environment for residents by fixing roads, plowing snow, creating infrastructure, and setting the rules for public behavior. Similarly, I have to
maintain this public commons I have created. And since I had the great
fortune of building the most successful political community online, it was
also my responsibility to continuously improve it, promote the movement
it has spawned, and protect the medium itself from unwarranted intru-
sions from government or corporate interests that would seek to undermine it. *That's* why I fought government regulations at the FEC (and
won). *That's* why I would talk to reporters and other media about the
movement and the medium.

The word still makes me feel a little weird, but it *is* leadership, just different than the traditional definition of the word. The conservative writer Dean Barnett gets the progressive netroots better than any writer I've seen to date, and he explained this "leadership" thing perfectly on July 2, 2007, at *Townhall.com*:

> "In the Beltway's eyes, Markos leads a movement of progressives in the blogosphere. But this is inaccurate, and Markos would be the first to tell you so. Markos doesn't lead the movement. He stands in front of it and is symbolic of it, but the movement's direction and interests flow directly from the people who compose it. The movement is a bottom-up thing, not something that a guy leads from the top.
>
> "It's probably comforting for Democratic politicians to believe that Markos leads the movement in the progressive blogosphere. That being the case, all they have to do is soothe the savage breasts of Markos and other rabble-rousing bloggers and then get back to business as usual. That's why Democratic politicians are so unfailingly solicitous of the liberal bloggers.
>
> "But it doesn't work like that. If Markos came out tomorrow and said he's supporting Hillary [Clinton], the people who read his blog would tell him to pound sand. They would keep reading his blog, but they wouldn't open their hearts or their wallets for Hillary."

So yeah, it *is* leadership in being a symbol for the movement. I loathe television interviews and traveling to conferences and events. It's not fun when my mother-in-law calls wondering why Bill O'Reilly just called me a Nazi. It's not pleasant when my wife loses a friend because the friend's boyfriend thinks I'm a horrible person. And worst of all, I despise the time it takes away from my wife and my family. As I write this, I've been holed up for a week in a cabin in the woods finishing up this manuscript. My four-year-old son has called several times asking why I can't come home. Now! His first sentence ever, in fact, was pointing to a plane during one of my frequent absences and saying, "Papy goes bye-bye." My ten-month-old daughter has been crying when hearing my voice on the phone. It breaks my heart.

And I'll confess to a streak of selfishness as I dedicate myself to expanding the depth and reach of this new movement, preaching that there are leadership roles for all of us: I want more leaders—the kind Barnett defined as being pushed from the ground up—to step up and spread the message, to be living examples themselves of the power of people willing to take charge of changing the world.

I look forward to help build this incredible progressive movement to the point where others can do the television punditry, are requested to speak at events, and can otherwise become the symbol for this people-powered movement we are building together. I dream of the day I can go back to focusing on my site's technology and writing a good rant about the latest injustice. But for now, at this moment in time, I've been dragged kicking and screaming into a more public role, and if that's the definition of "leader," then perhaps I *am* one of those after all . . . lack of diplomacy notwithstanding.

My guess is, there are thousands—hundreds of thousands, in fact—out there just like me. Tired of accepting a backseat. Tired of feeling powerless and voiceless. Tired of the squalid state of our public affairs. And at heart, more than ready, willing, and able to take on the system.

★ ACKNOWLEDGMENTS ★

I was nine years old when, watching the news on TV, I saw images of crowds marching in the street carrying banners that said "*Solidarność*." I turned to my father and asked, "What's going on?" He shrugged. "Politics." I watched those Polish protesters a few seconds more, then announced, "I like politics." So thanks to my parents, Maria and Markos (whom I miss every single day of my life), for encouraging me from the beginning to learn everything I could about "politics."

Now a decade strong, my partnership with Elisa is still the best thing to ever happen to me. Her support during the writing of this book was far more than any sane, rational, human being could ever expect.

My two children, Aristotle Alberto and his little sister, Elisandra Elexy, remind me every day why it's important to fight. This is their world, and I'll be damned if I won't fight to make it better than the mess I inherited.

I'd be nowhere without the *Daily Kos* community, one like none other. This wonderful group of users and readers keeps me real, reminding me every day that this is about *them*. I've been blessed with the honor of giving them voice. I forget that at my own peril.

My editor, Safir Ahmed, helped me say things much better than I ever could on my own. I wouldn't have done this book without him. Susan Gardner's advice and help during the editing process went above and beyond the call of duty. Barb Morrill turned the internet inside out digging up information and other research for the book.

The *Daily Kos* contributing editors didn't just mind the *Daily Kos* store while I was working on this book but served as a valued sounding board. A huge thanks to Joan McCarter, Dana Houle, Jake McEntyre, Mike Lazarro, Arjun Jaikumar, Tim Lange, Page Van Der Linden, DavidNYC, Steven Andrew, Mark Sumner, Georgia Logothetis, Jennifer Brunjes, Laura Clawson, David Waldman, and Greg Dworkin. Will Rockafellow, my friend and business manager, took care of business so I could focus on my writing. Jeremy Bingham kept the tubes unclogged so I could worry about book deadlines rather than website performance, especially during the craziest presidential primary season in generations.

The progressive blogosphere has taught me that when we work together and unite for a common cause we can move mountains. Big and small, all blogs play a critical role in something much grander than I could've ever imagined. We may be a sliver of the broader netroots, but damn, we're a fun part of it.

Thanks to everyone who offered advice, guidance and information that helped out with key portions of this book, such as the good folks at the Berkman Center for Internet & Society, Glenn Smith, Dante Zappala, Lowell Feld and Nate Wilcox, James Rucker, Dan Clawson, and those who chose to stay "on background" for professional or personal reasons. Gina Cooper is always an inspiration, as is Nolan Treadway. And speaking of inspirations, Alan Bean of Friends of Justice is my new hero.

Thanks to Penguin, and Raymond Garcia specifically, for trusting me with this project. They were far more patient than I would've ever been had the roles been reversed.

A special thanks to those people who are a personal inspiration in my life—Alexander Moulitsas, Morgan Rysdon, Lisa and Diego Batista, Jerome Armstrong, Tyler Bleszinski, Erika Chavez, Brent Copen, Hai Hoang, Amy Kiser, Nyran Pearson, Iara Peng, Sarah Van Laanen, Justin Krebs, the Drinking Liberally and Laughing Liberally folks, and everyone who gets off his or her ass to change the world.

Finally, thanks to this guy, who reminds us that everything is changing in this brand new digital world. Even bravery:

ASSOCIATED PRESS, DEC. 11, 2007

> ELMWOOD PARK, N.J.—When a robber started
> taking cash from his register over the weekend,

Dunkin' Donuts employee Dustin Hoffmann fought back by clobbering the man with a ceramic mug. But Hoffmann admits he was less worried about the stolen cash than how he might look on the video-sharing site YouTube.

"What was going through my mind at that point was that the security tape is either going to show me run away and hide in the office or whack this guy in the head, so I just grabbed the cup and clocked the guy pretty hard," Hoffmann told *The Record* of Bergen County for Tuesday's editions . . .

"There are only a few videos like that on YouTube now, so mine's going to be the best," he said. "That'll teach this guy."